1

7

9

# Ba Wei Di Huang Wan 八味地黃丸
## Rehmannia Eight Formula

### Indications:
Used to treat kidney *qi* and *yang* deficiency: aching and weakness of the lower back and knees, cold sensation in the lower half of the body, tenseness in the lower abdomen, either difficult urination or excessive urination (more severe at night), impotence, premature ejaculation, and chronic diarrhea.

**Tongue:** red and thin coating
**Pulse:** rapid and empty or frail (submerged and faint at the proximal position)

### Clinical Applications:
1. This is a classic presentation of kidney yang deficiency with insufficient *ming men* fire. It is often given to older patients.
2. Currently used for chronic nephritis, diabetes, hypothyroidism, anxiety during sexual performance, genital disorders, frequent urination, and menopause symptoms.

### Ingredients:

| | | | | | |
|---|---|---|---|---|---|
| 1. | shu di huang | 24.0 | 5. | mu dan pi | 9.0 |
| 2. | shan yao | 12.0 | 6. | ze xie | 9.0 |
| 3. | shan zhu yu | 12.0 | 7. | rou gui | 3.0 |
| 4. | fu ling | 9.0 | 8. | fu zi (pao) | 3.0 |

### Functions:
Warms and enriches the lower *jiao*, warms and tonifies kidney *yang*.

### Modifications:
1. For weakness and soreness in the lower back or knees, add *niu xi* and *du zhong*.
2. For dizziness, add *ju hua* and *gou qi zi*.
3. For low sexual performance, add *ren shen*, *lu rong*, and *rou cong rong*.
4. For blurry vision, combine with *Yi Qi Cong Ming Tang*.
5. For lower back pain, combine with *Fang Ji Huang Qi Tang*.
6. For *yin* deficiency weakness, combine with *Huang Qi Jian Zhong Tang*.

### Cautions and Contraindications:
Should not be used when patient has *yin* deficiency heat.

### Administration:
Take with warm water or lightly salted water, before meals.

Source: *Yi Fang Ji Jie* (醫方集解)

# Ban Xia Hou Po Tang 半夏厚朴湯
### Pinellia and Magnolia Combination

## Indications:
Plum pit *qi*: sensation of something caught in the throat that can neither be swallowed nor ejected, a stifling sensation in the chest and hypochondria, cough, shortness of breath, anxiety, periodic overactive palpitation, and sensation of tightness in throat.

| | |
|---|---|
| **Tongue:** | moist or greasy, white coating |
| **Pulse:** | wiry and slow or wiry and slippery |

## Clinical Applications:
1. This formula treats plum pit *qi*, which is phlegm obstruction and *qi* stagnation lodging in the throat; this combination of patterns arises from liver *qi* constraint causing the lungs and stomach to lose their ability to move *qi* downward, and *qi* disturbance of ascending and descending functions.
2. Currently used for hysteria, functional gastrointestinal disorders, esophageal spasms, chronic laryngitis, and edema of the vocal cords.

## Ingredients:
1. ban xia      16.0
2. hou po       9.0
3. fu ling       12.0
4. sheng jiang   15.0
5. zi su ye       6.0

## Functions:
Moves *qi*, dissipates clumps, descends rebellious *qi*, and transforms phlegm.

## Modifications:
1. For severe *qi* constraint, add *xiang fu* and *yu jin*.
2. For severe hypochondriac pain, add *chuan lian zi* and *yan hu suo*.
3. For severe throat spasm, add *zhi shi* and *jie geng*.
4. For accumulation of phlegm dampness, combine with *Er Chen Tang*.
5. For food stagnation, combine with *liu he tang*.
6. For depression, combine with *yue ju wan*.

## Cautions and Contraindications:
Should be not taken by patients with flushed face, a bitter taste in the mouth, or patients with a red tongue due to *qi* constraint transforming to fire and injuring *yin* and fluids.

## Administration:
Take with warm water, as needed.

Source: *Jin Gui Yao Lüe* (金匱要略)

# Ban Xia Xie Xin Tang 半夏瀉心湯
## Pinellia Combination

### Indications:
*Pi* obstruction pattern from disharmony of stomach and intestines: epigastric fullness and tightness with little or no pain, dry heaves or vomiting, borborygmus with diarrhea, and reduced appetite.

**Tongue**:     thin, yellow, and greasy coating
**Pulse**:     wiry and rapid

### Clinical Applications:
1. This formula is often used for *pi*-obstruction. "*Pi*" refers to a focused, localized sensation of discomfort, blockage, and distention due to spleen and stomach deficiency and external evil sinking in, which causes a combination of cold and heat, with a disorder of ascending and descending *qi*. Note: using purgatives prematurely in the stages of *shang han* causes localized distention and pain.
2. Currently used for chronic or acute gastroenteritis, chronic colitis, nervous gastritis, chronic hepatitis, early-stage cirrhosis, indigestion, or gastric ulcers due to excessive acid.

### Ingredients:
| | | | | | |
|---|---|---|---|---|---|
| 1. | ban xia | 15.0 | 5. | ren shen | 9.0 |
| 2. | huang lian | 3.0 | 6. | da zao | 9.0 |
| 3. | huang qin | 9.0 | 7. | zhi gan cao | 6.0 |
| 4. | gan jiang | 9.0 | | | |

### Functions:
Harmonizes the stomach, guides rebellious *qi* downward, disperses clumping, and eliminates distention.

### Modifications:
1. For severe vomiting without *qi* deficiency, or with thick and greasy tongue coating, omit *ren shen* and *da zao* and add *zhi shi* and *sheng jiang*.
2. For severe focal distention, add *zhi shi* and *jie geng*.
3. For nausea or regurgitation, add *fu ling* and *chen pi*.
4. For diarrhea and abdominal pain, add *mu xiang* and *shao yao*.
5. For vomiting with pain, combine with *San Huang Xie Xin Tang*.
6. For vomiting with fluid, combine with *Er Chen Tang*.
7. For vomiting with food, combine with *Ping Wei San*.

### Administration:
Take with warm water, as needed.

Source: *Shang Han Lun* (傷寒論)

# Bu Zhong Yi Qi Tang 補中益氣湯
### Ginseng and Astragalus Combination

## Indications:
Spleen and stomach *qi* deficiency pattern: intermittent fever (that worsens after exertion), spontaneous sweating, aversion to cold, unclear vision, laconic speech, a tendency to curl up, a thirst for warm beverages, shortness of breath, and loose or watery stool.
*Yang qi* deficiency and sinking *qi* pattern: prolapse of the rectum or uterus, chronic diarrhea, chronic dysentery, incontinence, and bleeding disorders.

**Tongue:**  pale with thin, white coating
**Pulse:**  flooding and deficient, or deficient and rootless at the middle position on the right-hand side

## Clinical Applications:
1. This formula tonifies *qi* and raises *yang*; it is very useful in treating organ prolapse and chronic low fever due to sunken *yang qi* of the middle *jiao*.
2. Currently used for chronic bronchitis, gastrointestinal prolapse, habitual miscarriage, functional uterine bleeding, leukorrhea, postpartum disorders, and 1ˢᵗ or 2ⁿᵈ degree prolapse of the uterus, rectum, or other internal organs.

## Ingredients:
| | | | | | |
|---|---|---|---|---|---|
| 1. huang *qi* | 12.0 | 5. chen pi | 4.0 | 9. sheng jiang | 6.0 |
| 2. ren shen | 8.0 | 6. dang gui | 4.0 | 10. da zao | 4.0 |
| 3. bai zhu | 4.0 | 7. sheng ma | 2.0 | | |
| 4. zhi gan cao | 8.0 | 8. chai hu | 2.0 | | |

## Functions:
Tonifies the middle *jiao*, benefits *qi*, raises *yang*, and lifts prolapsed organs.

## Modifications:
1. For abdominal pain, increase the dosage of *zhi gan cao* and add *bai shao*.
2. For dizziness with headache, add *bai zhi* and *chuan xiong*.
3. For herniations, add *ju he*, *xiao hui xiang*, and *li zhi he*.
4. For abdominal distention with pain, add *huang qin* and *bai shao*.
5. For *qi* deficiency fatigue, combine with *Bu Zhong Yi Qi Tang*.
6. For blood deficiency fatigue, combine with *Si Wu Tang*.
7. For cold fatigue, combine with *Xiao Chai Hu Tang*.

## Cautions and Contraindications:
Should not be used when patient has *yin* deficiency heat or a fever due to excess heat.

## Administration:
Take with warm water, between meals or on an empty stomach.

Source: *Pi Wei Lun* (脾胃論)

# Cang Er San 蒼耳散
Xanthium Formula
Xanthium Powder

## Indications:
Profuse nasal discharge (*bi yuan*) due to wind-heat.

Stuffy nose, running nose, foul-smelling nasal discharge and frontal headache.

## Clinical Applications:
1. This is the best formula for profuse nasal discharge caused by wind-heat attacking the head.
2. Currently used for acute/chronic, or allergic rhinitis or sinusitis.

## Ingredients:
1. bai zhi      2.4
2. bo he        1.2
3. xin yi hua   1.2
4. cang er zi   0.6
5. cong bai     0.3
6. cha          0.3

## Functions:
Disperses wind and opens the nasal orifices.

## Modifications:
1. For nasal clear discharge: add *fang feng* and *qiang huo*.
2. For nasal yellow discharge: add *chuan xiong* and *huang qin*.
3. For nasal turbid discharge: add *jing yin hua* and *lian qia*o.
4. For more heat in the *Lu*, add *sang bai pi, di gu pi* or *huang qin*.
5. For severe sinus infection, add *huang qin, shi gao, zhi zi, jin yin hua,* and *lian qiao*.
6. For allergic sinus, add *chan tui, xu chang qing, fang feng,* and *huang qi*.

## Administration:
Take with warm water, after meals.

Source: *Yi Fang Ji Jie*（醫方集解）

# Chai Ge Jie Ji Tang 柴葛解肌湯
### Bupleurum and Pueraria Combination
### Bupleurum and Kudzu Decoction to Release the Muscle Layer

## Indications:
Exterior wind-cold, stagnation turns to interior heat syndrome (*Tai Yang, Yang Ming, Shao Yang* combinations).

Increased fever, decreased aversion to cold, headache without sweat, orbital and eye pain, dry nasal passages, irritability and insomnia.

**Tongue:** thin yellow coating
**Pulse:** Floating, slightly flooding pulse

## Clinical Applications:
1. This formula is for unresolved, exterior wind-cold which has become constrained and transformed into heat.
2. The key symptoms are headache and fever, upset and insomnia, orbital pain and dry nose, dry throat and deafness, aversion to cold and no sweat.
3. Currently used for flu and toothache.
4. After using *Ma Huang Tang, Gui Zhi Tang,* or *Ge Gen Tang*, the patient still has not reached the sweating effect. Or the flu is not completely relieved, and there is still headache, nasal obstruction, thirst, and painful limbs.

## Ingredients:

| | | | | | | | | |
|---|---|---|---|---|---|---|---|---|
| 1. | chai hu | 2.5 | 5. | bai zhi | 2.5 | 9. | gan cao | 1.5 |
| 2. | ge gen | 2.5 | 6. | huang qin | 2.5 | 10. | sheng jiang | 2.0 |
| 3. | shi gao | 2.5 | 7. | bai shao | 2.5 | 11. | da zao | 2.0 |
| 4. | qiang huo | 2.5 | 8. | jie geng | 2.5 | | | |

## Functions:
Release the muscle layer and clear interior heat

## Modifications:
1. For wind-cold headache: add f*ang feng* and *chuan xiong.*
2. For damp-heat irritable heat: add *yin chen* and *bo he.*
3. For vomiting phlegm or saliva: add *ban xia* and *fu ling.*
4. For wind-cold attach: combine with *Sheng Ma Ge Gen Tang.*
5. For summer-heat pain: combine with *San Wu Xiang Ru Yin.*
6. For fever and thirst: combine with *Bai Hu Tang.*
7. For severe chills without sweating, substitute *ma huang* for *huang qin*; during the summer and fall, substitute *zi su ye* instead.

## Cautions and Contraindications:
Simple exterior wind-heat disorders.

## Administration:
Take with warm water, before meals.

Source: *Zhong Guo Yi Yao Da Ci Dian* （中國醫藥大辭典）

# Chai Hu Gui (Zhi) (Gan) Jiang Tang 柴胡桂枝乾姜湯
### Bupleurum, Cinnamon, and Ginger Combination
### Bupleurum, Cinnamon Twig and Ginger Decoction

## Indications:

1. The prolonged failure to expel the pathogen, combined with the damaging effects of the treatment for exterior resolution, leave the condition in a weakened state with the pathogen lodged in the *shao yang* stage.
2. Wind-cold pattern that after five or six days has not successfully resolved despite the repeated use of relieved exterior treatment.
3. Deficient physique with interior fluid accumulation combined with a *shao yang* pattern and fullness and glomus in the chest and flanks.

## Clinical Applications:

1. This formula is for treating internal and external *yang-qi* deficiency, residual pathogens and dryness, and those with *qi* rushing upward. This is complicated by fluid accumulation in the chest and abdomen that arises from the deficient body failing to properly metabolize fluids.
2. The key symptoms are fullness of chest and flanks, focal distention, difficulty urinating, thirst, sweating, alternative chill and fever, irritability, *qi* rushing upward, etc.
3. Currently used in treating cold, tuberculosis, pleurisy, scrofula, bronchitis, pneumonia and other in various febrile diseases; it can also be used for hepatitis, neurological weakness, menopausal disorders, hyperactive palpitations, insomnia and night sweats, etc.

## Ingredients:

| | | | | | | |
|---|---|---|---|---|---|---|
| 1. | chai hu | 8.0 | | 5. | mu li | 2.0 |
| 2. | gui zhi | 3.0 | | 6. | zhi gan cao | 2.0 |
| 3. | huang qin | 3.0 | | 7. | gua lou gen | 4.0 |
| 4. | gan jiang | 3.0 | | | | |

## Functions:

Expel cold and eliminate heat, move the *qi* and warm the middle.

## Modifications:

1. For irritability, focal distention: add *huang lian* and *zhi shi*.
2. For difficulty urination: add *fu ling* and *che qian zi*.
3. For headache and sweating: *chuan xiong* and *bai zhi*.
4. For urinary obstruction or difficulty urination caused by beriberi: add *wu zhu yu* and *fu ling*.
5. For nodules caused by tuberculous peritonitis: add *bie jiao* and *shao yao*.
6. For trouble urinating or sweating due to tuberculosis fever: add *huang qi* and *bie jiao*.

## Administration:

Take with warm water, after meals.

Source: *Shang Han Jin Kui* (傷寒金匱)

# Chai Hu Gui Zhi Tang 柴胡桂枝湯
Bupleurum and Cinnamon Combination
Bupleurum and Cinnamon Twig Decoction

## Indications:
1. *Shao yang* disorders where the exterior has not been completely released syndrome.
2. Fever with chills and aversion to wind; joint pain due to wind in the joints; and fullness in the hypochondriac area or any *shao yang* stage disorders.
3. Mild nausea, hypochondriac pain, and sudden chest pain (sudden pain in the lower part of the heart like angina attack).

**Tongue**: thin white
**Pulse**: floating, wiry

## Clinical Applications:
1. This formula is used for both *tai yang* stage to harmonize *ying* and *wei* – *Gui Zhi Tang* (Cinnamon Twigs Decoction) and *shao yang* stage to harmonize interior and exterior – *Xiao Chai Hu Tang* (Minor Bupleurum Decoction). *Tai yang* stage – fever, mild aversion to cold and joint pain and *shao yang* stage – mild nausea and fullness in the hypochondriac area.
2. Currently used for common cold, influenza, rhinitis, urticaria, or skin rashes triggered by exposure to cold, chronic hepatitis or pancreatitis.
3. Also for pneumonia, tuberculosis, pleurisy and other febrile diseases. Stomach pain, hyperacidity, hypoacidity, jaundice, malaria, liver dysfunction, etc. It can also be used to treat neurosis such as intercostal neuralgia, headache, joint pain, gynecomastia, hysteria, etc.

## Ingredients:
| | | | | | | | | |
|---|---|---|---|---|---|---|---|---|
| 1. chai hu | 5.6 | 4. bai shao | 2.1 | 7. zhi gan cao | 1.4 |
| 2. gui zhi | 2.1 | 5. ban xia | 3.5 | 8. sheng jiang | 2.1 |
| 3. huang qin | 2.1 | 6. ren shen | 2.1 | 9. da zao | 1.4 |

## Functions:
1. Releases *tai yang* and harmonizes *shao yang* stages and releases fever and chill disorder.
2. Release exterior and harmonize center, expel cold and eliminate heat, relive internal and external.

## Modifications:
1. For insomnia: add *dang gui, ye jiao teng,* and *suan zao ren.*
2. For fever and aversion to cold: add *ma huang* and *xing ren.*
3. For severe joint pain: add *ge gen* and *sheng ma.*
4. For fullness and distension in the hypochondriac area: add *zhi shi* and *jie geng.*
5. For amenorrhea with stagnation in hypochondriac area: add *da huang.*

## Cautions and Contraindications:
Excess sweating, *yang* collapse, or delirium conditions.

## Administration:
Take with warm water, any time needed.

Source: *Shang Han Lun* (傷寒論)

# Chai Hu Jia Long Mu Tang 柴胡加龍牡湯
### Bupleurum and Fossilized Minerals Combination

## Indications:
When purgatives have been given prematurely in *shang han* stages, it allows evils into the *yang ming* stage. Symptoms include fullness in the chest, fright, palpitation, constipation, delirious speech, inability to rotate the trunk, heaviness throughout the body, and difficult urination.

**Tongue:** red with a slippery coating
**Pulse:** wiry and rapid

## Clinical Applications:
1. This formula treats the key symptoms involved in the three *yang* stages of *shang han* diseases. This condition is due to premature application of purgatives.
2. Currently used for neurosis, depression, general anxiety disorder, schizophrenia, Parkinson's disease, and epilepsy. It has been used for hypertension, supraventricular tachycardia, hyperthyroidism, Meniere's disease, and menopausal syndromes.

## Ingredients:

| | | | | | |
|---|---|---|---|---|---|
| 1. | chai hu | 21.0 | 7. | ren shen | 21.0 |
| 2. | gui zhi | 21.0 | 8. | fu ling | 21.0 |
| 3. | huang qin | 21.0 | 9. | zhi ban xia | 21.0 |
| 4. | da huang | 28.0 | 10. | sheng jiang | 21.0 |
| 5. | long gu | 21.0 | 11. | da zao | 21.0 |
| 6. | mu li | 21.0 | | | |

## Functions:
Harmonizes *shao yang* and sedates and calms the spirit.

## Modifications:
1. For severe delirium, add *tian ma* and *gou teng*.
2. For difficult urination, add *mu tong* and *fang ji*.
3. For *pi* obstruction and irritability, add *huang lian* and *tian hua feng*.

## Cautions and Contraindications:
Should not be used when patient is deficient.

## Administration:
Take with warm or room temperature water, as needed.

Source: *Shang Han Za Bing Lun* (傷寒雜病論)

# Chai Hu Qing Gan Tang 柴胡清肝湯
Bupleurum and Rehmannia Combination
Bupleurum Decoction to Clear the Liver

## Indications:
Wind-heat fire in liver, gallbladder and *San Jiao* channels.

Blood-heat bleeding, red eyes, a propensity for anger, flank pain, alternating fever and chills, nose bleeding, hearing loss, infections of the outer or inner ear, sore throat, chronic inflammation of the uterus, swelling or itching of the genitals, upper body toxic swellings, or menstrual disorders.

## Clinical Applications:
1. This formula is effective for improving post-liver disease physique.
2. The key symptoms are thin and feeble physique in children, light black and blueish complexion, most likely tuberculosis constitution, or for epidemic hepatitis.
3. Currently used in long-term treatment of epidemic hepatitis.

## Ingredients:

| | | | | | |
|---|---|---|---|---|---|
| 1. | chai hu | 2.4 | 7. | lian *qi*ao | 1.6 |
| 2. | sheng di huang | 2.4 | 8. | huang *qi*n | 1.6 |
| 3. | dang gui | 3.2 | 9. | zhi zi | 1.6 |
| 4. | chi shao | 2.4 | 10. | tian hua fen | 1.6 |
| 5. | niu bang zi | 2.4 | 11. | gan cao | 1.6 |
| 6. | chuan xiong | 1.6 | 12. | fang feng | 1.6 |

## Functions:
Clear liver, disperse wind, purge fire and release toxins.

## Modifications:
For severe wind-heat evil in the liver, add *qiang huo* and *jing jie.*

## Cautions and Contraindications:
Excess heat in the stomach.

## Administration:
Take with warm water, after meals.

Source: *Yi Guan Tang* (一貫堂)

# Chai Hu Shu Gan Tang 柴胡疏肝湯
## Bupleurum and Cyperus Combination

### Indications:
Pain caused by liver *qi* stagnation with blood stasis patterns: hypochondriac pain, breast distention, a stifling sensation in the chest with pain that is relieved by deep sighs, belching, abdominal distention, and alternating chills and fever.

**Tongue:**   dark with a thin coating
**Pulse:**   wiry

### Clinical Applications:
1. Constraint and stagnation of liver *qi*, which manifests in symptoms such as: hypochondriac and flank pain; a stifling sensation in the chest that causes deep sighing; and tendency to vent frustration through anger.
2. This formula is *Si Ni San* (Frigid Extremities Powder) with the addition of *chen pi*, *xiang fu*, and *chuan xiong* and the transition of *zhi shi* to *zhi ke*.
3. Currently used for hepatitis, chronic cholecystitis, mastitis, chronic gastritis, chronic peptic ulcers, and intercostal neuralgia.

### Ingredients:
1. chai hu        32.0
2. chen pi        32.0
3. zhi ke         24.0
4. xiang fu       24.0
5. chuan xiong    24.0
6. bai shao       24.0
7. zhi gan cao     6.0

### Functions:
Soothes the liver *qi*, harmonizes the blood, and alleviates pain.

### Modifications:
1. For blood deficiency, add *dang gui*, *sheng di*, and *shu di*.
2. For severe blood stagnation, add *dan shen*.
3. For liver *qi* stagnation with fire, add *mu dan pi* and *zhi zi*.

### Cautions and Contraindications:
Should not be used when patient has liver *qi* stagnation pain due to *qi* or *yin* deficiency.

### Administration:
Take with warm water, before meals.

Source: *Tong Zhi Fang* (統旨方)

# Chai Ling Tang 柴苓湯
Bupleurum and Poria Combination

## Indications:
Malaria, more heat and less cold, dry mouth and irritabilities.

Residual heat from *shang han,* fullness and focal distention in chest and hypochondriac area, nausea and difficulty urinating, or immediate vomiting or diarrhea after drinking water, inability to sleep and thirsting and wasting syndromes.

## Clinical Applications:
1. This formula is for treating *shao yang* pattern and water metabolism dysfunction.
2. This formula is a combination of *Xiao Chai Hu Tang* (Minor Bupleurum Decoction) and *Wu Ling San* (Poria Five Herb Formula).
3. The key symptoms are common cold or summer heat, cold drinks injury to the internal organs, vomiting and thirst for drinking, dry retching and diarrhea.
4. Currently used to treat enteritis, nephritis, edema of skin and muscle, irregular urination, and chronic hepatitis and choleitis, etc. In Japan it has been used to treat liver cirrhosis with abdominal distention, fluid retention in the abdomen, and pressure in the area of the liver. Also thirst or summer heat patterns where the patient has consumed cold liquid.

## Ingredients:
| | | | | |
|---|---|---|---|---|
| 1. chai hu | 3.5 | | 7. huang qin | 1.5 |
| 2. fu ling | 2.2 | | 8. ren shen | 1.5 |
| 3. zhu ling | 2.2 | | 9. gan cao | 1.5 |
| 4. bai zhu | 2.2 | | 10. gui zhi | 1.5 |
| 5. ze xie | 3.0 | | 11. sheng jiang | 1.5 |
| 6. ban xia | 2.5 | | 12. da zao | 1.5 |

## Functions:
Eliminate cold and dispel heat, disinhibit water and transform phlegm.

## Modifications:
1. Irritability and thirst: add *mai men dong* and *huang lian.*
2. Nausea and vomit and thirst: add *zhi shi* and *zhu ru.*
3. Diarrhea and thirst: add *gan jiang* and *huang bai.*
4. Food retention and vomit and diarrhea: combine with *Ping Wei San.*
5. Summer heat and vomit and diarrhea: combine with *San Wu Xiang Ru Yin.*
6. Deficiency cold and vomit and diarrhea: combine with *Wu Zhu Yu Tang.*

## Administration:
Take with warm water, after meals.

Source: *Shen Shi Zung Sheng Shu* (沈氏尊生書)

# Chai Xian Tang 柴陷湯
## Bupleurum and Scute Combination
## Bupleurum and Trichosanthes Decoction

### Indications:

Heat and phlegm in the lungs in the *Shao Yang* pattern.

Wind-cold or wind-heat exterior pattern, the pathogen will sink into the lung, alternating fever and chills, cough, thoracic oppression, and bitter taste in the mouth.

| | |
|---|---|
| **Tongue:** | thin yellow coating |
| **Pulse:** | wiry and rapid pulse |

### Clinical Applications:

1. This formula is for treating heat and phlegm in the lungs that give rise to alternating fever and chills, cough, thoracic oppression, and bitter taste.
2. This formula is a modified version of *Xiao Chai Hu Tang* (Minor Bupleurum Combination) formed by increasing the dose of *ban xia* (pinellia) and adding *gua lou ren* (trichosanthes seed) and *huang lian* (coptis). These latter two ingredients comprise *Xiao Xian Xiong Tang* (Minor Trichosanthes Combination); therefore, the name of the formula, *Chai Xian Tang*, reflects the merging of the two root combinations.
3. The key symptoms are phlegm and heat combination, chest pain and cough.
4. Currently used to treat pleurisy, pneumonia, gallstones, fever, chest pain, or pain in the below epigastrium, cough.

### Ingredients:

| | | | | | | | | |
|---|---|---|---|---|---|---|---|---|
| 1. | ban xia | 6.0 | 4. | huang lian | 2.0 | 7. | gan cao | 1.0 |
| 2. | gua lou ren | 4.0 | 5. | huang qin | 2.0 | 8. | sheng jiang | 1.0 |
| 3. | chai hu | 4.0 | 6. | ren shen | 1.4 | 9. | da zao | 1.0 |

### Functions:

Expel cold and drain heat, move *qi* and phlegm, clear heat and eliminate phlegm, open the chest and dissipate lumps.

### Modifications:

1. Cough with hypochondriac pain: add *zhi shi* and *jie geng*.
2. Nausea vomit and chest pain: add *zhu ru* and *chen pi*.
3. Thirst with sore throat: add *shi gao* and *zhi mu*.
4. Phlegm cough pain: combine with *Wen Dan Tang*.
5. Oral sore and sore throat: combine *Qing Xin Li Ge Tang*.
6. Lung atrophy, palpitation, chest pain: take *Zhi Gan Cao Tang* afterwards.

### Administration:

Take with warm or cold water, after meals.

Source: *Shen Shi Zung Sheng Shu* (沈氏尊生書)

# Chuan Xiong Cha Tiao San 川芎茶調散
Ligusticum and Tea Formula
*Chuanxiong* Powder to be Taken with Green Tea

## Indications:
Headache due to wind-evil attack.

Headache or migraine in any part of the head accompanied by fever and aversion to cold, dizziness and nasal congestion.

**Tongue:** thin white coating
**Pulse:** floating

## Clinical Applications:
1. This is the best formula for a headache due to wind-cold.
2. Currently used for migraine headache, tension headache, neurogenic headache, and rhinitis or sinusitis etc. due to exterior wind.
3. Others: Influenza, nasal congestion and runny nose, severe cough. Cerebral neuralgia, increased brain pressure, dizziness, tearing disease, etc.

## Ingredients:

| | | | | | | | | |
|---|---|---|---|---|---|---|---|---|
| 1. bo he | 8.0 | 4. qiang huo | 2.0 | 7. xi xin | 1.0 |
| 2. chuan xiong | 4.0 | 5. gan cao | 2.0 | 8. bai zhi | 2.0 |
| 3. jing jie | 4.0 | 6. fang feng | 1.5 | 9. cha | 0.3 |

## Functions:
Disperses wind and alleviates pain.

## Modifications:
1. For wind-heat headache, omit *qiang huo and xi xin*, and add *ju hua* and *jiang can*.
2. For chronic headaches: add *tao ren, hong hua, jiang can* and *quan xie*.
3. For wind-phlegm headache: add *ban xia* and *fu ling*.
4. For dizziness headaches: add *tian ma* and *gao ben*.
5. For wind-cold headache: combine with *Yu Ping Feng San*.
6. For worried headaches: combine with *Xiao Yao San*.
7. To alter the focus of the formula in addressing headache along specific channels, add *gao ben* for *Tai Yang* (occipital, vertex) headache, *chai hu* for *Shao Yang* (temporal) headache, *ge gen* for *Yang Ming* (frontal) headache, and *wu zhu yu* and *di long* for *Jue Yin* (vertex) headache.

## Cautions and Contraindications:
This formula is inappropriate for treating headache due to *qi* and blood deficiency or due to liver wind and *yang* rising.

## Administration:
Take with green tea, after meals.

Source: *Tai Ping Hui Min He Ji Ju Fan* (太平惠民和劑局方)

# Da Bu Yin Wan 大補陰丸
## Rehmannia and Testudines Combination
### Great Tonify the *Yin* Pill

## Indications:
*Yin* deficiency fire rising syndromes.

Tidal fever and steaming bone, night sweats, spermatorrhea, coughing with blood, irritability, and weakness with sensation of heat or pain in the knees and legs.

**Tongue:**    red tongue, little coating
**Pulse:**    rapid and forceful in the "*chi*" position

## Clinical Applications:
1. This formula is used for flaring upward of fire due to liver and kidney deficiency.
2. The key symptoms are *yin* deficiency with excess fire, pulmonary dysfunction hemoptysis, hiccups and irritable heat; steaming bone, night sweats, feet and knees are heat-pain.
3. Currently used to treat tuberculosis (of lungs, kidneys, or bone), hyperthyroid conditions, diabetes mellitus and nervous exhaustion, anaphylactoid purpura, hyperthyroidism, neurasthenia, etc.

## Ingredients:
1. huang bai      6.0
2. zhi mu      6.0
3. shu di huang      9.0
4. gui ban      9.0

## Functions:
Enriches the *yin* and descends the fire.

## Modifications:
1. For coughing of blood: add *xian he cao, bai mao gen,* and *han lian cao.*
2. For severe *yin* deficiency: add *tian men dong* and *mai men dong.*
3. For night sweats: add *di gu pi.*
4. For severe night sweats: add *nuo dao gen, mu li,* and *fu xiao mai.*
5. For severe spermatorrhea: add *long gu, mu li,* and *lian xu.*
6. For deficiency, cough up blood: add *bai mao gen, san qi,* and *xian he cao.*
7. For irritability insomnia: *suan zao ren* and *bai zi ren.*

## Cautions and Contraindications:
Poor appetite, loose stool, or excess fire.

## Administration:
Take with warm, light-salty water on an empty stomach.

Source: *Dan Xi Xin Fa* （丹溪心法）

# Da Chai Hu Tang 大柴胡湯
### Major Bupleurum Combination
### Major Bupleurum Decoction

## Indications:
*Shao yang* and *yang ming* combination syndromes.

Alternative chill and fever, fullness in the chest and hypochondriac, continuous vomiting, slight irritability, fullness and pain or oppression and hardness in the epigastrium, constipation, or burning diarrhea, depression or irritability.

**Tongue**:   dry tongue, yellow coating
**Pulse**:   wiry, forceful pulse

## Clinical Applications:
1. This formula is used for *shao yang* and *yang ming* organ-stage disorders.
2. The key symptoms are alternative chills and fever; fullness and distention in hypochondriac area, nausea and vomit; either diarrhea (due to accumulation of heat in the intestines) or constipation; liver and gallbladder fire causing headache, tinnitus, or palpitation with anxiety.
3. Currently used for acute pancreatitis, hepatitis, cholecystitis, pleurisy, migraine headache, trigeminal neuralgia, malignant hypertension, peptic ulcer, and malaria.

## Ingredients:
| | | | | | | |
|---|---|---|---|---|---|---|
| 1. | chai hu | 4.8 | | 5. | zhi shi | 1.8 |
| 2. | huang qin | 1.8 | | 6. | da huang | 1.2 |
| 3. | ban xia | 4.8 | | 7. | sheng jiang | 3.0 |
| 4. | bai shao | 1.8 | | 8. | da zao | 1.8 |

## Functions:
Harmonizes and releases *shao yang* stages disorder and drains internal clumping heat.

## Modifications:
1. For cases with constipation, use *sheng da huang*; with diarrhea, use *zhi da huang*.
2. For cases with jaundice, add *yin chen* and *zhi zi*.
3. For gallstone, add *jin qian cao, yu jin,* and *ji nei jin*.
4. For *yangming* dry-heat: add *shi gao* and *zhi mu*.
5. For *shaoyang* chest-heat: add *huang lian*.

## Administration:
Take with room-temp water, after meals.

Source: *Shang Han Lun* (傷寒論)

0350

# Da Cheng Qi Tang 大承氣湯
Major Rhubarb Combination
Major Order the *Qi* Decoction

## Indications:
Severe pattern of *yang ming fu* organ excess syndrome

Excess heat with severe constipation and flatulence, focal distention and abdominal fullness, abdominal pain which increased upon pressure and a tense and firm abdomen. In severe cases, there may be tidal fever, unconsciousness, delirium, and constant sweating from the extremities. It is possible there may be diarrhea that is clear, watery and green.

**Tongue:** red tongue, dry yellow or dry black coating with prickles
**Pulse:** submerged, excessive pulse; deep. Slippery and forceful

## Clinical Applications:
1. This formula treats heat accumulation in the stomach and large intestine by carrying the stomach *qi* downward, thereby forcing open the obstruction to the orderly flow of *qi*.
2. The key symptoms are *yangming* excess heat, dry stool, hardness, firmness, and fullness in the abdomen.
3. Currently used for acute simple intestinal obstruction, adhesive intestinal obstruction, ascaris intestinal obstruction, acute cholecystitis, acute pancreatitis, postoperative constipation and distention.
4. For high fever and delirium, vague and restless consciousness, and fever that turns into tidal fever without aversion to cold.

## Ingredients:
| | | | | | |
|---|---|---|---|---|---|
| 1. | mang xiao | 6.0 | 3. | zhi shi | 3.0 |
| 2. | da huang | 8.0 | 4. | hou po | 16.0 |

## Functions:
Vigorously purges heat accumulation, dispersion distention and fullness.

## Modifications:
1. For cases with *qi* deficiency, add *ren shen*.
2. For *yin* and fluid deficiency, add *xuan shen* and *sheng di huang*.
3. For high fever, severe thirst with rapid and forceful pulse, add *shi gao* and *zhi mu*.

## Cautions and Contraindications:
1. Used only when necessary for weak patients with tonics.
2. Contraindicated during pregnancy.
3. Contraindications: abdominal fullness with weak, frequent pulse; water retention or distended with *qi* stagnation.

## Administration:
Take with room-temperature water, before meals; stop taking this formula after diarrhea occurs.

Source: *Shang Han Lun* (傷寒論)

# Da Fang Feng Tang 大防風湯
Major Siler Combination
Major Saposhnikovia Decoction

## Indications:
Dysentery wind: post-dysentery, pain in the feet, weak-atrophy and unable to walk.
Crane-knee wind: Both feet and knees are swollen and painful, but only skin and bones remain in the lower extremities, unable to bend or stretch.
Later-stage low-back injuries that coexist with a deficient constitution.

## Clinical Applications:
1. This formula is for treating chronic joint pain, arthritis, myelitis, and chronic low back pain in weak physique patients.
2. The key symptoms are chronic joint pain, arthritis, myelitis, and chronic low back pain in weak physique patients.
3. Currently used in treating chronic joint pain, myelitis, hemiplegia, beriberi, or postpartum dysfunction (paralysis of lower limbs), etc.

## Ingredients:
| | | | | | |
|---|---|---|---|---|---|
| 1. | fang feng | 3.0 | 8. | niu xi | 1.5 |
| 2. | bai zhu | 3.0 | 9. | dang gui | 1.5 |
| 3. | qiang huo | 3.0 | 10. | huang qi | 0.8 |
| 4. | ren shen | 3.0 | 11. | du zhong | 0.8 |
| 5. | chuan xiong | 2.4 | 12. | shu di huang | 0.8 |
| 6. | bai shao | 1.5 | 13. | zhi gan cao | 0.8 |
| 7. | fu zi | 1.5 | 14. | sheng jiang | 0.8 |

## Functions:
Dispel wind, remove cold dampness, and expel cold air, smooth *qi*, strengthen muscles and ligament, and tonify blood and nourish blood.

## Modifications:
1. For wind-cold damp *Bi:* add *qin jiao* and *cang zhu.*
2. For joint knee pain: add *xi xin* and *fang ji.*
3. For blood stagnation pain: add *tao ren* and *hong hua.*

## Cautions
Change to *Gui Zhi Shao Yao Zhi Mu Tang* if a patient, after taking this formula, starts to lose appetite or experience diarrhea.

## Administration:
Take with warm water, before meals.

Source: *Tai Ping Hui Min He Ji Ju Fang* (太平惠民和劑局方)

# Da Huang Mu Dang Tang 大黃牡丹湯
### Rhubarb and Moutan Combination
### Rhubarb and Moutan Decoction

## Indications:
Early stage of excess intestinal abscess syndromes.

Distention and pain that increase upon palpation with rebound tenderness usually over the right lower abdomen, limited extension of the right leg due to severe pain; therefore there may be irregular intermittent fever, spontaneous sweating with aversion to cold in the initial stage.

**Tongue:**    thin yellow, greasy
**Pulse:**    slow and tight – beginning; surging and rapid – later stage

## Clinical Applications:
1. This formula is used for damp-heat accumulating in the intestines and obstructing the flow of *qi* and blood.
2. The key symptoms are intestinal abscess, swollen lower abdomen, it will be painful upon palpation, smooth urination, always fever and spontaneous sweating, recurring aversion to cold, the pulse is slow and tight, but the pus is not formed, it can be purged, when there is blood.
3. Currently used in treating acute simple appendicitis, acute pelvic inflammation and/or fallopian tube infection; or colitis, proctitis, red dysentery, uterus and inflammation of the appendages, pelvic peritonitis.

## Ingredients:
1. da huang      6.0
2. mu dan pi     3.0
3. tao ren        4.0
4. mang xiao    4.0
5. dong gua ren  6.0

## Functions:
Purges heat, breaks stagnation, disperses clumping, reducing swelling.

## Modifications:
1. For severe toxin heat, add *pu gong yin, jin yin hua, hong teng,* and *bai jiang cao.*
2. For severe blood stasis, add *chi shao* and *ru xiang, mo yao.*
3. For red-swelling heat and thirst: add *huang lian* and *huang qin.*
4. For unformed pustules: add *zao jiao ci* and *bai zhi.*
5. For fire-heat swelling: combine with *Huang Lian Jie Du Tang.*
6. For unformed swelling: combine with *Pai Nong San.*
7. For formed pustulated swelling: combine with *Tuo Li Xiao Du Yin.*

### Cautions and Contraindications:
Necrotic appendicitis, appendicitis with peritonitis, appendicitis in infants, appendicitis during pregnancy; weak and senior patients.

For a surging big pulse or cases in which pus is already formed, this purging downward may cause peritonitis.

### Administration:
Take with room-temperature water, before meals.

Source: *Jin Kwi Yao Lue* (金匱要略)

# Da Jian Zhong Tang 大建中湯
Major Zanthoxylun Combination
Major Construct the Middle Decoction

## Indications:
Weak MJ (middle jiao) *yang* and interior excess *yin*-cold syndrome.
Severe cold pain in the chest, epigastrium and abdomen where the patient cannot tolerate being touched, unable to eat due to vomiting, cold extremities, and possible borborygmus.

**Tongue:**   white, slippery coating
**Pulse:**   thin, tight or slow, wiry pulse

## Clinical Applications:
1. This formula can be used for MJ *yang* deficiency with internal excess *yin*-cold, severe abdominal cold pain with vomiting.
2. The key symptoms are water retention between the diaphragm, fullness short of breath, focal distention below the heart.
3. Currently used for gastritis, gastric ulcer, duodenal ulcer, chronic pancreatitis, chronic cholecystitis and intestinal spasms.
4. For paroxysmal hypermotility of intestines with deficient cold symptoms and severe abdominal pain. And abdominal pain, gastroptosis, and achalasia caused by roundworms. It can also be applied to gastric dilatation.

## Ingredients:
1. chuan jiao     6.0
2. gan jiang     12.0
3. ren shen     6.0
4. yi tang     3.0

## Functions:
Warms the middle, tonifies MJ, guides rebellious *qi* downward and alleviates pain.

## Modifications:
1. For cold abdomen: add *fu ling* and *bai zhu.*
2. For vomit water fluid: add *ban xia* and *fu ling.*
3. For chest cold pain: add *fu zi* and *xi xin.*
4. For abdominal cold-pain: combine with *Li Zhong Tang.*
5. For vomit with abdominal pain: combine with *Ban Xia Xie Xin Tang.*

## Cautions and Contraindications:
1. Damp-heat or *yin* and blood deficiency.
2. Be cautious -- over-taking this formula may cause dry cough, edema or vomit.

## Administration:
Take with warm or hot water, before meals.

Source: *Jin Kwi Yao Lue* (金匱要略)

# Da Qin Jiao Tang 大秦艽湯
## Major Gentiana Macrophylla Combination
### Major Large Gentian Decoction

**Indications:**

Early stage of wind evil attacks the channels and collaterals or wind-stroke syndrome.

The eyes and mouth are awry, stiffness of the tongue, inability to move limbs or numbness and lack of sensation in the hands and feet, which is often accompanied by chills and fever, muscle spasms and joint ache.

| | |
|---|---|
| **Tongue:** | yellow or white coating |
| **Pulse:** | either floating and tight or wiry and thin |

**Clinical Applications:**

1. This is a formula used for the early and middle stages of wind stroke in the channels.
2. The key symptoms are hand and foot atrophy or paralysis caused by stroke, stiff tongue and aphasia.
3. This formula may be used to treat Bell's palsy, thrombotic strokes and rheumatoid arthritis.
4. Also used in treating anemic sensory motor nerve palsy.

**Ingredients:**

| | | | | | |
|---|---|---|---|---|---|
| 1. | qin jiao | 3.0 | 9. | fang feng | 1.5 |
| 2. | shi gao | 3.0 | 10. | huang qin | 1.5 |
| 3. | zhi gan cao | 1.5 | 11. | bai zhu | 1.5 |
| 4. | chuan xiong | 1.5 | 12. | bai zhi | 1.5 |
| 5. | dang gui | 1.5 | 13. | fu ling | 1.5 |
| 6. | bai shao | 1.5 | 14. | sheng di huang | 1.5 |
| 7. | qiang huo | 1.5 | 15. | shu di huang | 1.5 |
| 8. | du huo | 1.5 | 16. | xi xin | 0.8 |

**Functions:**

Disperses wind, clears heat, nourishes and invigorates the blood.

**Modifications:**

For no internal heat, omit *huang qin, shi gao,* and *sheng di.*

**Cautions and Contraindications:**

It should not be used in wind-stroke due to internal wind.

**Administration:**

Take with warm water, before meals.

Source: *Yi Fang Ji Jie* (醫方集解)

# Da Qing Long Tang 大青龍湯
### Major Blue Dragon Combination
### Major Bluegreen Dragon Decoction

## Indications:
For external wind-cold with internal heat.

Symptoms include fever, aversion to cold, vexation, cough, asthmatic breathing, absence of perspiration.

**Tongue:**   thin white coating
**Pulse:**   floating and tight

## Clinical Applications:
1. This formula is for treating *tai-yang* stage disorders that present with exterior cold and interior heat.
2. The key symptoms are for patients who suffer from deficient *yin* or middle burner *qi*.
3. Currently used in treating acute bronchitis, pneumonia, and cough and wheezing associated with an exterior wind-cold pattern. For those who have severe skin diseases with severe congestion or rash such as urticaria and pruritus.
4. Used for influenza, acute pneumonia, measles and other febrile diseases. Meningitis, acute arthritis, erysipelas, edema or acute nephritis and edema, even ascites, etc.

## Ingredients:
1. ma huang    4.5
2. gui zhi    1.5
3. gan cao    1.5
4. xing ren    3.8
5. sheng jiang    2.3
6. da zao    2.3
7. shi gao    7.5

## Functions:
Promote sweat, resolve the exterior, clear heat, and expel irritability.

## Modifications:
1. For headache and body ache: add *chuan xiong* and *bai zhi*.
2. For fever and body fatigue: add *mai men dong* and *wu wei zi*.
3. For lung heat and thirst: combine with *Xie Bai San*.

## Cautions and Contraindications:
Weak or soft pulse with spontaneous sweating.

## Administration:
Take with warm water to induce slight sweating; stop the formula if sweating heavily.

Source: *Shang Han Lun* (傷寒論)

# Dang Gui Bu Xue Tang 當歸補血湯
Tangkuei and Astragalus Combination
Tangkuei Decoction to Tonify the Blood

## Indications:
Blood deficiency heat syndrome.

Hot sensations in the muscles, red face, irritability, thirst with a desire for warm beverages, or sores refuse to heal for a long period of time after ulceration.

**Tongue:**    pale tongue
**Pulse:**    flooding, large, and deficient

## Clinical Applications:
1. This formula treats the consumptive fatigue due to internal injury, weakness of source *qi* and deficiency of blood.
2. This formula is also used for bleeding associated with deficient *qi* being unable to control the blood, and the *yin*-type ulcers caused by weakness of protective *qi* and blood that inhibits the normal healing process.
3. Currently used for anemia, allergic purpura, thrombocytopenic purpura, dysfunctional uterine bleeding, leukopenia, non-healing sores and postpartum fevers.

## Ingredients:
1. dang gui    4.0
2. huang qi    20.0

## Functions:
Tonify the *qi* and generate the blood.

## Modifications:
During periods, or postpartum cold with fever, headache: add *cong bai, dou shi, sheng jiang,* and *da zao*.

## Cautions and Contraindications:
Tidal fever from *yin* deficiency.

## Administration:
Take with warm water, before meals.

Source: *Nei Wai Shang Bian Huo Lun* (內外傷辨惑論)

# Dang Gui Liu Huang Tang 當歸六黃湯
Tangkuei and Six Yellow Combination
Tangkuei and Six-Yellow Decoction

## Indications:
*Yin* deficiency with excess fire and night sweats syndrome.

Fever, night sweats, red face, dry mouth, and parched lips, irritability, dry stools, and dark and scanty urine.

**Tongue**:     red, dry
**Pulse**:      rapid

## Clinical Applications:
1. This is a formula used for night sweats caused by *yin* deficiency with excess fire, particularly combined with night sweats, red face, irritability and dark and scanty urine with rapid pulse.
2. Currently used for tuberculosis, diabetes, hyperthyroidism, perimenopausal syndromes, and nervous exhaustion.

## Ingredients:
1. dang gui         3.5
2. sheng di huang   3.5
3. shu di huang     3.5
4. huang qin        3.5
5. huang bai        3.5
6. huang lian       3.5
7. huang qi         7.0

## Functions:
Nourishes *yin* and drains fire, stabilizes exterior and stops sweating.

## Modifications:
1. For severe sweating, add *ma huang gen* and *fu xiao mai*.
2. For *yin* deficiency without excess fire, remove *huang lian* and *huang qin* and add *zhi mu*.

## Cautions and Contraindications:
Sp and St deficiency, and/or diarrhea with poor appetite.

## Administration:
Take with warm water, before meals.

Source: *Lan Shi Mi Cang* (蘭室秘藏)

# Dang Gui Long Hui Wan 當歸龍薈丸
### Tangkuei, Gentiana, and Aloe Formula
### Tangkuei, Gentian, and Aloe Pill

## Indications:
Liver and gallbladder excess fire.

Palpitations, constipation and irritability, thirst.

## Clinical Applications:
1. This formula is for treating liver and gallbladder excess heat.
2. The key symptoms are frightened, irritability, itching, and constipation.
3. Currently used in treating acute rheumatic fever, hepatitis cholangitis, gastritis enteritis, pharyngitis, otitis, cystitis, urethritis, vaginitis, fever, swelling and pain, irritability and thirst, pruritus, cholelithiasis.

## Ingredients:
1. dang gui          3.00
2. long dan cao      3.00
3. zhi zi            3.00
4. huang qin         3.00
5. huang lian        3.00
6. huang bai         3.00
7. da huang          1.50
8. lu hui            1.50
9. mu xiang          0.75
10. qing dai         1.50

## Functions:
Purging excess liver and gallbladder heat, smooth the bowel movement.

## Modifications:
1. For irritable heat, thirst: add *mai men dong* and *wu wei zi*.
2. For difficulty urination: add *mu tong* and *sheng di*.
3. For severe constipation: add *zhi shi* and *hou po*.

## Cautions and Contraindications:
Pregnancy, or loose stool or diarrhea.

## Administration:
Take with warm water, before meals.

Source: *Dan Xi Xin Fa* （丹溪心法）

# Dang Gui Nian Tong Tang 當歸拈痛湯
## Tangkuei and Anemarrhena Combination
## Tangkuei Decoction to Pry Out Pain

## Indications:
Damp-heat attach the joints.

Whole-body joint irritable pain, heaviness on shoulder and upper back, discomforted in chest and diaphragm, swelling pain in lower legs and ankle.

All wind-damp-heat toxins, for all the sores and wounds have oozing fluids and itching or pain.

## Clinical Applications:
1. This formula is for treating damp-heat in the joints.
2. The key symptoms are whole-body joint pain, heat and pain of limbs and joints and itching swelling sores.
3. Currently used in treating acute rheumatism numbness, redness, beriberi swelling and pain, and any surgical sores, swelling and pain.

## Ingredients:
| 1. | dang gui | 1.0 | 9. | ge gen | 1.0 |
|----|----------|-----|-----|--------|-----|
| 2. | qiang huo | 2.5 | 10. | cang zhu | 1.0 |
| 3. | gan cao | 2.5 | 11. | bai zhu | 1.5 |
| 4. | huang qin | 2.5 | 12. | ze xie | 1.5 |
| 5. | yin chen hao | 2.5 | 13. | zhu ling | 1.5 |
| 6. | ren shen | 1.0 | 14. | fang feng | 1.5 |
| 7. | ku shen | 1.0 | 15. | zhi mu | 1.5 |
| 8. | sheng ma | 1.0 | | | |

## Functions:
Expel wind, eliminate damp, clear heat and stop pain.

## Modifications:
1. For severe red-swelling-heat pain: add *huang lian* and *shi gao*.
2. For whole body irritable pain: add *gui shi* and *shao yao*.
3. For skin itching pain: add *jin yin hua* and *lian qiao*.
4. For all sores, carbuncles swelling pain: combine with *Tuo Li Xiao Du Tang*.
5. For damp-heat swelling pain: combine with *Huang Lian Jie Du Tang*.
6. For a painful period: combine with *Si Wu Tang*.

## Administration:
Take with warm water, any time.

Source: *Li Dong Yuan Fang* (李東垣方)

# Dang Gui San 當歸散
Tangkuei Formula
Tangkuei Powder

## Indications:
Pregnancy blood deficiency with heat.

Unstable fetuses, or prone to miscarriage or difficult labor.

## Clinical Applications:
1. This formula is for treating pregnancy or postpartum weak and feeble conditions.
2. The key symptoms are blood deficiency heat, irritability, and thirst.
3. Currently used in treating habitual miscarriage, early labor, hysteria, abdominal pain or soreness of lower back.

## Ingredients:
1. dang gui        5.0
2. huang qin       5.0
3. bai shao        5.0
4. chuan xiong     5.0
5. bai zhu         2.5

## Functions:
Clear heat, expel dampness, nourishing blood, calm fetus.

## Modifications:
1. For wind-cold headache: add *chai hu* and *gui zhi.*
2. For lower back soreness and lower abdominal pain: add *zhi shi* and *xiang fu.*
3. For thirst irritable heat: add *huang lian* and *gan cao.*
4. For postpartum: combine with *Sheng Hua Tang.*

## Administration:
Take with warm water, before meals.

Source: *Jin Kwi Yao Lue* (金匱要略)

# Dang Gui Shao Yao San 當歸芍藥散
### Tangkuei and Peony Formula

## Indications:

Abdominal pain due to disharmony between the liver and spleen: mild pain of the abdomen pain that decreases with pressure, dizziness, difficult urination, and slight edema of the lower limbs. Such symptoms may occur during pregnancy.

**Tongue:** pink-red with white and greasy coating
**Pulse:** soggy, soft, and slow

## Clinical Applications:

1. This formula treats pain due to a mixed pattern of deficiency and excess where liver and spleen deficiency are complicated by blood stasis and accumulating dampness.
2. Currently used for dysmenorrhea, habitual miscarriage, postpartum depression, perimenopausal syndrome, pregnancy edema, polycystic ovaries, and infertility.
3. This formula has also been used for hypotension, benign prostatic hypertrophy, chronic appendicitis, chronic hepatitis, cholecystitis, and senile dementia.

## Ingredients:

| | | | | | |
|---|---|---|---|---|---|
| 1. | shao yao | 15.0 | 4. | bai zhu | 6.0 |
| 2. | dang gui | 5.0 | 5. | fu ling | 6.0 |
| 3. | chuan xiong | 5.0 | 6. | ze xie | 12.0 |

## Functions:

Nourishes the blood, regulates liver *qi*, strengthens the spleen, and resolves dampness.

## Modifications:

1. For kidney deficiency lower back soreness, add *shu di, du zhong,* and *sang ji sheng.*
2. For spleen deficiency loose stools, add *dang sheng, shan yao,* and *bai bian dou.*
3. For liver *qi* stagnation, add *chai hu* and *xiang fu.*
4. For prostatitis, add *dao chi san.*
5. For abdominal cramping pain, add *xiang fu* and *ai ye.*
6. For dizziness with headache, add *bai zhi* and *huang qi.*
7. For irritability and heat, add *huang qin* and *huang lian.*

## Cautions and Contraindications:

Caution during pregnancy, particularly in mothers who have deficient and weak kidney *qi.*

## Administration:

Take with warm water, after meals.

Source: *Jin Gui Yao Lüe* (金匱要略)

# Dang Gui Si Ni Tang 當歸四逆湯
### Tangkuei and Jujube Combination
### Tangkuei Decoction for Frigid Extremities

## Indications:
Lack of *yang qi* and blood deficiency syndrome.

Long-standing cold hands and feet that are cold to the touch and feel very cold to the patient. Cold invading the channels.

Pain in the lower back, thighs, legs, and feet due to cold invading the channels with blood stagnation and deficiency.

**Tongue**:     pale, white coating
**Pulse**:      submerged, thin pulse

## Clinical Applications:
1. This formula can be used for extremely cold hands and feet with a pulse that is thin to the point of being imperceptible.
2. The key symptoms are anemia, low back pain, spasm, sore limbs and coldness in limbs.
3. Currently used for thromboangitis, Raynaud's disease, rheumatoid arthritis, fibromyalgia, sciatica, peptic ulcer, chronic urticaria and frostbite.
4. A preventive agent for people who are prone to frostbite, can warm and move blood and improve peripheral circulation. Abdominal pain caused by the uterus and its appendages, the waist or kidney seems to be penetrated by cold wind; bloating and gassy under cold weather, and for intermittent diarrhea or early morning diarrhea.

## Ingredients:
| | | | | | |
|---|---|---|---|---|---|
| 1. dang gui | 4.0 | 4. xi xin | 4.0 | 7. mu tong | 2.7 |
| 2. bai shao | 4.0 | 5. gan cao | 2.7 | | |
| 3. gui zhi | 4.0 | 6. da zao | 2.7 | | |

## Functions:
Warms the channels, disperses cold, nourishes blood and unblocks the blood vessels.

## Modifications:
1. For cases with vomiting, add *wu zhu yu* and *sheng jiang*.
2. For pain in lower back and lower extremities due to blood deficiency and cold coagulation, add *xu duan, niu xi, ji xue teng,* and *mu gua*.
3. For hernia disorders due to cold, add *wu yao, xiao hui xiang,* and *gao liang jiang*.
4. For during period or postpartum: add *chuan xiong* and *di huang*.
5. For deficiency cold and limb frigid cold: combine with *Li Zhong Tang*.
6. For post-illness limbs frigid cold: combine with *Xiao Chai Hu Tang*.
7. For female frigid cold limbs: combine with *Si Wu Tang*.

## Cautions and Contraindications:

*Yin* deficiency heat.

**Administration:**
Take with warm or hot water, before meals.

Source: *Shang Han Lun* (傷寒論)

# Dang Gui Yin Zi 當歸飲子
## Tangkuei and Tribulus Combination
## Tangkuei Drink

## Indications:
Chronic itching skin due to blood deficiency syndrome.

Itching skin that worsens at night and may or may not be accompanied by rash and flaking skin.

**Tongue:**     pale, thin coating
**Pulse:**      wiry and thin.

## Clinical Applications:
1. This is a formula used for the external wind that has lodged in the body for a long time and has damaged the blood, or for those with a blood-deficient constitution who contract a wind pathogen leading to itchiness that worsens at night.
2. The key symptoms are skin itching caused by blood deficiency, blood dryness or wind-heat.
3. Currently used for treating dry skin caused by anemia, red and dry-itching skin or elderly dryness.
4. Scabies, chronic eczema, and other dry skin diseases, pustules with few secretions, with dryness and itching.

## Ingredients:
| | | | | | |
|---|---|---|---|---|---|
| 1. | dang gui | 2.0 | 6. | sheng di huang | 2.0 |
| 2. | bai shao (wine fried) | 2.0 | 7. | he shou wu | 2.0 |
| 3. | chuan xiong | 2.0 | 8. | jing jie | 2.0 |
| 4. | bai ji li | 2.0 | 9. | huang qi | 1.0 |
| 5. | fang feng | 2.0 | 10. | gan cao | 1.0 |

## Functions:
Nourishes the blood, moistens dryness, disperses wind and stops itching.

## Modifications:
1. For cases with more heat, add *huang qin, lian qiao,* and *zi hua di ding.*
2. For case with oozy pus, add *yi yi ren, che qian zi,* and *zhi zi.*

## Cautions and Contraindications:
Excess damp-heat.

## Administration:
Take with warm water, before meals.

Source: *Yi Zong Jin Jian* (醫宗金鑑)

# Dao Chi San 導赤散
Rehmannia and Armandi Formula
Guide Out the Red Powder

## Indications:
Heat in the heart and small intestine channels.

Irritability with a sensation of heat in the chest, thirst with a desire to drink cold beverages, red face, possible sores around the mouth and tongue.

**Tongue:**     red tongue
**Pulse:**       rapid pulse

## Clinical Applications:
1. This formula is used in treating urinary problems due to heat transferred from heart to small intestine; it may be used for dark, scanty, rough, and painful urination, or even clearly visible blood in the urine.
2. The key symptoms are mouth ulcers, red and hesitant urination, heat-*lin* syndromes.
3. Currently used for stomatitis, nightmares, morbid night crying of babies due to heart heat, urethritis, cystitis and acute UTI.
4. Acute cystitis, urethritis, red and difficul urination, and painful urination. Gastrointestinal mucositis with loose stools. Use this formula to guide out the heat from urine.

## Ingredients:
| | | | | |
|---|---|---|---|---|
| 1. sheng di | 6.0 | | 3. gan cao | 6.0 |
| 2. mu tong | 6.0 | | 4. dan zhu ye | 6.0 |

## Functions:
Clears heat and brings down fire, cools blood, clears heart fire, nourishes the *Yin* and promotes urination.

## Modifications:
1. For cases with excess heat, add *huang lian.*
2. For heart fire transfers to the small intestine channel, urinary difficulty, add *che qian zi* and *chi fu ling.*
3. For severe ulceration in the mouth and tongue: add *jing yin hua* and *lian qiao.*
4. For fever and thirst: add *hua shi* and *shi gao.*
5. For bad breath and tongue sores: combine with *Gan Lu Yin.*
6. For edema with difficulty urination: combine with *Wu Ling Sa*n.

## Cautions and Contraindications:
Spleen and stomach deficiency.

## Administration:
Take with warm water, before meals.

Source: *Xiao Er Yao Zheng Zhi Jue* (小兒藥證直訣)

# Dao Shui Fu Ling Tang 導水茯苓湯
## Poria, Atractylodes, and Areca Combination

### Indications:
Whole body edema.

Heavy breathing, hard to lie down, no desire for eating or drinking and difficulty urinating.

### Clinical Applications:
This formula is for treating whole body edema with difficult urination.
1. The key symptoms are water edema, fullness in the chest, difficulty breathing and hastened urination.
2. Currently used in treating chronic nephritis, edema, skin edema, ascites, cardiac edema, wheezing; swelling all over the body with difficulty to urinate.

### Ingredients:
1. chi fu ling       4.8
2. mai men dong   4.8
3. ze xie             4.8
4. bai zhu            4.8
5. sang bai pi       1.6
6. zi su ye           1.6
7. bing lang         1.6
8. mu gua            1.6
9. da fu pi           1.2
10. chen pi           1.2
11. sha ren          1.2
12. mu xiang        1.2
13. deng xin cao    1.0

### Functions:
To promote *qi* to transform dampness, move water to relieve swelling, relieve lung and harmonize spleen.

### Modifications:
1. For deficiency water edema: add *di gu pi* and *fu ling*.
2. For fullness of cough, asthma: add *ho pu* and *xing ren*.
3. For difficulty urination: add *mu tong* and *che qian zi*.

### Administration:
Take with warm water, before meals.

Source: *Qi Xiao Lian Fang* (奇效良方)

# Ding Chuan Tang 定喘湯
Ephedra and Ginkgo Combination
Arrest Wheezing Decoction

## Indications:
Asthma due to exterior wind-cold constraint and interior phlegm-heat syndrome.

Coughing and wheezing with copious, thick, and yellow sputum, labored breathing, and slight aversion to wind-cold.

**Tongue:**     greasy, yellow coating
**Pulse:**      slippery, rapid

## Clinical Applications:
1. This is a formula used for the patients with constitutional excessive phlegm after contracting wind-cold and the constrained lung *qi* transforms into heat.
2. The key symptoms are heat syndrome with coughing and asthma.
3. Currently used for chronic bronchitis, bronchial asthma, and bronchiolitis.
4. Common cold wind, cough and shortness of breath.

## Ingredients:
| | | | | | | |
|---|---|---|---|---|---|---|
| 1. | ma huang | 4.0 | | 6. | ban xia | 4.0 |
| 2. | bai guo | 4.0 | | 7. | sang bai pi | 4.0 |
| 3. | xing ren | 2.0 | | 8. | huang qin | 2.0 |
| 4. | zi su zi | 2.5 | | 9. | gan cao | 1.5 |
| 5. | kuan dong hua | 4.0 | | | | |

## Functions:
Facilitates the lung *qi*, clears heat, transforms the phlegm and calms asthma.

## Modifications:
1. For a severe stifling sensation in the chest, add *hou po* and *zhi shi.*
2. For thick, yellow sputum that is difficult to expectorate, add *gua lou pi* and *qian hu.*
3. For rapid *qi* asthma: add *hou po* and *bei me.*
4. For watery phlegm cough: add *fu ling* and *chen pi.*
5. For wind-cold asthma: combine with *Ma Huang Tang.*
6. For damp-heat asthma: combine with *Liang Ge San.*
7. For watery phlegm asthma: combine with *Er Chen Tang.*

## Cautions and Contraindications:
Chronic lung and kidney *yin* deficiency asthma.

## Administration:
Take with warm water, after meals.

Source: *Zheng Zhi Zhun Sheng* (證治準繩)

# Ding Xian Wan 定癇丸
Gastrodia and Amber Combination
Arrest Seizure Pill

## Indications:
Phlegm-heat with liver wind seizures syndromes.

Recurrent vertigo, sudden loss of consciousness with falling down, upward rolling of the eyes, deviation of the mouth, spitting up of mucus with loud, raspy sound, and in severe cases, convulsions with shrieking sound or incontinence of stool or urine.

| | |
|---|---|
| **Tongue:** | white greasy coating |
| **Pulse:** | wiry, slippery pulse |

## Clinical Applications:
1. This formula is used for epilepsy and/or seizures.
2. The key symptoms are internal heat and phlegm that give rise to seizures that occur suddenly and cause the person to lose balance and fall.
3. Currently used in treating primary and secondary epilepsy, or multi-infarct dementia.
4. The condition with epileptic-type disorders, dizziness (with falling), schizophrenia, hysteria, and compulsive disorders when these are part of a pattern of phlegm obstruction of the channels and connection vessels.

## Ingredients:
| | | | | | |
|---|---|---|---|---|---|
| 1. dan nan xing | 1.0 | 7. dan shen | 4.0 | 13. fu shen | 2.0 |
| 2. ban xia | 2.0 | 8. shi chang pu | 1.0 | 14. deng xin cao | 1.0 |
| 3. chen pi | 1.5 | 9. quan xie | 1.0 | 15. yuan zhi | 1.5 |
| 4. fu ling | 2.0 | 10. jiang can | 1.0 | 16. sheng jiang zhi | 1.0 |
| 5. zhe bei mu | 2.0 | 11. tian ma | 2.0 | | |
| 6. mai men dong | 4.0 | 12. hu po | 1.0 | | |

## Functions:
Scours out phlegm, opens the orifices, clears heat, extinguishes wind, alleviates convulsions.

## Modifications:
1. For constipation, add *da huang* and *mang xiao.*
2. For persistent convulsions, add *gou teng* and *ling yang jiao.*
3. For weak constitution, add *ren shen.*
4. For "yin:deficiency", add *gou teng.*
5. For heat signs, add *shi gao, zhi mu,* and *mu dan pi.*
6. For liver *qi* binding, add *yu jin* and *bai shao.*
7. For supporting the righteous *qi:* add *ren shen* 9g.
8. For completion of epilepsy: *He Che Wan.*

## Cautions and Contraindications:
This formula focuses on removing phlegm, extinguishing wind, and treating the symptoms first. Once the epilepsy is calmed down, it should still expel phlegm, extinguish wind, and support the righteous root and strengthen the body. Pay attention to diet and consolidate the mind to achieve full results.

## Special Note:
People with epilepsy have a sudden onset, vertigo and fall to the ground, unconscious, and even convulsions, slanting eyes, phlegm and salivation, and yelling as animal sounds. The doctor listens to the five sounds and divides them into five internal organs. For example, those who bark like dogs have issues with lungs; those who bleat like goats have issues with livers; neighing like horses is heart; lowing like ox is spleen; snorting like pigs is kidneys. Although there are differences in the five internal organs, for phlegm and salivation, one is the main reason for *Ding Xian Wan*.

## Administration:
Take with warm water, before meals.

Source: *Yi Xue Xin Wu* (醫學心悟)

# Du Huo Ji Sheng Tang 獨活寄生湯
### Tuhuo and Loranthus Combination
### Angelica Pubescens and Sangjisheng Decoction

## Indications:
Chronic *Bi* syndrome, damp obstructing the channels due to liver, kidney, *qi* and blood deficiency.

Heavy and fixed pain in lower back and extremities with weakness, stiffness, and numbness, limited range of motion; aversions to cold, better with warmth, palpitations or shortness of breath.

**Tongue:**     pale, white coating
**Pulse:**     thin, weak, slow

## Clinical Applications:
1. This formula is used for chronic *Bi* syndrome with righteous *qi* deficiency. This condition is commonly due to cold-predominant painful obstruction, which is indicated by the fixed pain.
2. The key symptoms are cold and pain in the lower back and knees and limited movement.
3. Currently used in treating rheumatoid arthritis, osteoarthritis, chronic lower back pain, sciatica, periarthritis of the shoulder, lumbar disc disease and lumbar muscle strain.

## Ingredients:
| | | | | | | | |
|---|---|---|---|---|---|---|---|
| 1. | du huo | 3.0 | 6. | rou gui | 2.0 | 11. chuan xiong | 2.0 |
| 2. | sang ji sheng | 2.0 | 7. | du zhong | 2.0 | 12. sheng di huang | 2.0 |
| 3. | fang feng | 2.0 | 8. | niu xi | 2.0 | 13. ren shen | 2.0 |
| 4. | qin jiao | 2.0 | 9. | dang gui | 2.0 | 14. fu ling | 2.0 |
| 5. | xi xin | 2.0 | 10. | bai shao | 2.0 | 15. gan cao | 2.0 |

## Functions:
Expels wind-damp, disperses painful obstruction, benefits liver and kidney and tonifies *qi* and blood.

## Modifications:
1. For severe pain, add *chuan wu, bai hua she, di long,* and *hong hua.*
2. For severe cold attacks, add *fu zi* and *gan jiang.*
3. For severe damp evil attacks, omit *shu di,* add *fang ji, yi yi ren* and *cang zhu.*
4. For mild righteous *qi* deficiency, reduce dosage of *ren shen* and *shu di.*
5. For severe soreness in lower back and knee pain: add *qiang huo* and *xu duan.*
6. For cold-*Bi* weakness: add *huang qi* and *bai zhu.*

## Cautions and Contraindications:
Excess damp-heat *Bi* syndrome; and caution for hypertension or pregnancy.

## Administration:
Take with warm water, as needed.

Source: *Qian Jin Fang* (千金方)

# Dun Sou San 頓嗽散
## Mulberry Bark and Platycodon Formula
## Immediately Relieve Cough Powder

### Indications:
For heat cough or dry cough.

Febrile, spasmodic dry cough with less phlegm, or agitated strong cough.

### Clinical Applications:
1. This formula is for treating the cough caused by heat syndromes.
2. The key symptoms are spasmodic dry cough with less phlegm or agitated strong cough.
3. Currently used in treating common cough, whooping cough, and bronchitis.

### Ingredients:
1. shi gao          6.0
2. chai hu          6.0
3. jie geng         3.0
4. sang ji sheng    3.0
5. huang qin        3.0
6. gan cao          1.2
7. zhi zi           1.2

### Functions:
Clear lungs, release the heat, transform phlegm, and stop the cough.

### Modifications:
1. For excess liver fire: add *mu dan pi, sheng di huang* and *bai shao*.
2. For blood in the phlegm: add *sheng di huang* and *di gu pi*.
3. For a combination of external symptoms, aversion to cold: add *ma huang* and *xing ren*.

### Cautions and Contraindications:
Cold cough with clear watery phlegm.

### Administration:
Take with warm water, after meals.

Source: *Zheng Zhi Zhun Sheng* (證治準繩)

# Er Chen Tang 二陳湯
Citrus and Pinellia Combination
Two-Cured Decoction

## Indications:
Damp-phlegm accumulation in middle *jiao*, causing coughing. Coughing with copious, white phlegm which is easily expectorated, distention and stifling sensation in the chest and diaphragm, palpitations, retching, nausea or vomiting, or dizziness.

**Tongue:**  thick white coating
**Pulse:**  slippery pulse

## Clinical Applications:
1. This formula is widely used for phlegm-fluid syndrome caused by water accumulation in the stomach.
2. Assists *qi* in the spleen and stomach in the transformation and transportation (T/T) of fluids.
3. The key symptoms are coughing with white phlegm that is easily expectorated; phlegm obstructs the *qi* in the middle *jiao*, which may cause nausea or retching.
4. Currently used in treating upper respiratory tract infections, nausea, vomiting, dizziness, *qi* stagnation, hangovers, goiters, chronic gastritis, peptic ulcers and Meniere's disease.

## Ingredients:
1. ban xia       6.0       3. fu ling       6.0       5. sheng jiang       1.5
2. chen pi       6.0       4. zhi gan cao   3.0       6. wu mei           1.5

## Functions:
Dries dampness, transforms phlegm, regulates *qi*, and harmonizes the MJ (middle jiao).

## Modifications:
1. For wind-phlegm, add *zhi nan xing* and *zhi fu zi.*
2. For heat-phlegm, add *huang qin* and *gua lou.*
3. For cold-phlegm, add *gan jiang* and *xi xin.*
4. For damp-phlegm, add *cang zhu* and *hou po.*
5. For food-phlegm, add *shan zha, mai ya,* and *shen qu.*
6. For hangover vomit: add *sha ren* and *wu mei.*
7. For elderly pulmonary emphysema, add *zi wan, kuan dong hua,* and *sha ren.*
8. For general vomiting and abdominal pain: add *huang lian tang.*
9. For pregnancy morning sickness: add *sha ren, lian qiao,* and *huang qin.*
10. For any stagnations from food, combine with *Yue Ju Wan.*
11. For indigestion, combine with *Ping Wei San.*

## Note:
All phlegm is caused by dampness. *Er Chen Tang* is the basic formula to dry internal dampness. Wind phlegm: color is greenish-shiny; cold phlegm: opaque in color (clear-watery); damp phlegm: white color; heat phlegm: yellow color.

## Administration:
Take with warm water between meals; if the person has nausea, cold water may be used.

Source: *Tai Ping Hui Min He Ji Ju Fang* (太平惠民和劑局方)

# Er Miao San 二妙散
## Two-Marvel Powder

## Indications:

Damp-heat flowing downward; pain in the sinews and bones; or red, swollen, hot and painful knees and feet; or weakness and atrophy in the lower extremities or thick, yellow and foul-smelling vaginal discharge; or sores on the lower extremities due to dampness and scanty and yellow urine.

**Tongue:**   yellow, greasy coating
**Pulse:**   slippery rapid

## Clinical Applications:

1. This formula is commonly used for damp heat in the lower *jiao*, causing painful sinews and swollen joints.
2. The key symptoms are scanty and yellow urine.
3. Currently used in treating arthritis, UTI, vaginitis, cervicitis, beriberi, gouty arthritis, and scrotal eczema.

## Ingredients:

1. huang bai      10.0
2. cang zhu      10.0

## Functions:

Clears heat and dries dampness.

## Modifications:

1. For severe symptoms of atrophy add: *xi xian cao, mu gua, wu jia pi,* and *bei xie.*
2. For sores on the lower extremities, add: *yi yi ren, mu gua, bing lang,* and *chi xiao dou.*
3. For yellow, foul-smelling vaginal discharge, add *tu fu ling* and *qian shi.*
4. Associated Formulas:
   - ***San Miao Wan*** 三妙丸 (Three-Marvel Powder) (***Er Miao San + niu xi***):
     1. **Indications**: For damp-heat in the lower *jiao* with numbness, weakness and burning sensation in the feet.
   - ***Si Miao Wan*** 四妙丸 (Four-Marvel Powder) (***San Miao Wan + yi yi ren***):
     1. **Indications**: For atrophy due to damp-heat. This formulation stretches the sinews and strengthens the bones.

## Cautions and Contraindications:

Not to be used in the presence of excessive lung heat or liver or kidney deficiency.

## Administration:

Take with warm water, between meals.

Source: *Dan Xi Xin Fa* (丹溪心法)

# Er Xian Tang 二仙湯
Curculigo and Epimedium Combination
Two Immortals Decoction

## Indications:
Both kidney *yin* and *yang* deficiencies with a flaring-up of the *ming men* fire syndrome.

Menopause symptoms including hypertension, irregular menstruation, hot flashes, night sweats, nervousness, fatigue, sluggishness, depression, irritability, insomnia, heart palpitations, and frequent urination.

**Tongue:**    thin, yellow coating
**Pulse:**    thin, rapid pulse

## Clinical Applications:
1. This formula nourishes kidney *yin* and tonifies kidney *yang*. It also purges deficiency fire, most often seen in the elderly and those suffering from menopause.
2. Currently used for perimenopausal syndrome, essential hypertension, polycystic kidneys, renal vascular disease, hyperthyroidism, UTI and hypofunction of the anterior pituitary.

## Ingredients:
| | | |
|---|---|---|
| 1. xian mao | 20.0 |
| 2. xian ling pi (yin yang huo) | 20.0 |
| 3. ba ji tian | 15.0 |
| 4. huang bai | 15.0 |
| 5. zhi mu | 15.0 |
| 6. dang gui | 15.0 |

## Functions:
Warms the kidney *yang*, tonifies the essence, drains the kidney fire and regulates *chong* and *ren* channels.

## Modifications:
1. For high blood pressure related to menopause: add *du zhong*.
2. For hot flashes: add *yin chai hu* and *hu huang lian*.
3. For insomnia: add *yuan zhi* and *suan zao ren*.

## Administration:
Take with warm or salt water, before meals.

Source: *Fu Chan Ke Xue* (婦產科學)

# Er Zhi Wan 二至丸

Ligustrum and Eclipta Combination
Two-Ultimate Pill

## Indications:
For the treatment of kidney and liver *yin* deficiency syndromes.

May also be used for patients with bitter taste and dry mouth, dizziness, insomnia with vivid dreams, soreness and weakness in the knees and lower back, spermatorrhea, nocturnal emission, spontaneous sweating, night sweats, and premature gra*ying* or loss of hair.

| | |
|---|---|
| **Tongue:** | red, crimson coating |
| **Pulse:** | thin, rapid pulse |

## Clinical Applications:
1. This formula is widely used both by itself and as an addition to other formulas when liver and kidney *yin* need to be tonified.
2. Currently, it is considered by some to be superior in treating premature gra*ying* or loss of hair, essential hypertension, systemic lupus erythematosus (SLE), and neurasthenia.

## Ingredients:
1. nü zhen zi      50.0
2. han lian cao    50.0

## Functions:
Tonifies the kidney and benefits the liver.

## Modifications:
1. For a slightly stronger effect, add *sang shen zi.*
2. For pain in the lower back: add *du zhong* and *xu duan.*
3. For premature gra*ying* or hair loss: add *he shou wu.*
4. For sleep disturbance: add *suan zao ren*, and *he huan hua.*

## Administration:
Take with warm water or wine before meals.

Source: *Yi Fang Ji Jie* (醫方集解)

# Fu Yuan Huo Xue Tang 復元活血湯
Tangkuei and Persica Combination
Revive Health by Invigorating the Blood Decoction

## Indications:
For the treatment of physical traumatic injury syndrome.

Excruciating pain associated with traumatic injury, especially in the chest or flanks, hypochondria.

| | |
|---|---|
| **Tongue:** | Red, crimson coating |
| **Pulse:** | Thin, rapid |

## Clinical Applications:
1. This formula is used in treating the trauma syndrome with severe hypochondriac pain with bruising and swelling.
2. Currently used for traumatic injuries, intercostal neuralgia, costochondritis, acute lower back sprains, or post-surgical pain, especially thoracic pain from surgeries in the chest or abdominal area.

## Ingredients:
1. da huang        2.3
2. chai hu         3.8
3. dang gui wei    2.3
4. tao ren         3.0
5. hong hua        1.5
6. tian hua fen    2.3
7. gan cao         1.5

## Functions:
Invigorates blood, dispels blood stasis, soothes the liver *qi*, and opens the collateral vessels.

## Modifications:
1. For cases with *qi* and blood stagnation, add *mu xiang* and *xiang fu.*
2. For moving *qi* and blood stasis, add *chuan xiong, yu jin, san qi* powder, *ru xiang,* or *mo yao.*

## Cautions and Contraindications:
Contraindicated for pain from chronic skin lesions; caution should be used for pregnant patients or patients on their period.

## Administration:
Take with warm water, after meals.

Source: *Yi Xu Fa Ming* (醫學發明)

# Gan Cao Xie Xin Tang 甘草瀉心湯
Pinellia and Licorice Combination
Licorice Decoction to Drain the Epigastrium

## Indications:
For the treatment of *pi* syndrome due to stomach *qi* deficiency cold accumulation.

May also be used for *hu huo* (fox delusion) syndrome, epigastric focal distention, fullness and tightness of the stomach area, dry heaves or nausea, loud borborygmus, diarrhea with undigested food in stool, irritability, throat or oral white mucous.

**Tongue:**       pale, yellow and greasy coating
**Pulse:**        wiry and rapid with forceless pulse

## Clinical Applications:
1. This formula is often used for *pi*. "*Pi*" refers to a focused, localized sensation of discomfort, blockage, and distention due to stomach *qi* deficiency and external exogenous sinking internal (because of the early stage of purging) and cold accumulation (due to ascending and descending *qi* dysfunction).
2. Currently used for chronic or acute gastroenteritis. Behcet's disease, gingivitis, stomatitis, stomach or mouth ulcers, difficulty sleeping or sleep talking. Pediatric diarrhea or roundworm vomit.

## Ingredients:
1. zhi gan cao      5.6
2. huang qin        4.2
3. gan jiang        4.2
4. ban xia          5.6
5. huang lian       1.4
6. da zao           2.8

## Functions:
Clears heat, drains fire, strengthens the *qi* to harmonize the stomach, dissipates clumping, and stops nausea.

## Modifications:
1. For nausea, vomiting and thirst: add *sheng jiang* and *zhu ru*.
2. For wind-cold or alternating heat and cold: add *chai hu* and *gui zhi*.
3. For more chronic diarrhea: add *rou dou kou* and *chi shi zhi*.
4. For vomit and abdominal pain: add *huang lian tang*.
5. For vomiting undigested food: add *wei ling tang*.

## Administration:
Take with warm water as needed.

Source: *Shang Han Lun* (傷寒論)

# Gan Mai Da Zao Tang 甘麥大棗湯
### Licorice and Jujube Combination
### Licorice, Wheat, and Jujube Decoction

## Indications:
Restless organ disorder (*zang zao* syndrome).

Disorientation, frequent attacks of melancholy and crying spells, inability to control oneself, frequent yawning; insomnia or pediatric night crying; and in severe cases, behavior and speech may become abnormal.

**Tongue**:　　red, minimal coating
**Pulse**:　　thin, rapid

## Clinical Applications:
1. This formula is used to nourish heart *yin*, settle ethereal and corporeal souls, tonify spleen *qi,* and for heart *qi* deficiencies for when the heart fails to nourish blood.
2. Currently used for hysteria, neurosis, menopausal syndrome, anxiety, schizophrenia, sleep walking, autonomic dystonia and enuresis (bed wetting).

## Ingredients:
1. xiao mai　　16.0
2. gan cao　　4.0
3. da zao　　4.6

## Functions:
Nourishes the heart, calms the *shen*, harmonizes the middle *jiao*, and moderates anxiety.

## Modifications:
1. For severe *yin* deficiency, with irritability and insomnia, add *sheng di* and *bai he.*
2. For liver blood deficiency with dizziness, add *suan zao ren* and *dang gui.*
3. For wind-cold, add *sheng jiang* and, *cong bai.*
4. For irritability and thirst: add *mai men dong* and *wu wei zi.*
5. For palpitations and unsettled feelings: add *ren shen* and *huang qi.*

## Administration:
Take with warm water, as needed.

Source: *Jin Gui Yao Lue* (金櫃要略)

# Ge Gen Huang Lian Huang Qin Tang 葛根黃連黃芩湯
## Pueraria, Coptis, and Scute Combination
## Kudzu, Coptis, and Scutellaria Decoction

## Indications:
For the treatment of exterior heat sinks into the interior *yang ming* channel (*shang han* stage).
May also be used for fever, sweating, thirst, dysenteric diarrhea characterized by especially foul-smelling stools and burning sensation around the anus, a sensation of irritability and heat sensation in the chest and epigastrium and wheezing.

| | |
|---|---|
| **Tongue:** | red with yellow coating |
| **Pulse:** | floating and rapid |

## Clinical Applications:
1. Formula to be used when exterior heat has not been completely released but the interior is already ablaze with heat. This is when an external pathogen attacks the interior. This transition is known as the *tai yang – yang ming* pattern.
2. This formula was originally used for diarrhea and dysentery due to large intestine heat with external pathogens but may also be used for cases without external pathogens.
3. Currently used for fever with dysentery, acute enteritis, bacillary dysentery, measles, stomach flu, conjunctivitis, red eyes, mouth ulcers, or frozen shoulder caused by hypertension.

## Ingredients:
1. ge gen         12.0
2. huang lian      4.5
3. huang qin       4.5
4. zhi gan cao     3.0

## Functions:
Clears heat, releases external pathogens and harmonizes the middle *jiao* and purges heat.

## Modifications:
1. For cases with abdominal pain, add *zhi shi* and *shao yao*.
2. For alcohol heat asthma, add *zhi ju zi* and *bai dou kou*.
3. For dysentery with tenesmus, add *mu xiang* and *bing lang*.

## Cautions and Contraindications:
Contraindicated for dysenteric disorders due to deficiency-cold without fever with a deep, slow or weak pulse.

## Administration:
Take with warm water, after meals.

Source: *Shang Han Lun* (傷寒論)

# Ge Gen Tang 葛根湯
Pueraria Combination
Kudzu Decoction

## Indications:
For the treatment of external wind-cold excess syndrome (*tai yang shang han* syndrome).

May also be used for fever, aversion to cold, and headache without sweating, stiff and rigid neck and upper back at *tai yang* pattern or diarrhea at *taiyang – yangming* combination patterns.

**Tongue:**     normal or white coating
**Pulse:**      floating, tight

## Clinical Applications:
1. This is the best formula to promote sweating and resolves the exterior in acute-stage *ma huang tang* syndrome with rigid neck and upper back.
2. Currently used for the common cold, flu, acute cervical myositis, tendonitis or bursitis of the shoulder and allergic rhinitis; also for enteritis and early-stage red dysentery with fever and aversion to cold.

## Ingredients:
1. ge gen          6.0
2. ma huang        4.5
3. gui zhi         3.0
4. bai shao        3.0
5. sheng jiang     4.5
6. da zao          4.0
7. zhi gan cao     3.0

## Functions:
Releases the exterior wind-cold from the muscle layer and generates fluids.

## Modifications:
1. For severe nasal blockage, add *chuan xiong, huang qin, xin yi hua,* and *jie geng.*
2. For vomiting with rebelling stomach *qi*: add *ban xia* and *fu ling.*
3. For fever with thirst: add *zhi mu* and *shi gao.*
4. For abdominal pain diarrhea or dysentery: add *huang qin* and *huang lian.*

## Administration:
Take with warm water after meals.

Source: *Shang Han Lun* (傷寒論)

# Ge Xia Zhu Yu Tang 膈下逐瘀湯
## Tangkuei and Corydalis Combination
## Drive Out Blood Stasis Below the Diaphragm Decoction

## Indications:

For the treatment of blood and *qi* stagnation below the diaphragm.

For blood stasis and liver *qi* stagnation in the area below the diaphragm accompanied by fixed pain or abdominal masses, which are visible when lying down.

**Tongue:** purple, with purple spots
**Pulse:** hesitant or choppy

## Clinical Applications:

1. This formula is used to treat blood stasis in the area below the diaphragm. The key symptoms are fixed pain and palpable masses that are visible when lying down.
2. This formula is an anti-coagulant and an anti-inflammatory; it dilates the blood vessels, relieves smooth muscle spasms, and some analgesia.
3. Currently used to treat chronic hepatitis, liver cirrhosis, colon cancer, chronic leukemia, ectopic pregnancy, chronic pelvic inflammatory disease, adhesive pleurisy, peritonitis, chronic pancreatitis, infertility, dysmenorrhea, irregular menstruation, and trauma.

## Ingredients:

| | | | | | |
|---|---|---|---|---|---|
| 1. dang gui | 3.0 | 5. mu dan pi | 2.0 | 9. wu yao | 2.0 |
| 2. chuang xiong | 2.0 | 6. chi shao | 2.0 | 10. zhi ke | 1.5 |
| 3. tao ren | 3.0 | 7. yan hu suo | 1.0 | 11. wu ling zhi | 2.0 |
| 4. hong hua | 3.0 | 8. xiang fu | 1.5 | 12. gan cao | 3.0 |

## Functions:

Invigorates the blood, dispels blood stasis, moves the *qi*, alleviates pain.

## Modifications:

1. For cases with constipation: add *da huang*.
2. For cases with blood deficiency: add *bai shao* and *dan shen*.
3. For cases with painful menstruation: add *yi mu can* and *dan shen*.

## Cautions and Contraindications:

Contraindicated for women who are pregnant or persons with weak constitution without stagnation or those taking anti-coagulant medication.

## Administration:

Take with warm water, before meals.

Source: *Yi Lin Gai Cuo* (醫林改錯)

# Gu Jing Wan 固經丸
## Stable Menstruation Pill

## Indications:
For the treatment of *beng lou* syndrome.

May be used for continuous menstruation or uterine bleeding that alternates between trickling and heavy flow of blood; the blood is red and may contain dark-purple clots. Accompanying signs include a heat sensation in the chest and irritability, abdominal pain, and dark urine.

**Tongue**:    red
**Pulse**:    rapid, wiry

## Clinical Applications:
1. This formula is used for liver and kidney *yin* deficiencies with vigorous fire disturbing the *chong* and *ren* channels, leading to abnormal uterine bleeding.
2. Currently used for functional uterine bleeding and chronic pelvic inflammatory disease (PID).

## Ingredients:
1. gui ban (zhi)        30.0
2. bai shao (chao)      30.0
3. huang qin (chao)     30.0
4. huang bai (chao)      9.0
5. chun gen pi          21.0
6. xiang fu              6.0

## Functions:
Enriches the *yin*, clears the heat, stabilizes the menses, and stops bleeding.

## Modifications:
For chronic bleeding, add *long gu, mu li, hai piao xiao,* and *qian cao gen.*

## Administration:
Take with warm wine or water on an empty stomach.

Source: *Yi Xue Ru Men* (醫學入門)

# Gui Pi Tang 歸脾湯
### Ginseng and Longan Combination

## Indications:

Dual *qi* and blood deficiency of the spleen and heart: symptoms include palpitations (with or without anxiety), anxiety and phobia, forgetfulness, insomnia, night sweating, feverishness, withdrawal, reduced appetite, and a pallid and wan complexion.

Spleen failing to control the blood: symptoms include blood in the stool, purpura, severe uterine bleeding (*beng lou* pattern), shortened menstrual cycle with copious, pale blood, or prolonged period with scant flow or leukorrhea.

**Tongue:**　　pale with thin white coating
**Pulse:**　　thin and frail

## Clinical Applications:

1. This formula treats many common clinical disorders: restless heart spirit, *qi* and blood deficiency, and inability of the spleen to control the blood.
2. Currently used for stomach or peptic bleeding ulcer, functional uterine bleeding, aplastic anemia, thrombocytopenic or allergic purpura, and cervicitis.

## Ingredients:

| | | | | | |
|---|---|---|---|---|---|
| 1. huang qi | 6.0 | 5. dang gui | 6.0 | 9. mu xiang | 3.0 |
| 2. long yan rou | 6.0 | 6. suan zao ren | 6.0 | 10. zhi gan cao | 3.0 |
| 3. ren shen | 6.0 | 7. fu shen | 6.0 | 11. sheng jiang | 4.0 |
| 4. bai zhu | 6.0 | 8. yuan zhi | 6.0 | 12. da zao | 4.0 |

## Functions:

Augments *qi*, nourishes blood, strengthens the spleen, and nourishes the heart.

## Modifications:

1. For tonifying the blood to stop bleeding, add *shu di huang* and *e jiao*.
2. For palpitation with insomnia, add *gou teng* and *bai zi ren*.
3. For poor appetite with fatigue, add *sha ren* and *cang zhu*.
4. For excessive thinking, combine with *Tian Wang Bu Xin Dan*.
5. For deficiency fatigue, combine with *Huan Shao Dan*.

## Cautions and Contraindications:

Should not be used when patient has tidal fever from *yin* deficiency or internal-heat bleeding.

## Administration:

Take with warm water, as needed.

Source: *Jiao Zhu Fu Ren Liang Fang* (校註婦人良方)

# Gui Zhi Fu Ling Wan 桂枝茯苓丸
## Cinnamon and Hoelen Formula

**Indications:**
Uterine blood stasis: mild and persistent uterine bleeding of purple or dark blood during pregnancy accompanied by abdominal pain that is worse when pressure is applied.

**Pulse:** choppy

**Clinical Applications:**
1. This formula treats dysmenorrhea, amenorrhea, lochia retention, and prevents difficult labor, and fetal death due to blood stasis in the uterus.
2. Currently used for dysmenorrhea, leiomyoma, cervical erosion, ovarian cysts, endometriosis, lochioschesis, ectopic pregnancy, and polycystic ovaries.

**Ingredients:**
1. gui zhi        6.0
2. tao ren        6.0
3. mu dan pi      6.0
4. bai shao       6.0
5. fu ling        6.0

**Functions:**
Invigorate the blood, transform blood stasis, and reduce fixed masses in the abdomen.

**Modifications:**
1. For irregular menstruation, add *dang gui* and *chuan xiong*.
2. For menstrual stagnation, add *zhi shi* and *hong hua*.
3. For dysmenorrhea, add *chen pi* and *xiang fu*.

**Cautions and Contraindications:**
Caution during pregnancy or postpartum.

**Administration:**
Take with warm water, before meals.

Source: *Jin Gui Yao Lüe* (金匱要略)

# Gui Zhi Shao Yao Zhi Mu Tang 桂枝芍藥知母湯
## Cinnamon and Anemarrhena Combination
### Cinnamon Twig, Peony, and Anemarrhena Decoctio

## Indications:
Wind-cold-damp *bi* syndrome with local heat.

Swollen and painful joints that are warm to the touch, with pain worsening at night, reducing range of motion in the affected joints. Symptoms also include chills without sweat, emaciation, dizziness, irritability, and nausea.

**Tongue:**   white, greasy coating
**Pulse:**   wiry, slippery

## Clinical Applications:
1. This formula is used for painfully localized wind-cold-damp obstructions in the joints, with constraint of motion that generates heat.
2. The key symptoms are painful joints that are warm to touch, with symptoms worsening at night.
3. Currently used in treating rheumatoid arthritis, connective tissue disorders, arthrosis of the knee joint or gouty arthritis.

## Ingredients:
| | | | | | |
|---|---|---|---|---|---|
| 1. | gui zhi | 3.2 | 6. | bai zhu | 3.2 |
| 2. | bai shao | 2.4 | 7. | fang feng | 3.2 |
| 3. | zhi mu | 3.2 | 8. | sheng jiang | 4.0 |
| 4. | ma huang | 1.6 | 9. | gan cao | 1.6 |
| 5. | fu zi (pao) | 1.6 | | | |

## Functions:
Expels wind, overcomes dampness, moves the *yang qi*, removes obstructions, nourishes *yin* and clears heat.

## Modifications:
1. For severe pain with limited range of motion which gets better with warmth, increase the dosage of *fu zi, ma huang,* and *gui zhi.*
2. For a heavy sensation in the body, swollen and numb joints which worsen in cold and damp conditions, increase the dosage of *fu zi* and *bai zhu.*
3. For painful and hot joints which worsen at night, increase the dosage of *shao yao, zhi mu,* and *gan cao,* or add *sheng di huang* and *ren dong teng.*

## Administration:
Take with warm water, as needed.

Source: *Jin Gui Yao Lue* (金櫃要略)

# Gui Zhi Tang 桂枝湯
## Cinnamon Combination

**Indications:**
Exterior wind-cold deficiency pattern (wind stroke disorder of the *tai yang* channel): headache and fever, aversion to wind and sweating, nasal congestion, dry heaves, and lack of thirst.

**Tongue:**     thin and white coating
**Pulse:**     floating or superficial pulse that is either moderate or frail

**Clinical Applications:**
1. This is a commonly used formula for exterior wind-cold or wind attack deficiency pattern with disharmony of *ying* and *wei*.
2. Currently used for common cold, flu, upper respiratory tract infection, postpartum fever, allergic rhinitis, cerebrovascular spasm, eczema, and urticaria.

**Ingredients:**

| | | | | |
|---|---|---|---|---|
| 1. gui zhi | 6.0 | | 4. da zao | 5.0 |
| 2. bai shao | 6.0 | | 5. zhi gan cao | 4.0 |
| 3. sheng jiang | 6.0 | | | |

**Functions:**
Releases Exterior wind-cold from the muscle layer and regulates *ying qi* and *wei qi*.

**Modifications:**
1. For stiff neck and back, add *ge gen*.
2. For coughing and wheezing, add *hou po* and *xing ren*.
3. For profuse sweating, increase the dosage of *bai shao*, reduce by one-third the dosage of *gui zhi*, *sheng jiang*, and *zhi gan cao*, and add *huang qi* and *fang feng*.
4. For severe vomiting, increase the dosage of *sheng jiang* and add *chen pi* and *hou po*.
5. For aversion to cold without sweat, add *ma huang* and *ge gen*.
6. For more heat and less cold, add *zhi mu* and *shi gao*.
7. For proclivity to catching wind-cold, combine with *Yu Ping Feng San*.
8. For proclivity to catching cold after an illness, combine with *Xiao Chai Hu Tang*.

**Cautions and Contraindications:**
This formula should not be used for exterior cold with interior heat characterized by fever, thirst, and rapid pulse, or for exterior excess cold without sweating and febrile disease in the early stages characterized by fever with thirst, sore throat, and rapid pulse.

**Administration:**
Take with warm water, before meals, and follow with hot rice porridge to induce sweat.

Source: *Shang Han Lun* (傷寒論)

# Huai Hua San 槐花散
Sophora Flower Formula
Sophora Japonica Flower Powder

## Indications:
For the treatment of rectal bleeding due to intestinal wind or organ toxicity disorders.

May be used for patients with bright-red bleeding from rectum that precedes or follows defecation, blood in the stool, and hemorrhoids with either bright-red or dark-red bleeding.

**Tongue**:     red
**Pulse**:      wiry and rapid or soggy and rapid

## Clinical Applications:
1. This formula treats intestinal wind disorder or damp heat in the intestines and stomach where it forms toxin.
2. Currently used for amebic dysentery, ulcerative colitis, hemorrhoids, anal fissures, prolapsed rectum, colitis, and colon cancer.

## Ingredients:
1. huai hua (chao)    6.0
2. ce bai ye          6.0
3. jing jie           6.0
4. zhi ke             6.0

## Functions:
Cools the intestines, stops bleeding, disperses wind, and moves the *qi* downward.

## Modifications:
1. For vigorous heat in lower intestine (LI), add *huang lian* and *huang bai*.
2. For excessive bleeding, add *di yu* and *xian he cao*.
3. For damp heat in the lower limbs, add *cang zhu* and *huang bai*.

## Cautions and Contraindications:
*Huai Hua San* should not be taken long-term; contraindicated for chronic bleeding due to *qi* or *yin* deficiency.

## Administration:
Take with warm water, after meals.

Source: *Pu Ji Ben Shi Fang* (普濟本事方)

# Huang Lian E Jiao Tang 黃蓮阿膠湯
### Coptis and Donkey Hide Gelatin Decoction

## Indications:
For use when the heat transformation pattern is in *shao yin* stage.

Irritability with a sensation of heat in the chest, insomnia, and heart palpitations with anxiety. There may also be sores on the tongue or in the mouth.

**Tongue**:     red, dry, yellow coating
**Pulse**:      thin, rapid

## Clinical Applications:
1. This formula is used for nourishing *yin* and treating excessive and blood deficiencies in patients whose symptoms predominantly manifest in the heart *shao yin* stage.
2. Currently used for nervous exhaustion, the recuperative stage of an infectious disease, autonomic dystonia, erectile dysfunction, and hypertension.

## Ingredients:
1. huang lian       12.0
2. e jiao           9.0
3. huang qin        6.0
4. bai shao         6.0
5. ji zi huang      2 yolks

## Functions:
Nourishes *yin*, helps fire descend, adds moisture to dryness, and calms the spirit.

## Modifications:
1. For severe *yin* deficiencies, with injured fluids and dry throat, add *xuan shen, mai dong,* and *shi hu.*
2. For heat in the five centers, add *zhi zi* and *dan zhu ye.*

## Administration:
Take with warm water between meals.

Source: *Shang Han Zu Bing Lun* (傷寒卒病論)

# Huang Lian Jie Du Tang 黃連解毒湯
### Coptis and Scute Combination

## Indications:
Used to treat symptoms caused by fire toxin obstructing the three *jiao*:
1. High fever, irritability, dry mouth and throat, incoherent speech, insomnia, and dark urine.
2. Febrile illness that causes nosebleed or vomiting of blood, or for severe heat that causes macular rash and erythema.
3. Diarrhea and jaundice due to damp heat.
4. Carbuncles, deep-rooted boils, and sores due to toxic heat.

**Tongue**:   red tongue with yellow coating
**Pulse**:   rapid and forceful

## Clinical Applications:
1. This formula can be used for all types of fire toxin obstructing the three *jiao*.
2. Currently used for encephalitis, meningitis, septicemia, toxemia, dysentery, pneumonia, urinary tract infection (UTI), and infectious inflammation due to toxic heat.

## Ingredients:
1. huang lian   6.0
2. huang qin   6.0
3. huang bai   6.0
4. zhi zi   6.0

## Functions:
Clears fire heat and relieves toxins.

## Modifications:
1. For constipation, add *da huang*.
2. For jaundice due to blood stasis and heat accumulation, add *da huang* and *yin chen hao*.
3. For nosebleed, vomiting blood, macular rash, and erythema, add *xuan shen*, *sheng di huang*, and *mu dan pi*.
4. For fever with thirst, add *shi gao* and *zhi mu*.
5. For dry throat, add *mai men dong* and *wu wei zi*.
6. For hemorrhoids, combine with *Pai Nong San*.

## Cautions and Contraindications:
Should not be used long term and should only be used in cases with excess heat.

## Administration:
Take with warm water, as needed.

Source: *Wai Tai Mi Yao* (外台秘要)

# Huo Xiang Zheng Qi San 藿香正氣散
## Agastache Formula

### Indications:
Sudden turmoil (*huo luan*) symptoms and exterior wind-cold with interior dampness stagnation patterns: fever and chills, headache, a sensation of fullness and stifling oppression in the chest, pain in the epigastrium and abdomen, nausea and vomiting, borborygmus, diarrhea, and loss of taste.

**Tongue**:     white with greasy coating
**Pulse**:      moderate and soggy

### Clinical Applications:
1. This formula is better for transforming dampness and harmonizing the stomach than for releasing exterior wind-cold. The symptoms are chills with fever, vomiting, and diarrhea, with a white and greasy tongue coating.
2. Currently used for acute gastroenteritis, common cold causing dyspepsia, and stomach flu due to middle *jiao* injury by wind-cold-dampness during summer or autumn. Also for sudden turmoil disorders or malarial disorders.

### Ingredients:

| | | | | | | | |
|---|---|---|---|---|---|---|---|
| 1. | huo xiang | 3.0 | 6. | bai zhu | 2.0 | 11. sheng jiang | 3.0 |
| 2. | zi su ye | 3.0 | 7. | fu ling | 3.0 | 12. da zao | 1.0 |
| 3. | bai zhi | 3.0 | 8. | hou po | 2.0 | 13. zhi gan cao | 1.0 |
| 4. | ban xia | 2.0 | 9. | da fu pi | 3.0 | | |
| 5. | chen pi | 2.0 | 10. jie geng | 2.0 | | |

### Functions:
Releases the exterior, transforms dampness, regulates the *qi*, and harmonizes the middle *jiao*.

### Modifications:
1. For cases during summer, add *pei lan*.
2. For severe cases with exterior chills and fever and no sweating, add *xiang ru* and cover the patient with a blanket to promote sweating.
3. For food stagnation, omit *gan cao* and *da zao* and add *shan zha*, *ji nei jin*, or *shen qu*.
4. For severe dampness, omit *bai zhu* and add *cang zhu*.
5. For abdominal pain with diarrhea, add *cang zhu* and *huang lian*.
6. For nausea and vomiting, add *zhi shi* and *zhu ru*.
7. For summer-heat stroke with vomiting and diarrhea, combine with *San Wu Xiang Ru San*.

### Cautions and Contraindications:
Should not be used when patient has wind-heat or deficiency fire.

### Administration:
Take with warm water, as needed.

Source: *Tai Ping Hui Ming He Ji Ju Fang* (太平惠民合劑局方)

# Ji Chuan Jian 濟川煎
Flowing River Decoction

## Indications:
For the treatment of constipation due to kidney *yang* deficiency syndrome.

May be used for constipation, clear and copious urine, lower back pain and a cold sensation in the back.

**Tongue:**     pale, white coating
**Pulse:**       deep, slow

## Clinical Applications:
1. This formula tonifies kidney and facilitates the distribution of fluid in order to move the stool.
2. Currently used for habitual atonic constipation and reduced bowel activity, especially in the elderly, due to kidney *qi* deficiency.

## Ingredients:
1. rou cong rong     8.0
2. dang gui          12.0
3. niu xi            6.0
4. zhi ke            3.0
5. ze xie            5.0
6. sheng ma          3.0

## Functions:
Warms the kidney, lubricates the intestines and unblocks the bowels.

## Modifications:
1. For cases with *qi* deficiency, add *ren shen.*
2. For severe kidney deficiency, add *shu di huang.*

## Administration:
Take with warm water, before meals,

Source: *Jing Yue Quan Shu* (景岳全書)

# Ji Sheng Shen Qi Wan 濟生腎氣丸
## Cyathula and Plantago Formula

## Indications:
Kidney *yang* deficiency and edema: water retention, heaviness around the waist with edema in the feet, difficult urination, cold limbs, aversion to cold, and soreness and weakness in the lower back and knees.

| | |
|---|---|
| **Tongue**: | pale tongue with white coating |
| **Pulse**: | deep |

## Clinical Applications:
1. This is the standard formula for kidney *yang* deficiency with soreness and heaviness in the lower back and difficult urination.
2. Currently used for chronic nephritis, renal functional atrophy, edema, geriatric deficiency, diabetes, wasting and thirsting (*xiao ke*) patterns, and frequent urination.

## Ingredients:

| | | | | | |
|---|---|---|---|---|---|
| 1. | shu di huang | 8.0 | 6. | fu ling | 6.0 |
| 2. | shan zhu yu | 4.0 | 7. | fu zi (pao) | 1.0 |
| 3. | shan yao | 4.0 | 8. | rou gui | 1.0 |
| 4. | ze xie | 3.0 | 9. | chuan niu xi | 2.0 |
| 5. | mu dan pi | 3.0 | 10. | che qian zi | 2.0 |

## Functions:
Tonifies *qi* and supplements *yang*, nourishes *yin* and blood, warms kidney and transforms *qi*, regulates water and eliminates water retention.

## Modifications:
1. For severe *yang* atrophy, add *gui ban* and *lu jiao shuang*.
2. For severe swelling pain and back soreness, add *du zhong* and *gou qi zi*.
3. For abdominal distention, add *huang qi* and *fang ji*.

## Cautions and Contraindications:
Should not be used when patient has *yin* deficiency with excess fire or body fluid injured by excess heat.

## Administration:
Take with warm water or lightly salted warm water, before meals.

Source: *Ji Sheng Fang* (濟生方)

# Jia Jian Wei Rui Tang 加減葳蕤湯
## Modified Solomon's Seal Decoction

## Indications:

For the treatment of exterior wind-heat with preexisting *yin* deficiency syndrome.

May also be used for fever with slight chills, little or no sweating, headache, dry throat, cough, irritability, and thirst.

**Tongue:**    dark, red
**Pulse:**    rapid

## Clinical Applications:

1. This is the formula for exterior wind-heat with underlying *yin* deficiency and internal heat.
2. Used for the common cold in the elderly, postpartum treatment, acute tonsillitis and pharyngitis due to exterior disorders along with *yin* deficiency.

## Ingredients:

1. yu zhu (wei rui)    9.0
2. cong bai    10.0
3. dan dou chi    12.0
4. bo he    5.0
5. jie geng    5.0
6. bai wei    3.0
7. zhi gan cao    2.0
8. da zao    2 pcs

## Functions:

Nourishes the *yin*, clears heat, promotes sweating and releases the exterior wind-heat.

## Modifications:

1. For severe exterior disorders, add *fang feng* and *ge gen.*
2. For cough, dry mouth, phlegm that is difficult to expectorate, add *niu bang zi* and *gua lou pi.*
3. For severe irritability and thirst, add *zhu ye* and *tian hua fen.*

## Administration:

Take with warm water, as needed.

Source: *Chong Ding Tong Su Shang Han Lun* (重訂通俗傷寒論)

# Jia Wei Xiao Yao San 加味逍遙散
Bupleurum and Peony Powder

## Indications:
Liver *qi* stagnation, blood deficiency, and deficiency heat: hypochondriac pain, headache, dizziness, dry mouth and throat, fatigue, poor appetite, irritability, and irregular menstruation or mood swings.

**Tongue**:     pale red tongue
**Pulse**:       wiry and deficient

## Clinical Applications:
1. This formula is often used for regulating menstruation and menopausal patterns.
2. This formula is for early-stage liver cirrhosis and hypochondriac pain, particularly patients who have liver enlargement, distended abdomen, dry or bitter taste in the mouth, headache, yellow urine, nosebleed, and bleeding gums without water retention.
3. Currently used for chronic hepatitis, cirrhosis, gallstones, neurosis, fibrocystic breasts, PMS, pelvic inflammation, postpartum eczema, irritability, and constipation.

## Ingredients:
| | | | | |
|---|---|---|---|---|
| 1. chai hu | 8.0 | | 6. zhi gan cao | 4.0 |
| 2. bai shao | 8.0 | | 7. wei jiang | 8.0 |
| 3. dang gui | 8.0 | | 8. bo he | 4.0 |
| 4. bai zhu | 8.0 | | 9. mu dan pi | 5.0 |
| 5. fu ling | 8.0 | | 10. zhi zi | 5.0 |

## Functions:
Spreads liver *qi*, releases constraint, clears heat, and cools the blood.

## Modifications:
1. For severe blood deficiency heat, add *chuan xiong* and *di huang*.
2. For severe *qi* deficiency fatigue, add *ren shen* and *huang qi*.
3. For severe irritability, add *mai men dong* and *wu wei zi*.
4. For alternating chills and fever, combine with *Xiao Chai Hu Tang*.
5. For steaming bone fever, combine with *Qin Jiao* and *Bie Jiaoo San*.
6. For hand eczema, add *di gu pi* and *jing jie*.
7. For female dermatitis, add *chuan xiong* and *di huang*.

## Administration:
Take with warm water, as needed.

Source: *Zheng Zhi Zhun Sheng* (證治準繩)

# (Jin Gui) Shen Qi Wan (金匱) 腎氣丸
Kidney *Qi* Pill (from the Golden Cabinet)

## Indications:
For the treatment of kidney *qi* and *yang* deficiency syndromes.

May be used for patients with aching and weakness of the lower back and knees, a cold sensation in the lower half of the body, tenseness in the lower abdomen, either difficulty with urination or excessive urination that increases in severity at night, impotence, premature ejaculation, or chronic diarrhea.

**Tongue**:     pale, swollen with thin, white and moist coating
**Pulse**:     empty or frail (submerged and faint at the proximal position)

## Clinical Applications:
1. One of the most used and effective preparations of kidney *yang* deficiency with insufficient *ming men* fire.
2. Currently used for chronic nephritis, diabetes, hyperaldosteronism, hypothyroidism, sexual neurosis, various genital disorders, chronic asthma, and menopause symptoms.

## Ingredients:
1. fu zi (zhi)      3.0
2. gui zhi      3.0
3. gan di huang      24.0
4. shan zhu yu      12.0
5. shan yao      12.0
6. ze xie      9.0
7. mu dan pi      9.0
8. fu ling      9.0

## Functions:
Warms and tonifies the kidney *yang*.

## Modifications:
1. For stronger result, omit *gan di huang* and *gui zhi*, and add *shu di huang* and *rou gui*.
2. For impotence, add *yin yang huo, bu gu zhi* and *ba ji tian*.

## Cautions and Contraindications:
Contraindicated in the presence of *yin* deficiency heat.

## Administration:
Take with warm or even salted water before meals.

Source: *Shang Han Zu Bing Lun* (傷寒卒病論)

# Jin Ling Zi San 金鈴子散
## Melia Toosendan Powder

### Indications:
For the treatment of liver *qi* stagnation, especially that which turns to heat syndrome.

May be used for intermittent epigastric and hypochondriac pain, hernia pain, or menstrual pain that becomes worse when eating hot foods, or which is accompanied by a bitter taste in the mouth.

**Tongue:** red and yellow coating
**Pulse:** wiry or rapid

### Clinical Applications:
1. This formula is used to treat various pain symptoms due to liver *qi* stagnation turning into heat syndrome.
2. Currently used for peptic ulcers, chronic gastritis, hepatitis, and cholecystitis.

### Ingredients:
1. jin ling zi     9.0
2. yan hu suo     9.0

### Functions:
Soothes the liver *qi*, drains heat, regulates the blood, and generally alleviates pain.

### Modifications:
1. For menstrual pain, add *dang gui, yi mu cao* and *xiang fu.*
2. For hernia pain, add *ju he* and *li zhi he.*

### Cautions and Contraindications:
Not to be taken during pregnancy.

### Administration:
Take with warm water, as needed.

Source: *Tai Ping Sheng Hui Fang* (太平聖惠方)

# Jin Suo Gu Jing Wan 金鎖固精丸
### Lotus Stamen Formula
### Golden Lock to Stabilize the Essence

## Indications:
For the treatment of kidney deficiency and spermatorrhea syndrome.

May be used for chronic spermatorrhea without sexual dreams, impotence, fatigue and weakness, lower back pain, tinnitus, and soreness and weakness of the lower back and limbs.

**Tongue**:    pale, white coating
**Pulse**:    thin, frail

## Clinical Applications:
1. This is a formula used for spermatorrhea due to kidney *qi* deficiency causes inability to stabilize the essence.
2. Currently used for spermatorrhea, premature ejaculation, chronic prostatitis, and myasthenia gravis.

## Ingredients:
1. sha yuan zi    6.0
2. qian shi    6.0
3. lian zi    6.0
4. lian xu    6.0
5. long gu    3.0
6. mu li    3.0

## Functions:
Stabilizes the kidney and binds up the essence.

## Modifications:
1. For constipation with dry stool, add *shu di* and *rou cong rong*.
2. For diarrhea, add *tu si zi* and *wu wei zi*.
3. For soreness of lower back and knees, add *du zhong* and *xu duan*.

## Cautions and Contraindications:
Contraindicated for damp-heat in the lower *jiao*.

## Administration:
Take with warm or even salted water, before meals.

Source: *Yi Fang Ji Jie* (醫方集解)

# Ju Pi Zhu Ru Tang 橘皮竹茹湯
## Citrus and Bamboo Combination
### Tangerine Peel and Bamboo Shavings Decoction

**Indications:**
For the treatment of stomach deficiency or heat hiccup syndrome.

May be used for excessive hiccupping, nausea, dry heaves, or retching.

**Tongue:**  tender and red
**Pulse:**  deficient and rapid

**Clinical Applications:**
1. This formula is used to treat the up-flushing of *qi* or *qi* stagnation syndrome due to stomach deficiency.
2. Currently used for partial pyloric obstructions, post-surgical hiccups and morning sickness.

**Ingredients:**
1. ju pi         1.6
2. zhu ru        0.8
3. ren shen      0.4
4. sheng jiang   1.6
5. gan cao       0.8
6. da zao        0.8

**Functions:**
Directs the rebellious *qi* downward, stops excessive hiccupping, augments the *qi* and clears heat.

**Modifications:**
1. For cases with stomach *yin* deficiency, add *mai men dong* and *shi hu.*
2. For hiccups due to stomach heat without deficiency, omit *ren shen, gan cao,* and *da zao*, and add *shi di.*

**Cautions and Contraindications:**
Not to be used for patients with excess heat.

**Administration:**
Take with warm water before meals.

Source: *Jin Gui Yao Lue* (金櫃要略)

# Juan Bi Tang 蠲痹湯
### Remove Painful Obstruction Decoction

## Indications:
For the treatment of wind-cold-damp *bi* syndrome with *ying* and *wei* deficiency.
May be used for stiffness and pain in the shoulder, neck, arms and upper back, numbness in extremities, general difficulty moving.

**Tongue:**     thick, white coating
**Pulse:**      moderate

## Clinical Applications:
1. This formula is used for wind-cold-damp *bi* syndrome with *ying* and *wei* deficiency. This is joint pain due to local obstruction of *qi* from wind, dampness, and cold. This is painful obstruction (*bi*) and focuses on upper part of body.
2. The key symptoms are pain in the head, arms, and upper back.
3. Currently used in treating osteoarthritis, rheumatoid arthritis and bursitis.

## Ingredients:
1. qiang huo                 4.0
2. fang feng                 4.0
3. dang gui                  4.0
4. chi shao                  4.0
5. huang qi (honey fried)    4.0
6. jiang huang               4.0
7. zhi gan cao               1.5
8. sheng jiang               3.0
9. da zao                    2.0

## Functions:
Expels wind-dampness, alleviates painful *qi* obstruction, tonifies *qi* and activates blood.

## Modifications:
1. For more severe cold, add *gui zhi* and *xi xin.*
2. For pain in the lower extremities, add *du zhong, niu xi,* and *xu duan.*
3. For more severe damp, add *cang zhu, fang ji* and *yi yi ren.*

## Cautions and Contraindications:
Not to be used for wind-damp-heat condition.

## Administration:
Take with warm water, after meals.

Source: *Zhong Guo Yi Xue Da Ci Dian* (中國醫學大辭典)

# Li Zhong Wan 理中丸
### Regulate the Middle Pill

## Indications:
For the treatment of middle *jiao* deficiency-cold syndrome.

May also be used for diarrhea with watery stool, nausea and vomiting, lack of thirst, loss of appetite and abdominal pain.

**Tongue**: pale, white coating
**Pulse**: submerged, thin

## Clinical Applications:
1. This formula may be used for sudden turmoil disorder with cold marked by an absence of thirst. May be prescribed when a patient spits up fluids due to cold in the chest when recovering from a chronic illness.
2. It may also be used for chronic bleeding and chronic convulsions in childhood, emaciation, cold hands and feet, vomiting, and diarrhea.
3. Currently used for chronic or acute gastritis, gastric or duodenal ulcers, gastroptosis, irritable bowel syndrome, chronic colitis, chronic bronchitis, and oral herpes.

## Ingredients:
1. gan jiang   1.2
2. ren shen   1.6
3. bai zhu   1.6
4. zhi gan cao   1.6

## Functions:
Warms the middle *jiao*, dispels cold, tonifies *qi* and strengthens the spleen.

## Modifications:
1. For severe vomiting, add *sheng jiang*.
2. For bleeding due to *yang* deficiency, substitute *pao jiang* or *gan jiang*, add *huang qi, dang gui,* or *e jiao*.
3. For palpitations, add *fu ling*.

## Cautions and Contraindications:
Fever due to external pathogenic influences or *yin* deficiency.

## Administration:
Take with warm, as needed.

Source: *Shang Han Jin Gui* (傷寒金櫃)

# Liang Fu Wan 良附丸
Galangal and Cyperus Pill

## Indications:
For the treatment of epigastric pain, especially that favors warmth, bringing about a stifling sensation in the chest and pain in the hypochondrium.

**Tongue:**    white coating
**Pulse:**    wiry

## Clinical Applications:
1. This formula is used for painful epigastric or hypochondriac disorder with cold marked by attraction to warmth.
2. Currently used for chronic gastritis, peptic ulcers, and dysmenorrhea.

## Ingredients:
1. gao liang jiang    3.0
2. xiang fu    12.0

## Functions:
Regulates *qi* to soothe the liver, warm the middle *jiao* to alleviate pain.

## Modifications:
1. For more severe cold, increase the dosage of *gao liang jiang* and add *gan jiang*.
2. For more severe pain, increase the dosage of *xiang fu* and add *qing pi, mu xiang* or *chen xiang*.
3. For painful menstruation, add *dang gui*.

## Cautions and Contraindications:
Contraindicated when there is excessive heat in the liver and stomach or a bleeding ulcer.

## Administration:
Take with warm or salted water, before meals.

Source: *Liang Fang Ji Ye* (良方集腋)

# Liang Ge San 凉膈散
## Cool the Diaphragm Powder

### Indications:
For the treatment of accumulated heat in upper and lower *jiao* syndrome.

May be used for patient with a sensation of heat and irritability in the chest and abdomen, thirst, red face, dry lips, mouth and tongue sores, sore throat, nosebleeds, constipation, and scanty urine.

**Tongue:**    red in the center, with a dry, yellow or white coating around the edges.
**Pulse:**    rapid, possibly slippery

### Clinical Applications:
1. This formula cools the diaphragm by clearing heat from the upper *jiao* and draining heat from the middle *jiao*. (The UJ and MJ straddle the diaphragm).
2. Currently used for pharyngitis, acute tonsillitis, biliary tract infection, and acute hepatitis.

### Ingredients:
1. lian qiao    8.0
2. huang qin    2.0
3. zhi zi    2.0
4. bo he    2.0
5. da huang    4.0
6. mang xiao    4.0
7. gan cao    4.0
8. dan zhu ye    2.0

### Functions:
Drains heat, unblocks the bowels, clears the upper *jiao* and purges the lower *jiao*.

### Modifications:
1. For cases with severe toxic heat in upper *jiao*, omit *mang xiao*, add *shi gao* and *jie geng*.
2. For severe thirst, add *tian hua fen*.
3. For severe mouth sores, add *huang lian*.

### Cautions and Contraindications:
Not to be taken during pregnancy or by particularly weak patients.

### Administration:
Take with warm or cool water after meals.

Source: *Tai Ping Hui Ming He Ji Ju Fang* (太平惠民和劑局方)

# Ling Gui Zhu Gan Tang 苓桂术甘湯
Poria and Atractylodes Combination
Poria, Cinnamon Twig, Atractylodes Macrocephala and Licorice Decoction

## Indications:
For the treatment of congested thin fluid *(tan-yin)* in the epigastrium.

Also treats fullness in the chest and hypochondrium, palpitations, shortness of breath, coughing up clear and watery phlegm, and dizziness or vertigo.

**Tongue:**    pale, swollen with white slippery or greasy coating
**Pulse:**     deep and tight

## Clinical Applications:
1. This formula is used for deficiency thin water fluid retention in the epigastrium.
2. The key symptoms are dizziness or vertigo, body shivering sensation, standing vertigo, labored breathing, coughing, palpitations, and headaches.
3. Symptoms may also include reduced urination, cold feet, soft and weak abdominal region, water retention or bloating in stomach caused by spleen *yang* deficiency and difficulty for the spleen to transport fluid.
4. Currently used in treating Meniere's disease, neurosis, rheumatoid arthritis, chronic nephritis, pleurisy, chronic gastritis, chronic bronchitis, and water in the inner ear.

## Ingredients:
1. fu ling        8.0
2. gui zhi        6.0
3. bai zhu        6.0
4. zhi gan cao    4.0

## Functions:
Warms the *yang*, transforms phlegm and water, strengthens the spleen, and dries dampness.

## Modifications:
1. For dizziness and headache: add *dang gui* and *chuan xiong.*
2. For thin fluid retention and rebellious water: add *ban xia* and *sheng jiang.*
3. For irritability palpitations: add *ren shen* and *huang qi.*
4. For severe coughing and profuse phlegm, add *Er Chen Tang.*
5. For fatigue, add *xiao jian zhong tang.*

## Cautions and Contraindications:
Not to be used in the instance of damp-heat or *yin* deficiency, or liver *yang* rising.

## Administration:
Take with warm water, as needed.

Source: *Jin Gui Yao Lue* (金櫃要略)

# Ling Jiao Gou Teng Tang 羚角鉤藤湯
## Antelope Horn and Uncaria Decoction

### Indications:
For the treatment of excess liver channel heat, which generates internal wind.

May also be used for patients with a persistent high fever, irritability, restlessness, spasms of the extremities, and convulsions. In severe cases, there may also be loss of consciousness.

**Tongue:**    deep red, dry, or burnt with prickles
**Pulse:**    wiry and rapid

### Clinical Applications:
1. This formula is used for excess heat in the liver channel, stirring up internal movement of wind.
2. Headache, dizziness, vertigo, and tics or spasms caused by "yin:deficiency"-heat.
3. Currently used for hypertension, hypertensive encephalopathy, cerebrovascular disease, encephalitis, meningitis, eclampsia and puerperal convulsions, facial spasms, and hysterical psychosis.

### Ingredients:
1. ling yang jiao     4.5
2. gou teng     9.0
3. sang ye     6.0
4. ju hua     9.0
5. sheng di huang (fresh)     15.0
6. bai shao     9.0
7. chuan bei mu     12.0
8. zhu ru (fresh)     15.0
9. fu shen mu     9.0
10. gan cao     3.0

### Functions:
Cools the liver, extinguishes internal wind, generates the fluids and relaxes the sinews.

### Modifications:
For internal evil heat obstructions and loss of consciousness or coma, combine with *An Gong Niu, Huang Wan,* or *Zi Xue Dan.*

### Cautions and Contraindications:
Not to be used for internal wind due to deficiency.

### Administration:
Take with warm water, after meals.

Source: *Tong Su Shang Han Lun* (通俗傷寒論)

# Liu He Tang 六和湯
Amomum Combination
Harmonize the Six Decoction 695

## Indications:
1. Summer-heat with inappropriate diet: internal damage by raw cold food or drink, external damage by summer-heat, alternative hot and cold, fatigue with tendency to sleep, and thirstiness.
2. Sudden turmoil disorder: a cholera-like disorder, severe vomiting and diarrhea.

**Tongue:**   white, glossy coating

## Clinical Applications:
1. This formula is for treating a summertime diet that is intemperate or replete with uncooked food, compounded by the invasion of a summer-heat pathogen.
2. The key symptoms are vomiting, diarrhea, fullness and distention in the chest and diaphragm, head and eye pain, clouded vision, fatigue, fever, and aversion to cold.
3. Currently used in treating flu cold, food damage in summer, hangover and vomiting, thirst, and heat-stroke.
4. Gastrointestinal disease caused by exogenous infection, and gastrointestinal flu during summertime.

## Ingredients:

| | | | | | |
|---|---|---|---|---|---|
| 1. | sha ren | 1.0 | 8. | huo xiang | 2.0 |
| 2. | ban xia | 1.0 | 9. | bai bian dou | 2.0 |
| 3. | xing ren | 1.0 | 10. | hou po | 2.0 |
| 4. | ren shen | 1.0 | 11. | mu gua | 2.0 |
| 5. | gan cao | 1.0 | 12. | bai zhu | 2.0 |
| 6. | chi fu ling | 2.0 | 13. | sheng jiang | 2.0 |
| 7. | da zao | 2.0 | | | |

## Functions:
Expel summer-heat, transform accumulation, tonify *qi*, and harmonize the center.

## Modifications:
1. For cases with cold damage summer cold: add *zi su* and *xiang fu*.
2. For cases with summer damage thirst: add *xiang ru* and *shi gao*.
3. For cases with hangover: add *gen gen* and *shen qu*.
4. For cases with summer heat, and cold damage: combine with *San Wu Xiang Ru Yin*.
5. For cases suddenly turmoil vomit and diarrhea: combine with *Huo Xiang Zheng Qi San*.

## Administration:
Take with warm water, as needed.

Source: *Tai Ping Hui Min He Ji Ju Fang* (太平惠民和劑局方)

# Liu Jun Zi Tang 六君子湯
## Major Six Herb Combination

## Indications:

Spleen and stomach *qi* deficiency with phlegm damp: loss of appetite, nausea or vomiting, localized distention and a stifling sensation in the chest and epigastrium, and coughing of copious, thin, and white sputum.

**Tongue**:    pale tongue with a white coating
**Pulse**:    soggy and slow

## Clinical Applications:

1. This formula tonifies *qi* and increases the appetite.
2. It combines Four Gentlemen Decoction (*Si Jun Zi Tang*) with Two-Aged (Herb) Decoction (*Er Chen Tang*).
3. Currently used for chronic stomatitis, stomach prolapse, and poor appetite.

## Ingredients:

1. ren shen      10.0
2. bai zhu      10.0
3. fu ling      10.0
4. zhi gan cao      5.0
5. chen pi      5.0
6. ban xia      10.0
7. sheng jiang      5.0
8. da zao      5.0

## Functions:

Benefits *qi* and strengthens the spleen, dries damp and transforms phlegm.

## Modifications:

1. For severe deficiency cold with abdominal pain, add *xiang fu* and *sha ren*.
2. For severe spleen deficiency diarrhea, add *shan yao* and *qian shi*.
3. For wind-cold or wind-heat, add *chai hu* and *shao yao*.
4. For indigestion and abdominal distention, combine with *Ping Wei San*.
5. For post-illness deficiency, combine with *Xiao Chai Hu Tang*.
6. For deficiency in women, combine with *Si Wu Tang*.

## Administration:

Take with warm water, after meals.

Source: *Tai Ping Hui Min He Ji Ju Fang* (太平惠民合劑局方)

# Liu Wei Di Huang Wan 六味地黃丸
### Rehmannia Six Formula

## Indications:
For kidney and liver *yin* deficiency patterns: soreness and weakness in the lower back, dizziness, vertigo, headache, tinnitus, diminished hearing, night sweats, and spontaneous or nocturnal emission. Symptoms may also include hot palms and soles of feet, chronic dry and sore throat, toothache, heel pain, or wasting and thirsting (*xiao ke*) disorder.

**Tongue**: red tongue with little or no coating
**Pulse**: rapid and thin

## Clinical Applications:
1. This is the basic formula for kidney and liver *yin* deficiency.
2. Research shows this formula reduces renal hypertension and improves renal function, decreases blood fat and cholesterol and prevents fatty liver, and boosts the immune system. It also has anti-fatigue, anti-hypothermia, and anti-hypoxia functions.
3. Currently used for chronic nephritis, hypertension, diabetes, pulmonary or renal tuberculosis hyperthyroidism, menopausal syndrome, dysfunctional uterine bleeding, optic nerve atrophy, optic neuritis, central retinitis, cataracts, glaucoma, and chronic prostatitis.

## Ingredients:
| | | | | |
|---|---|---|---|---|
| 1. shu di | 24.0 | | 4. ze xie | 9.0 |
| 2. shan zhu yu | 12.0 | | 5. mu dan pi | 9.0 |
| 3. shan yao | 12.0 | | 6. fu ling | 9.0 |

## Functions:
Enriches *yin*, nourishes the kidney.

## Modifications:
1. For spleen *qi* deficiency and *qi* stagnation, add *chao bai zhu*, *chen pi*, and *sha ren*.
2. For *yin* deficiency cold, add *rou gui* and *fu zi*.
3. For *yin* deficiency add *zhi mu* and *huang bai*.
4. For weakness with soreness of the lower back and knees, combine with *Jin Suo Gu Jing Wan*.

## Cautions and Contraindications:
This formula has cloying properties and should be used with caution if the patient has indigestion, diarrhea due to spleen deficiency, or a white and greasy tongue coating.

## Administration:
Take with warm water or lightly salted warm water, before meals.

Source: *Xiao Er Yao Zheng Zhi Ju* (小兒藥證直局)

# Liu Wei Gu Jing Wan 六味固精丸
## Rehmannia Six and Stamen Formula

## Indications:
Seminal emission, mental issues and fatigue.

## Clinical Applications:
1. This formula is for treating seminal emission and fatigue.
2. It also might treat deficiency vaginal discharge and any other chronic disorders that present with symptoms characterized by an inability to retain fluids.
3. Currently used in treating seminal efflux, sexual dysfunction, neurological disorders, hypersensitivity, and lassitude of the spirit (*shen*).

## Ingredients:
1. shu di huang     3.0
2. shan zhu yu      1.5
3. shan yao         1.5
4. fu ling          1.5
5. mu dan pi        1.1
6. ze xie           1.1
7. qian shi         2.2
8. lian xu          2.2
9. sha yuan zi      2.2
10. long gu         1.1
11. mu li           1.1
12. wu wei zi       0.8
13. jin ying zi     1.1

## Functions:
Tonify the kidney, enrich *yin*, restrain seminal emission, and consolidate essence.

## Modifications:
1. For case with incontinence: add *yi zhi ren*.
2. For case with vaginal discharge: add *chun gen pi* and *bai guo*.
3. For case with early morning diarrhea: add *bu gu zhi* and *rou dou kou*.

## Note:
This formula is combination of *Jin Suo Gu Jing Wan* and *Liu Wei Di Huang Wan*.

## Administration:
Take with warm water, after meals.

Source: *Tai Ping Hui Min He Ji Ju Fang* (太平惠民和劑局方)

# Liu Yi San 六一散
## Six-to-One Powder

### Indications:
For the treatment of summer heat accompanied by dampness.

May also be used for fever, sweating, excessive thirst, irritability, urinary difficulties, or diarrhea.

**Tongue:**  thin, yellow greasy coating
**Pulse:**  soggy, rapid

### Clinical Applications:
1. This formula is commonly used for summer-heat-damp syndrome, a damp-heat syndrome of the middle *jiao* and lower *jiao*, heat-*lin* syndrome or stone-*lin* syndrome.
2. Currently used for upper respiratory tract infections or urinary tract infections.

### Ingredients:
1. hua shi    30.0
2. gan cao    5.0

### Functions:
Clears summer heat, resolves dampness and augments the *qi*.

### Modifications:
1. For cases with palpitations, anxiety, insomnia, or excessive dreams, add *zhu sha*.
2. For cases with constrained heat in the liver and gallbladder, add *qing dai*.
3. For cases with mild exterior syndrome marked by slight aversion to wind and cold, distention headache, or coughing with difficult expectoration, add *bo he*.

### Cautions and Contraindications:
Contraindicated for *yin* deficiency with no dampness, or for patients with copious and clear urine.

### Administration:
Take with warm water any time.

Source: *Shang Han Biao Ben* (傷寒標本)

# Long Dan Xie Gan Tang 龍膽瀉肝湯
### Gentiana Combination

## Indications:
Treats excess heat in the liver and gallbladder channels: headache, red and sore eyes, hypochondriac pain, bitter taste in the mouth, deafness, swelling in the ears, irritability, swelling, itching, and sweating of the pudendum, difficult and painful urination with a burning sensation in the urethra, dark and scanty or turbid urine, and leukorrhea due to damp-heat.

**Tongue:**   red tongue with yellow coating
**Pulse:**   wiry, rapid, and forceful

## Clinical Applications:
1. This formula treats various patterns due to excess liver and gallbladder fire rising or damp-heat descending.
2. Currently used for migraine, eczema, hypertension, acute conjunctivitis, corneal ulcer, acute glaucoma, central retinitis, iridocyclitis, furuncle of external auditory canal, rhinitis, acute hepatitis, acute cholecystitis, UTI, episioitis, orchitis, epididymitis, acute pelvic inflammation, herpes simplex, shingles (herpes zoster), and intercostal neuralgia.

## Ingredients:
| | | | | |
|---|---|---|---|---|
| 1. long dan cao | 8.0 | | 6. che qian zi | 4.0 |
| 2. huang qin | 4.0 | | 7. sheng di | 4.0 |
| 3. zhi zi | 4.0 | | 8. dang gui | 4.0 |
| 4. ze xie | 8.0 | | 9. chai hu | 8.0 |
| 5. mu tong | 4.0 | | 10. gan cao | 4.0 |

## Functions:
Drains excess fire from liver and gallbladder, clears and drains damp-heat from the lower *jiao*.

## Modifications:
1. For excess fire of the liver and gallbladder, replace *mu tong* and *che qian zi* with *huang lian*.
2. For more damp than heat, replace *huang qin* and *sheng di* with *hua shi* and *yi yi ren*.
3. For sores on the penis, infected hemorrhoids, or swelling, pain, redness, and heat of the scrotum, replace *chai hu* with *lian qiao*, *huang lian*, and *da huang*.
4. For severe difficult urination, add *yin chen* and *fu ling*.
5. For swollen, painful red eyes, add *bai ju hua* and *chuan xiong*.
6. For turbid vaginal discharge, combine with *Wen Qing Yin*.

## Cautions and Contraindications:
Caution with pregnancy, this formula should not be used for a long time or in large doses or by patients with spleen yang deficiency.

## Administration:
Take with warm water, before meals.

Source: *Li Dong Yuan Fang* (李東垣方)

# Ma Huang Tang 麻黃湯
Ephedra Combination
Ephedra Decoction

## Indications:
For the treatment of exterior wind-cold excess (*tai-yang shang-han* disorder).

*Tai-yang* pattern: fever, headache, body and lower back pain, aching joints, aversion to wind, no sweat and wheezing.

*Tai-yang* and *yang ming* combination patterns: wheezing with chest fullness, wind-cold attacks, fever with no sweating and aversion to cold, headache and body soreness.

**Tongue:**    thin and white coating
**Pulse:**    floating, superficial, and tight

## Clinical Applications:
1. This is a common formula used for exterior wind-cold excess.
2. The key symptoms are chills and fever without sweating, wheezing, and a superficial and tight pulse.
3. Currently used for the common cold (no sweating), flu, acute bronchitis, bronchial asthma, nerve pain, and rheumatism. According to research, it can also be used for influenza or rheumatoid influenza.

## Ingredients:
1. ma huang    9.0
2. gui zhi    6.0
3. xing ren    5.0
4. zhi gan cao    3.0

## Functions:
Promotes sweating to release exterior cold; opens the liver *qi* and calms wheezing.

## Modifications:
1. For wind, cold and dampness, add *bai zhu*.
2. For fever and aversion to cold, add *shi gao* and *sheng jiang*.
3. For headache with body ache, add *qiang huo* and *chuan xiong*.
4. For cough with thin phlegm, add *gan jiang, xi xin,* and *zi wan*.
5. For exterior cold with interior heat, add *shi gao*.
6. For concurrent *yang* deficiency, add *huang qi*.
7. For sore throat, reduce the dosage of *gui zhi* by half, and add *tian hua fen* and *she gan*.

## Cautions and Contraindications:
*Ma Huang Tang* should not be used in cases with fever, thirst, or rapid pulse; or with *qi,* blood, or body fluid deficiency;, or if a patient is prone to bleeding (especially from the nose). Use only for patients with strong constitution in colder climates. Use caution for patients with hypertension.

## Administration:
Take with warm or hot water, after meals.

Source: *Shang Han Lun* (傷寒論)

# Ma Xing Gan Shi Tang 麻杏甘石湯
Ephedra and Apricot Seed Combination
Ephedra, Apricot Kernel, Gypsum and Licorice Decoction

## Indications:
For the treatment of coughing and wheezing due to constrained interior lung heat.

May also be used for fever with or without sweating, excessive thirst, shortness of breath, and nasal flaring.

**Tongue**: yellow coating
**Pulse**: slippery and rapid, or superficial and rapid

## Clinical Applications:
1. This formula is commonly used for a wide variety of lung disorders. For example, it may be used in treating children with frequent or poorly controlled urination accompanied by coughing and wheezing.
2. Currently used for upper respiratory tract infections, acute bronchitis, bronchial pneumonia, labored pneumonia, whooping-cough pneumonia, bronchial asthma, measles pneumonia, bronchiolitis, pertussis and mild diphtheria; hemorrhoids or testitis.

## Ingredients:
1. ma huang        8.0
2. shi gao         16.0
3. xing ren        6.0
4. zhi gan cao     4.0

## Functions:
Pungent-cold to ventilate the lung *qi*, clear lung heat and calm wheezing.

## Modifications:
1. For phlegm that is difficult to cough up, add *jie geng.*
2. For fever and aversion to wind, add *chai hu* and *shao yao.*
3. For irritability and thirst, add *zhi mu* and *huang bai.*
4. For coughing with shortness of breath: add *sang bai pi, di gu pi,* and *bai bu.*
5. For pediatric cough, add *Er Chen Tang.*
6. For cases with excess heat in the lungs, high fever with sweating, increase the dosage of *shi gao.*
7. For cases with more exterior chills and fever without sweating, add *jing jie, bo he, su ye,* and *sang ye.*

## Cautions and Contraindications:
Contraindicated for wheezing due to cold or normal *qi* deficiency.

## Administration:
Take with warm water, after meals.

Source: *Shang Han Lun* (傷寒論)

# Ma Zi Ren Wan 麻子仁丸
Apricot Seed and Linum Formula

## Indications:
Spleen constraint pattern: dry-heat in the stomach and intestines with deficiency of *jin ye* fluids, constipation with hard stool that is difficult to expel, and frequent urination.

**Tongue**:     dry yellow coating
**Pulse**:      submerged and rapid or floating and choppy

## Clinical Applications:
1. This formula treats heat-induced dryness in the stomach and intestines. Heat and dryness in the stomach depletes spleen fluids. The excess in the stomach binds the fluid-depleted spleen, which is then unable to distribute fluids to the extremities.
2. Currently used for habitual, postpartum, or post-surgical constipation and hemorrhoids.

## Ingredients:
1. ma zi ren     7.5
2. da huang      5.0
3. xing ren      2.5
4. bai shao      2.5
5. zhi shi       2.5
6. hou po        2.5

## Functions:
Moistens the intestines, purges heat, moves *qi*, and unblocks the bowels.

## Modifications:
1. For severe difficulty passing stool, add *dang gui* and *mang xiao*.
2. For frequent urination, add *huang qin* and *huang bai*.
3. For hemorrhoid constipation, add *huang lian* and *sheng ma*.

## Cautions and Contraindications:
Should not be used to treat very weak patients without modification, nor should it be used for constipation solely due to blood deficiency. It is contraindicated during pregnancy.

## Administration:
Swallow with cold water, before meals.

Source: *Shang Han Lun* (傷寒論)

# Mai Men Dong Tang 麥門冬湯
Ophiopogon Combination
Ophiopogonis Decoction

## Indications:
For the treatment of lung atrophy or lung wilting (*fei wei*) due to heat syndrome.

Also may be used for fire-heat flaring upward; inhibited throat; coughing up of thick, sticky, and difficult to expectorate phlegm; nausea; dryness; and hoarseness. Lung atrophy (TB), short cough (whooping cough), or laboring cough (chronic bronchitis), and pregnancy cough.

| | |
|---|---|
| **Tongue:** | dry, red and scanty coating |
| **Pulse:** | deficiency and rapid |

## Clinical Applications:
1. This is a formula used for lung wilting (*fei wei*) caused by heat generated from stomach deficiency, which rises and scorches the lung *yin*.
2. Currently used for chronic bronchitis, bronchiectasis, chronic pharyngitis, laryngitis and TB due to lung *yin* deficiency. Also used for peptic ulcers or chronic atrophic gastritis due to stomach *yin* deficiency.

## Ingredients:
| | | | | | |
|---|---|---|---|---|---|
| 1. | mai men dong | 8.0 | 4. | da zao | 2.4 |
| 2. | ren shen | 1.6 | 5. | zhi gan cao | 1.6 |
| 3. | jing mi | 4.0 | 6. | ban xia | 4.0 |

## Functions:
Enrich the fluid to tonify the lung *qi*, clear heat to expel phlegm, benefits stomach and directs rebellious *qi* downward.

## Modifications:
1. For irritability, add *shi gao ,zhi mu.*
2. For dry throat, add *zhu ru, wu wei zi.*
3. For cough with blood, add *huang lian, e jiao, sheng di huang.*
4. For dry throat with hoarseness, add *jie geng, zi wan,* and *xuan shen.*
5. For brain hemorrhage with surging, big pulse with flaring, add *shi gao.*
6. For severe *yin* deficiency, add *bei sha shen, yu zhu.*
7. For tidal fever, add *di gu pi, yin chai hu.*

## Cautions and Contraindications:
Not to be used for lung atrophy that is due to deficient cold or dampness.

## Administration:
Take with warm water, after meals.

Source: *Jin Gui Yao Lue* (金櫃要略)

# Mai Wei Di Huang Wan 麥味地黃丸
## Ophiopogon and Schizandra Formula
# (Ba Xian Chang Shou Wan 八仙長壽丸)
### (Eight-Immortal Pill for Longevity)

## Indications:
Lung and kidney *yin* deficient consumptive disorders with cough.

Coughing of blood, tidal fevers, and night sweats.

## Clinical Applications:
1. This formula is for treating lung and kidney *yin* deficiency syndromes.
2. The key symptoms are muscles and bones are weak and atrophied, body is thin, cough and *qi* rebelling, cough with deficiency asthma, hot flashes and night sweats.
3. Currently used in treating lung-kidney *yin* deficiency asthma, dry cough without phlegm, or hemoptysis.
4. This formula can tonify weakness of elderly persons or children.

## Ingredients:
1. shu di huang    8.0
2. shan zhu yu    4.0
3. shan yao    4.0
4. fu ling    3.0
5. mu dan pi    3.0
6. ze xie    3.0
7. wu wei zi    2.0
8. mai men dong    3.0

## Functions:
Astringent the lungs *qi*, nourish the kidney *yin*.

## Modifications:
1. For nourishing lung-kidney, bring down fire and benefit the throat: combine with *Bai He Gu Jin Tang*
2. For nourishing *yin*, generate fluid; for *yin* deficiency irritable heat: combine with *Yu Quan Wan.*

## Note:
This formula is a modification of *Liu Wei Di Huang Wan* and adding *mai men dong* and *wu wei zi.*

## Administration:
Take with warm water, after meals.

Source: *Shou Shi Bao Fang* (壽世保方)

# Mu Fang Ji Tang 木防己湯
Stephania and Ginseng Combination

## Indications:
Water-fluid retention in the diaphragm area.

Gasping, fullness, glomus lump in the epigastrium, and dark facial color.

**Tongue:** light-dark tongue, greasy coating
**Pulse:** tight, deep

## Clinical Applications:
1. This formula is for treating diaphragmatic branch water retention, fullness and asthma, and focal distention in epigastrium area.
2. The key symptoms are *yang qi* deficiency and caused water-fluid accumulation in heart valve disease, cardiac insufficiency, and cardiac dyspnea.
3. Currently used in treating nephritis, edema, pregnancy nephritis, beriberi, bronchial wheezing, ascites, uremia, lower extremity edema.

## Ingredients:
1. mu fang ji     6.0
2. shi gao     12.0
3. gui zhi     4.0
4. ren shen     8.0

## Functions:
Move water, dissipate binds, recover *yin*, and calm rebelling.

## Modifications:
1. For cases with severe water accumulations: add *fu ling, zhu ling* and *mang xiao.*
2. For cases with severe heat evil damage *yin*: add *sha shen, mai men dong , chuan bai,* and *gua lou.*
3. For cases with cardiac asthmatic condition: add s*ang bai pi, zi su zi* and *sheng jiang.*

## Administration:
Take with warm water, after meals.

Source: *Jin Gui Yao Lue* (金匱要略)

# Mu Li San 牡蠣散
## Oyster Shell Powder

## Indications:
For the treatment of night sweats and/or spontaneous sweating syndrome.

May be used for spontaneous sweating that worsens at night, palpitations, patients who are easily startled, experience shortness of breath, irritability, or lethargy.

**Tongue:**  pale red
**Pulse:**  thin, frail

## Clinical Applications:
1. This formula is used for night sweats and/or spontaneous sweating associated with *wei qi* not binding the *yin* fluids.
2. Currently used for spontaneous sweating or night sweats occurring postpartum, post-surgery, or post-illness.

## Ingredients:
1. mu li (duan)      30.0
2. huang qi          30.0
3. xiao mai          30.0
4. ma huang gen      30.0

## Functions:
Augments the *qi*, stabilizes the exterior, gathers *yin*, and stops sweating.

## Modifications:
1. For *yang* deficiency sweating, add *fu zi.*
2. For *qi* deficiency sweating, add *ren shen* and *bai zhu.*
3. For *yin* deficiency sweating, add *sheng di* and *bai shao.*
4. For severe spontaneous sweating, increase *huang qi* dosages.

## Cautions and Contraindications:
Not for treatment of the profuse, oily sweating associated with exhaustion of the *yin* or *yang*.

## Administration:
Take with warm or hot water, as needed.

Source: *Tai Ping Hui Min He Ji Ju Fang* (太平惠民和劑局方)

# Mu Xiang Bing Lang Wan 木香檳榔丸
Vladimiria and Areca Seed Formula
Aucklandia and Betel Nut Pill from Zhu Dan-Xi 833

## Indications:
Food stagnation in the middle burner and dysenteric diarrhea syndromes.

Focal distention, fullness and pain in the epigastrium and abdomen, dysentery with red-and-white diarrhea with tenesmus or may be constipation.

**Tongue:**      yellow, greasy
**Pulse:**       submerged and excessive (deep and forceful).

## Clinical Applications:
1. This formula is used for food accumulation with *qi* stagnation that generated damp-heat in the middle *jiao*.
2. The key symptoms are distention and pain in the epigastrium and abdominal, constipation or dysentery with tenesmus.
3. Currently used in treating bacterial dysentery, acute and chronic cholecystitis, and acute gastroenteritis.
4. Indigestion, constipation, dysentery, acute and chronic gastroenteritis; an appropriate amount can strengthen the stomach, stop diarrhea, reduce inflammation and relieve pain.

## Ingredients:

| | | | | | | |
|---|---|---|---|---|---|---|
| 1. mu xiang | 1.0 | 6. huang bai | 1.0 | 11. xiang fu | 4.0 |
| 2. bin lang | 1.0 | 7. huang lian | 1.0 | 12. qian niu zi | 4.0 |
| 3. qing pi | 1.0 | 8. san leng | 1.0 | 13. mang xiao | 2.0 |
| 4. chen pi | 1.0 | 9. e zhu | 1.0 | | |
| 5. zhi ke | 1.0 | 10. da huang | 2.0 | | |

## Functions:
Moves *qi,* guides out stagnation, purges accumulation, and drains heat.

## Modifications:
1. For cases with phlegm fluid accumulation: add *ban xia* and *fu ling.*
2. For cases with damp-heat, *qi* stagnation: add *yin chen* and *zhi zi.*
3. For cases with female blood stagnation: add *dang gui* and *chuan xiong.*

## Cautions and Contraindications:
*Qi* deficiency.

## Administration:
Take with room-temp water or with warm ginger water, before meals.

Source: *Dan Xi xin Fa* (丹溪心法)

# Ning Sou Wan 寧嗽丸
## Fritillaria and Platycodon Formula
## Calm Coughing Pill

## Indications:
Cough or asthmatic breathing.

Acute wind-cold attack, stuffy or running nose; or chronic productive cough.

## Clinical Applications:
1. This formula is for treating cough or asthmatic breathing when these are acute wind-cold patterns or chronic productive coughs.
2. The key symptoms are congestion and runny nose, headache and fever, cough with phlegm or wheezing, *qi* rebelling cough, or sneezing and aversion to wind.
3. Currently used in treating cough and calming cough, a powerful formula for clearing heat and eliminating phlegm, and it is effective for long-term cough.

## Ingredients:
1. jie geng       2.4
2. shi hu        2.4
3. ban xia       2.4
4. bei mu        2.4
5. zi su zi       2.4
6. fu ling       2.4
7. bo he         1.8
8. xing ren      1.8
9. sang bai pi    1.8
10. ju hong      1.2
11. gu ya        1.2
12. gan cao      0.6

## Functions:
Ventilate stagnation, transform phlegm; benefit *qi* and tonify lungs.

## Modifications:
1. For cases with stuffy and running nose: add *fang fen* and *jing jie*.
2. For cases with phlegm, saliva and cough: add *di gu pi* and *zhu ru*.
3. For cases with dry throat and thirst: add *mai men dong* and *wu wei zi*.
4. For cases with common cold and cough: combine with *Hua Gai San*.
5. For cases with cough: combine with *Xie Bai San* or *Er Chen Tang*.

## Administration:
Take with warm water, after meals.

Source: *Shi Yi Jing Yan Fang* (世醫經驗方)

# Nu Ke Bai Zi Ren Wan 女科柏子仁丸
Biota and Cyathula Formula
Arborvitae Seed Pill for Women's Disorders

## Indications:
Blood deficiency and weakness of *shen* (spirit).

Irregular menstruation or amenorrhea and blood deficiency and hot flashes.

## Clinical Applications:
1. This formula is for treating weakness of the spirit caused by blood deficiency and is accompanied by irregular menstruation or amenorrhea.
2. The key symptoms are lumbar soreness, afternoon fevers, low spirit, abdominal pain, dizziness, and blurred vision.
3. Currently used in treating women with chronic painful conditions accompanied by disturbance of the spirit.

## Ingredients:
1. bai zhi ren        1.8
2. niu xi             1.8
3. huang bai          1.8
4. ze lan             7.2
5. xu duan            7.2
6. shu di huang       3.6

## Functions:
Calm the *shen*, tonify *qi*, nourish blood; activate blood, free the channel.

## Modifications:
1. For cases with blood deficiency headache: add *dang gui* and *chuan xiong*.
2. For cases with *qi* deficiency lower back pain: add *ren shen* and *huang qi*.
3. For cases with stagnation pain: add *tao ren* and *hong hua*.
4. For cases with blood deficiency amenorrhea: combine with *Si Wu Tang*.
5. For cases with over-fatigue amenorrhea: combine with *Xiao Chai Hu Tang*.
6. For cases with blood stagnation amenorrhea: combine with *Tao Ren Cheng Qi Tang*.

## Administration:
Take with warm water, before meals.

Source: *Fu Ren Da Quan Liang Fang* (婦人大全良方)

# Nuan Gan Jian 暖肝煎
### Warm the Liver Decoction

## Indications:
For the treatment of liver and kidney deficiency-cold syndrome.

May be used for lower abdominal pain that is sharp, localized, and is aggravated by the local application of cold. Also used for swelling, distention and pain of the scrotum.

**Tongue**: pale, white coating
**Pulse**: slow, deep and tight

## Clinical Applications:
1. This formula is used for liver blood and kidney *yang* deficiency cold, lower abdominal pain, or hernia pain caused by liver *qi* stagnation. It generally occurs in those who crave warmth and are averse to cold.
2. This formula may be used to treat a variety of disorders including varicocele, hydrocele and inguinal hernia.

## Ingredients:
1. rou gui — 3.0
2. xiao hui xiang — 6.0
3. dang gui — 9.0
4. gou qi zi — 9.0
5. wu yao — 6.0
6. chen xiang — 3.0
7. fu ling — 12.0
8. sheng jiang — 5.0

## Functions:
Warms and tonifies liver and kidneys, moves the *qi* and alleviates pain.

## Modifications:
1. For severe cold, add *yu, gan jiang.*
2. For severe abdominal pain, add *xiang fu.*
3. For severe scrotum pain, add *qing pi* and *ju he.*

## Cautions and Contraindications:
Not to be used for patients with heat, redness, swelling, or pain of the scrotum due to damp-heat in the lower *jiao.*

## Administration:
Take with warm water, after meals.

Source: *Jing Yue Quan Shu* (景岳全書)

# Pai Nong San 排膿散

### Platycodon and Aurantium Immaturus Formula
### Powder to Outburst Pus

## Indications:
Painful purulent disease.

Stomach or intestine abscess with pus that is about to erupt or beginning to erupt.

Abdominal fullness and spasm, lower abdominal pain, there is hardness underneath, or pus and blood in stool, dry mouth.

**Tongue:**  purple spots, thin yellow coating
**Pulse:**  slippery and rapid

## Clinical Applications:
1. This formula is for treating painful purulence, or pus and blood in stool.
2. The key symptoms are toxic swellings that are slow to suppurate, or swellings in which the flesh surrounding the post-suppuration sore remains hard and tight.
3. Currently used in treating mastitis, carbuncles, boils, infected lymph nodes, infected cysts.

## Ingredients:
1. zhi shi      1.8
2. bai shao     6.0
3. jie geng     2.0

## Functions:
Drain out pus, resolve toxin, disperse binds, and dissipate stagnation.

## Modifications:
1. For cases with hard, unform pus: add *jin yin hu* and  *lian qiao.*
2. For cases with formed pus erupted: *huang qi* and *dang gui.*
3. For cases with red, hot, swollen pain: add *huang lian* and *zhi zi.*
4. For cases with sore, ulcerated swollen pain: combine with *Zhen Ren Huo Ming Yin.*
5. For cases with carbuncle swelling: combine with *Tuo Li Xiao Du Yin.*

## Administration:
Take with warm water, before meals.

Source: *Jin Gui Yao Lue* (金櫃要略)

# Ping Wei San 平胃散
## Magnolia and Ginger Formula

## Indications:
Dampness obstructing the spleen and stomach: distention and fullness in the epigastrium and abdomen, loss of taste and appetite, heavy sensation in the limbs, loose stool or diarrhea, fatigue, increased desire to sleep, nausea and vomiting, and belching and acid regurgitation.

**Tongue**:  swollen with thick, white, and greasy coating
**Pulse**:  moderate or slippery

## Clinical Applications:
1. This formula is bitter and dry and used to treat damp cold in the middle *jiao*. Symptoms include distention and fullness in the epigastrium and abdomen, heavy sensation in the limbs, and fatigue.
2. Currently used for chronic gastritis, dysfunction of the digestive tract, colitis, and peptic ulcers due to dampness accumulating.

## Ingredients:
1. cang zhu   18.0
2. hou po   9.0
3. chen pi   9.0
4. gan cao   9.0
5. sheng jiang   9.0
6. da zao   9.0

## Functions:
Dries dampness, strengthens the spleen, rectifies *qi*, and harmonizes the middle.

## Modifications:
1. For damp heat, add *huang lian* and *huang qin*.
2. For severe cold damp, add *gan jiang* and *cao dou kou*.
3. For food stagnation, add *shan zha*, *mai ya*, and *shen qu*.
4. For *qi* stagnation, add *xiang fu* and *sha ren*.
5. For cold uterus, add *rou gui*.
6. For retained placenta, add *mang xiao*.
7. For phlegm dampness, add *ban xia* and *fu ling*.
8. For abdominal distention and pain, add *mu xiang* and *sha ren*.
9. For coldness of the lower limbs, add *niu xi*.

## Cautions and Contraindications:
This formula is contraindicated when the patient has *yin* and blood deficiency, has no symptoms of dampness, or is pregnant.

## Administration:
Swallow with warm water, before meals.

Source: *Tai Ping Hui Min He Ji Ju Fang* (太平惠民合劑局方)

# Pu Ji Xiao Du Yin 普濟消毒飲

Scute and Cimicifuga Combination
Universal Benefit Decoction to Eliminate Toxins

## Indications:

Used to treat wind-heat and epidemic toxicity affecting the head and face (*da tou wen*).

May be used to treat fever and chills, redness, swelling, and burning pain on the head and face, especially when the patient's eyes are not able to open due to swelling, dysfunction of the throat, dryness and thirst.

**Tongue**:     red , yellow coating
**Pulse**:       superficial, rapid and forceful

## Clinical Applications:

1. This formula is used to treat an acute and massive febrile disorder of the head due to a seasonal epidemic toxin associated with wind-heat and wind phlegm.
2. Currently used for erysipelas, mumps, acute tonsillitis, lymphangitis with lymphatic systems dysfunction due to toxic wind-heat evil.

## Ingredients:

| | | | | | |
|---|---|---|---|---|---|
| 1. | huang *qin* | 5.0 | 8. | niu ban zi | 1.0 |
| 2. | huang lian | 5.0 | 9. | jiang can | 0.7 |
| 3. | lian *qiao* | 1.0 | 10. | chai hu | 2.0 |
| 4. | xuan shen | 2.0 | 11. | jie geng | 2.0 |
| 5. | sheng ma | 0.7 | 12. | gan cao | 2.0 |
| 6. | ban lan gen | 1.0 | 13. | ma bo | 1.0 |
| 7. | bo he | 1.0 | 14. | chen pi | 2.0 |

## Functions:

Expels wind, disperses evil, clears heat and relieves toxins.

## Modifications:

1. For cases with constipation, add *jiu zhi da huang*.
2. For mumps or orchitis, add *chuan lian zi* and *long dan cao*.

## Cautions and Contraindications:

Use caution with patients who have *yin* deficiency.

## Administration:

Take with warm water, after meals.

Source: *Dong Yuan Shi Xiao Fang* (東垣試效方)

# Qi Bao Mei Ran Dan 七寶美髯丹
Seven Treasures Formula
Seven-Treasure Special Pill for Beautiful Whiskers 409

## Indications:
Liver and kidney deficiency symptoms.

Premature gra*ying* of the hair or hair loss, loose teeth, spontaneous and nocturnal emissions, infertility caused by kidney deficiency; and soreness and weakness of the lower back and knees.

**Tongue:** thin white coating
**Pulse:** deep, thin and forceless

## Clinical Applications:
1. This formula is used primarily to treat premature gra*ying* hair, hair loss, loose teeth, weakness and soreness of the lower back and knees, and degenerated anemia.
2. Currently used for alopecia, premature gra*ying* of the hair, impotence and infertility in male.
3. Prevent arteriosclerosis, physical fatigue, mental weakness, hair loss, sparse sperm and poor mobility.
4. Adrenal insufficiency and hypogonadism manifested by *yang* deficiency, which has the function of promoting and regulating kidney hormones.

## Ingredients:

| | | | | | | |
|---|---|---|---|---|---|---|
| 1. | zhi he shou wu | 5.0 | | 5. | tu si zi | 2.5 |
| 2. | huai niu xi | 2.5 | | 6. | gou *qi* zi | 2.5 |
| 3. | bu gu zhi | 2.5 | | 7. | dang gui | 2.5 |
| 4. | fu ling | 2.5 | | | | |

## Functions:
Tonifies the kidney *yin* and nourishes the liver blood, blackens the hair and replenishes the essence *(jing)*

## Modifications:
1. For cases with hair gray and dry: add *huang qi* and *shu di huang*.
2. For cases with *yang* rising and *yin* deficiency: add *zhi mu, huang bai, mai men dong,* and *wu wei zi.*
3. For cases with blood *yin* deficiency: add *nu zhen zi, han lian cao,* and *fu pen zi.*
4. For cases with cholesterol: add *dan shen* and *sang shen.*
5. For cases with soreness and weakness of lower back and knee: combine with *Ji Sheng Shen Qi Wan.*

## Cautions and Contraindications:
Spleen *qi* deficiency.

## Administration:
Take with warm water, as needed.

Take one pill with warm wine in the morning, one pill with ginger water at noon and one pill with salt water before bedtime.

Source: *ShaoYing Jie Fang* (邵應節方)

# Qi Ju Di Huang Wan 杞菊地黃丸
Lycium, Chrysanthemum and Rehmannia Formula

## Indications:
Kidney and liver *yin* deficiency: dry eyes, photophobia, tearing of the eye when exposed to drafts, painful eyes, dizziness, headache, diminished vision, and blurry vision.

**Tongue**:     red tongue with little or no coating
**Pulse**:      thin and rapid

## Clinical Applications:
1. This is the standard formula used for kidney and liver *yin* deficiency with blurry vision.
2. Currently used for menopausal syndrome, optic nerve atrophy, optic neuritis, central retinitis, cataracts, glaucoma, keratitis and scleritis.

## Ingredients:
1. shu di         24.0
2. shan zhu yu    12.0
3. shan yao       12.0
4. ze xie          9.0
5. mu dan pi       9.0
6. fu ling         9.0
7. gou qi zi        6.0
8. ju hua           6.0

## Functions:
Enriches *yin*, nourishes the kidneys.

## Modifications:
1. For red eyes with swelling and pain, add *zhi mu* and *huang bai*.
2. For severe tearing when exposed to drafts, add *sheng ma* and *ge gen*.
3. For diminished vision, add *dang gui* and *huang qi*.
4. For blurry vision, combine with *yi qi cong ming tang*.

## Cautions and Contraindications:
This formula has cloying properties and should be used cautiously when the patient has indigestion, diarrhea due to spleen deficiency, or a white and greasy tongue coating.

## Administration:
Swallow with warm water, after meals.

Source: *Zhong Guo Yi Xue Da Ci Dian* (中國醫學大辭典)

# Qi Pi Wan 啟脾湯
## Lotus and Citrus Formula
## Open the Spleen Pill

## Indications:
Chronic diarrhea, pediatric *gan* accumulation.

Indigestion, diarrhea, improper diets, abdominal pain.

## Clinical Applications:
1. This formula is for treating vomit and diarrhea caused by weakness of spleen and stomach.
2. The key symptoms are indigestion, diarrhea, vomit, jaundice, distention, abdominal pain, weak spleen and stomach.
3. Currently used in treating chronic enteritis, improper diet in children, dyspepsia, chronic debilitating diarrhea, gastrointestinal weakness after illness, low appetite.
4. This formula is especially suitable for pediatric patients - infants and small children.

## Ingredients:
1. ren shen     3.0
2. bai zhu      3.0
3. fu ling       3.0
4. shan yao    3.0
5. lian zi       3.0
6. chen pi      1.5
7. ze xie       1.5
8. shan zha    1.5
9. gan cao     1.5

## Functions:
Strengthen the spleen, harmonize the stomach, disperse accumulation, and supplement *qi,* stop diarrhea.

## Modifications:
1. For cases with low appetite: add *mai ya* and *shen qu.*
2. For cases with abdominal pain and diarrhea: add *mu xiang* and *sha ren.*
3. For cases with nausea, vomit, and focal distention: add *zhi shi* and *ban xia.*
4. For cases with indigestion: combine with *Ping Wei San.*
5. For cases with wind-cold vomit, diarrhea: combine with *Xiao Chai Hu Tang.*
6. For cases with post-illness and physique deficiency: combine with *Yu Ping Feng San.*

## Administration:
Take with warm water, before meals.

Source: *Wan Bing Hui Chun* (萬病回春)

# Qi Wei Bai Zhu San 七味白朮散
### Pueraria and Atractylodes Formula
### Seven-Ingredient Powder with White Atractylodes

## Indications:
Persistent vomiting and diarrhea due to spleen and stomach deficiency.

Improper digestion in children, vomiting and diarrhea caused by the common cold.

## Clinical Applications:
1. This formula is for treating pediatric indigestion, vomit and diarrhea caused by weakness of spleen and stomach.
2. The key symptoms are the long-term reduction in food intake leading to exhaustion of the essence and fluids with emaciation, which in turn leads to severe thirst, irritability, and in extreme cases, seizures.
3. Currently used in treating vomiting, diarrhea, pediatric diarrhea, chronic gastritis.
4. This formula is especially suitable for pediatric patients - infants and small children - to stimulate the stomach *qi* upward to help stop the diarrhea.

## Ingredients:
1. ge gen       6.0
2. ren shen     3.0
3. bai zhu      3.0
4. gan cao      3.0
5. fu ling      3.0
6. huo xiang    3.0

## Functions:
Strengthen the spleen and tonify the *qi*; harmonize stomach and generate fluid; stop diarrhea.

## Note:
This formula is a modification of *Si Jun Zi Tang* with the addition of *huo xiang* – aromatically transform the damp; *mu xiang* – move the *qi,* stop the pain; and *ge gen* – stimulate stomach *qi* rising and stop diarrhea.

## Administration:
Take with warm water, as needed.

Source: *Xiao Er Yao Zheng Zhi Jue*（小兒藥證直訣）

# Qian Jin Nei Tuo San 千金內托散
### Astragalus and Platycodon Formula
### Powder to Support the Interior Worth a Thousand Gold Pieces

## Indications:
Carbuncle sores and furuncles; those that are not built up or formed will quickly disperse, and those that have matured will quickly erupt.

## Clinical Applications:
1. This formula is for treating skin lesions such as carbuncles and boils. This formula disperses lesions that are not yet fully formed and causes sores that have already formed to suppurate.
2. The key symptoms are dermal swellings or infections that exist for some time and do not come to a head (or sores that suppurate but continue to produce pus) because of the patient's constitutional deficiencies.
3. Currently used in treating welling abscesses, flat abscesses, peri-anal inflammation, mastitis, lymphadenitis, or external and internal ear infections.
4. Carbuncle, hemorrhoid fistula, gangrene, transverse carbuncle, suppurative mastitis, bone tuberculosis, tendonitis, empyema, suppurative otitis media and skin ulcer.

## Ingredients:
1. dang shen     4.8
2. dang gui      2.4
3. huang *qi*    4.8
4. chuan xiong   1.8
5. fang fen      1.8
6. jie geng      2.4
7. hou po        1.8
8. rou gui       1.2
9. bai zhi       2.4
10. gan cao      1.2

## Functions:
Move blood, tonify the deficiency; expel foulness and generate flesh; quicken the blood to release toxin.

## Modifications:
1. For cases with severe pain: add *ru xiang* and *mo yao*.
2. For cases with constipation: add *da huang* and *zhi ke*.
3. For cases with short hesitant urination: add *mai men dong, che qian zi, mu tong,* and *deng xin cao*.
4. For cases with swelling pain and no appetite: add *sha ren* and *xiang fu*.

## Administration:
Take with warm water, after meals.

Source: *Wan Bing Hui Chun Fang* (萬病回春)

# Qiang Huo Sheng Shi Tang 羌活勝濕湯
Notopteryguim and Tuhuo Combination
Notopterygium Decoction to Overcome Dampness

## Indications:
For the treatment of exterior wind-damp evil attacks, causing pain. Common symptoms may include heavy and painful head, stiffness of the neck and shoulders, back pain, a generalized sensation of heaviness, difficulty rotating or bending the trunk, and mild fever and chills.

**Tongue:** white coating
**Pulse:** floating

## Clinical Applications:
1. This formula is used for wind-damp in the superficial aspects of the body, or the exterior and muscle levels. This most often occurs in those who have caught a cold after sweating profusely, or who live in damp environments.
2. The key symptoms are heaviness and pain in the head, neck, shoulders, and back, along with difficulty rotating or bending the trunk, and mild fever and chills.
3. Currently used in treating influenza, rheumatic fever, muscular headache, or upper respiratory tract infections.

## Ingredients:
1. qiang huo    5.0
2. du huo       5.0
3. fang feng    5.0
4. gao ben      5.0
5. chuan xiong  1.0
6. man jing zi  1.5
7. zhi gan cao  2.5

## Functions:
Expels wind and overcomes dampness.

## Modifications:
1. For heat and pain in the joints with heavy body, add *cang zhu, huang bai, fang ji,* and *yi yi ren.*
2. For severe heaviness and pain in the lower back, especially with white tongue coat and cold abdomen: add *fang ji* and *fu zi.*

## Cautions and Contraindications:
*Yin* deficiency or heat condition.

## Administration:
Take with warm water, as needed.

Source: *Li Dong Yuan Fang* (李東垣方)

# Qing Fei Tang 清肺湯
Platycodon and Fritillaria Combination
Clear the Lungs Decoction

## Indications:
Cough with phlegm accumulation in upper *jiao* (burner).

Chronic bronchitis, pneumonia, chest residual heat caused cough or cough with excessive phlegm.

## Clinical Applications:
1. This formula is for treating chronic disorders where fire has damaged the lung.
2. The key symptoms are in cough, phlegm, chronic incessant cough, chronic hoarseness, or throat sores.
3. Currently used in treating chronic bronchitis, chronic sore throat, pneumonia, pulmonary tuberculosis, chronic pharyngitis, bronchiectasis, and bronchial asthma, cardiac wheezing.

## Ingredients:

| | | | | |
|---|---|---|---|---|
| 1. gan cao | 0.6 | | 9. tian men dong | 1.5 |
| 2. huang qin | 3.0 | | 10. zhi zhi | 1.5 |
| 3. jie geng | 2.0 | | 11. xing ren | 1.5 |
| 4. fu ling | 2.0 | | 12. mai men dong | 1.5 |
| 5. chen pi | 2.0 | | 13. wu wei zi | 0.4 |
| 6. dang gui | 2.0 | | 14. sheng jiang | 3.0 |
| 7. bei mu | 2.0 | | 15. da zao | 2.0 |
| 8. sang bai pi | 2.0 | | 16. zhu ru | 2.0 |

## Functions:
Clear lung, transform phlegm, and stop cough.

## Modifications:
1. For cases with dry and painful throat: add *shi gao* and *zhi mu.*
2. For cases with hoarseness voice and cough: add *di gu pi.*
3. For irritable and swollen pain: add *jin yin hua* and *lian qiao.*

## Administration:
Take with warm water, after meals.

Source: *Zeng Bu Wan Bing Hui Chun*（增補萬病回春）

# Qing Fei Yin 清肺飲
Platycodon and Apricot Seed Formula
Clear the Lungs Drink

## Indications:
Cough caused by damp-phlegm *qi* rebelling.

## Clinical Applications:
1. This formula is for treating almost all types of lung-phlegm coughs.
2. The key symptoms are cold, flu cough, bronchitis cough.
3. Currently used in treating influenza cough, bronchitis wheezing, tuberculosis cough, and chronic pharyngitis cough.

## Ingredients:
1. xing ren      4
2. bei mu        4
3. fu ling       4
4. jie geng      2
5. gan cao       2
6. wu wei zi     2
7. ju hong       2
8. sheng jiang   2

## Functions:
Clear lungs, transform phlegm, benefit the *qi* and moisten the dryness.

## Modifications:
1. For cases with dry throat and thirst: add *mai men dong* and *ren shen*.
2. For cases with phlegm cough or asthma: add *sang bai pi* and *di gu pi*.
3. For cases with clear running nose: add *bo he* and *fang fen*.

## Cautions and Contraindications:
Dry cough.

## Administration:
Take with warm water, after meals.

Source: *Yi Fang ji Jie* (醫方集解)

# Qing Gu San 清骨散

Cool the Bones Powder

## Indications:

For the treatment of steaming bone disorder, due to liver and kidney *yin* deficiency syndromes. Also used to treat *xu lao* and *yin* deficiencies caused by heat.

Symptoms may include afternoon or night tidal fever or unremitting chronic low-grade fever, a sensation of internal heat, feeling as if bones are steaming, accompanied by irritability, dry throat, emaciation, red lips and dark-red cheeks, fatigue and night sweats.

**Tongue:**       Red color, little coating
**Pulse:**        Thready, rapid pulse

## Clinical Applications:

1. This formula was commonly used for steaming bone disorder.
2. Currently used in the treatment of tuberculosis, chronic wasting diseases caused by fever due to *yin* deficiency and interior heat.

## Ingredients:

1. yin chai hu          4.5
2. zhi mu               3.0
3. hu huang lian        3.0
4. di gu pi             3.0
5. qin jiao             3.0
6. qing hao             3.0
7. bie jiao  (cu zhi)   3.0
8. gan cao              1.5

## Functions:

Clears heat and improves *yin* deficiency in the liver and kidney.

## Modifications:

1. For severe blood deficiency: add *dang gui, bai shao,* and *sheng di.*
2. For frequent coughing: add *e jiao, mai men dong,* and *wu wei zi.*

## Administration:

Take with warm water, before meals.

Source: *Zheng Zhi Zhung Sheng* (證治準繩)

# Qing Hao Bie Jiao Tang 青蒿鱉甲湯
Artemisia and Turtle Shell Combination
Artemisia Annua and Soft-Shelled Turtle Shell Decoction

## Indications:
For the treatment of patients in the late stages of *wen bing*, which depletes the fluids. Addresses hidden evil lingering in *yin* region of body.

Indicated if night fever reduces in the morning, with an absence of sweating as the fever recedes. Patient may be emaciated, despite an adequate appetite and nutrition.

**Tongue**:     Red color, little coating
**Pulse**:      Thready, rapid

## Clinical Applications:
1. This formula was originally used for deficient heat syndrome due to lingering heat with *yin* and fluid deficiency in the late stage of febrile disease. It is used to treat tidal fevers with liver *yin* deficiency characterized by afternoon fever, fatigue, sweating and emaciation.
2. Currently used for the advanced stages of various infectious diseases, chronic nephritis, fevers of unknown origin, and post-surgical fevers.

## Ingredients:
1. bie jiao      15.0
2. qing hao       6.0
3. sheng di      12.0
4. zhi mu         6.0
5. mu dan pi      9.0

## Functions:
Nourishes *yin* and vents heat.

## Modifications:
1. For low-grade fevers of unknown origin: add *bai wei, shi hu* and *di gu pi.*
2. For steaming bones: add *sha shen* and *han lian cao.*
3. For post-operative fevers: add *bai wei, yin chai hu,* and *pu gong ying.*
4. For hot, itching skin rashes that are worse at night: combine with *Dang Gu Yin Zi.*
5. For herpes zoster (shingles) of the conjunctiva: add *ju hua, xuan shen, ban lan gen, chai hu,* and *che qian zi.*

## Cautions and Contraindications:
Not to be used for cases with spasms or convulsions.

## Administration:
Take with warm water, after meals.

Source: *Jin Gui Yao Lue* (溫病條辨)

# Qing Kong Gao 清空膏
Scute, Siler and Notopterygium Formula

## Indications:
Wind-heat headache, migraine headache.

Bitter taste in mouth, red eyes, short dark urine.

**Tongue**: red, yellow coating.
**Pulse**: floating

## Clinical Applications:
1. This formula is for treating headache or migraine headache from wind-damp-heat blazing upward.
2. The key symptoms are head-wind (*tou feng* 頭風) and excruciating pain.
3. Currently used in treating wind-heat neuralgia, vascular headache. Also, eye pain of acute conjunctivitis and glaucoma caused by wind-heat in liver channel.

## Ingredients:
1. huang qin        7.2
2. gan cao          3.6
3. fang fen         2.4
4. qiand huo        2.4
5. huang lian       2.4
6. chai hu          1.8
7. chuan xiong      1.2

## Functions:
Expel wind, clear heat.

## Modifications:
1. For severe wind-heat: add *ju hua* and *man jing zi.*
2. For long-lasting chronic headache: add few *xi xin.*

## Cautions and Contraindications:
1. Caution for pregnant women, or during menstruation cycle.
2. Do not take long-term with a weak spleen and stomach.

## Administration:
Take with warm water, after meals; or mix with tea and make a syrup.

Source: *Li Dong Yuan Fang* (李東垣方)

# Qing Liang *Yin* 清涼飲
## Scute and Mint Combination
## Clearing and Cooling Drink

## Indications:
Dryness in the upper *jiao* (burner).

## Clinical Applications:
1. This formula is for treating upper body heat accumulation.
2. The key symptoms are treating dry mouth, tongue, throat, and nose. This heat could be left over from a hot pathogen or could be the result of internal damage.
3. Currently used in treating sore throat, blood-heat nosebleed, conjunctivitis, and mouth sores.

## Ingredients:
1. huang qin       2.0
2. huang lian      2.0
3. bo he           1.5
4. xuan shen       1.5
5. dang gui        1.5
6. bai shao        1.5
7. zhi gan cao     1.0

## Functions:
Drains and clears upper burner heat and cools blood.

## Modifications:
1. For cases with mouth or tongue sores: add *mu tong*.
2. For cases with sore throat: add *niu bang zi*.
3. For cases with eye disorders: add *man jing zi, ju hua* and *che qian zi*.

## Administration:
Take with warm water, before meals.

Source: *Zheng Zhi Zhun Sheng* (證治準繩)

# Qing Qi Hua Tan Wan 清氣化痰丸
Pinellia and Scute Formula
Clear the *Qi* and Transform Phlegm Pill

## Indications:
This formula is primarily used in the treatment of congested, phlegmy coughs caused by heat.

Symptoms may include coughing with yellow, sticky sputum that is difficult to expectorate, pressure and fullness in the chest and diaphragm, and possibly nausea or vomit; in severe cases, there may also be difficulty breathing.

**Tongue:** red, greasy, yellow coating
**Pulse:** rapid, slippery or wiry

## Clinical Applications:
1. This formula is used for phlegm-heat that occurs when fire heats the stagnated fluids due to spleen deficiency.
2. The key symptoms are coughing with yellow, viscous sputum and focal distention and feeling of fullness in the chest and diaphragm, feeling unsettled with irritability, short and dark-colored, even reddish urination.
3. Currently used in treating pneumonia, bronchitis and bronchiectasis.

## Ingredients:

| | | | | | |
|---|---|---|---|---|---|
| 1. | dan nan xing | 3.0 | 6. | fu ling | 2.0 |
| 2. | gua lou ren | 2.0 | 7. | ban xia | 3.0 |
| 3. | huang qin | 2.0 | 8. | xing ren | 2.0 |
| 4. | zhi shi | 2.0 | 9. | sheng jiang | 1.0 |
| 5. | chen pi | 2.0 | | | |

## Functions:
Clears heat, transforms phlegm, directs rebellious *qi* downward, and stops coughing.

## Modifications:
1. For severe heat with thick phlegm, tight chest and thirst: add *shi gao, zhi mu,* and *huang qin.*
2. For hot phlegm which is difficult to expectorate: add *dong gua zi, jie geng,* and *sang bai pi.*

## Cautions and Contraindications:
Not to be used for coughs due to *yin* deficiency.

## Administration:
Take with warm ginger water, after meals.

Source: *Yi Fang Kao* (醫方考)

# Qing Shang Fang Fen Tang 清上防風湯

### Siler Combination
### Clear the Upper (Burner) Decoction with Saposhnikovia

## Indications:
Upper burner fire.

Wind-heat-toxin sores and swellings on the head and face.

## Clinical Applications:
1. This formula is for treating upper burner fire; wind-heat-toxin sores and swellings on the head and face, and dark yellow urination.
2. The key symptoms are headache, facial sores and swellings, upper body acne or boils, infantile fetal heat, red swollen eyes, red face and neck.
3. Currently used in treating sties, red, swollen eyelids, miscellaneous red facial rashes and brandy nose.

## Ingredients:
| | | | | | |
|---|---|---|---|---|---|
| 1. | fang fen | 3.0 | 7. | huang lian | 1.5 |
| 2. | lian qiao | 2.4 | 8. | jing jie | 1.5 |
| 3. | bai zhi | 2.4 | 9. | zhi zi | 1.5 |
| 4. | jie geng | 2.4 | 10. | zhi ke | 1.5 |
| 5. | huang qin | 2.1 | 11. | bo he | 1.5 |
| 6. | chuan xiong | 2.1 | 12. | gan cao | 0.9 |

## Functions:
Clear heat, resolve toxin, and dispel wind and damp.

## Modifications:
1. For cases with acne: add *yi yi ren*.
2. For cases with constipation: add *da huang*.
3. For cases with swollen pain head sore: add *sheng ma* and *ge geng*.
4. For cases with itching head sore: add *jin yin hua* and *tu fu ling*.
5. For cases with swollen hot head sore: add *zhi mu* and *shi gao*.
6. For cases with heat-toxin sore or ulcer: combine with *Huang Lian Jie Du Tang*.

## Note:
If the stool is blocked, be sure to add *da huang* (rhubarb) to purge heat-toxin.

## Administration:
Take with warm or room-temp water, after meals.

Source: *Wan Bing Hui Chun* (萬病回春)

# Qing Shu Yi Qi Tang 清暑益氣湯
### Astragalus and Atractylodes Combination
### Clear Summer-Heat and Augment the *Qi* Decoction

## Indications:
Summer or late summertime with damp-heat patterns.

Drowsiness and fatigue of limbs, body heat and irritability, spontaneous sweating and thirst, yellow stool, and dark-yellow urine.

| Tongue: | yellow coating |
|---|---|
| Pulse: | deficiency rapid |

## Clinical Applications:
1. This formula is for treating summer-heat disorder that has damaged *qi* and fluids.
2. The key symptoms are fever, profuse sweating, vexation, thirst, no desire for food, heaviness in the limbs, short and dark urination, fatigue, shallow breathing, lassitude of the spirit.
3. Currently used in treating whole body fatigue and general internal weakness caused by long summer dampness.

## Ingredients:

| | | | | | |
|---|---|---|---|---|---|
| 1. | huang qi | 3.0 | 10. ge gen | 1.0 |
| 2. | cang zhu | 3.0 | 11. qi pi | 1.0 |
| 3. | sheng ma | 3.0 | 12. dang gui | 1.0 |
| 4. | ren shen | 1.5 | 13. mai men dong | 1.0 |
| 5. | bai zhu | 1.5 | 14. wu wei zi | 0.5 |
| 6. | chen pi | 1.5 | 15. sheng jiang | 3.0 |
| 7. | shen qu | 1.5 | 16. da zao | 2.0 |
| 8. | zhi gan cao | 1.0 | 17. ze xie | 1.5 |
| 9. | huang bai | 1.0 | | |

## Functions:
Clear heat, dispel damp, boost *qi*, and strengthen the spleen.

## Modifications:
1. For cases with thirst and aversion to food: add *shi gao, zhi mu*.
2. For cases with difficulty urinating: add *mu tong, sheng di*.
3. For cases with irritability heat: add *yin chen, zhi zi*.
4. For cases with cold drink and abdominal pain: combine with *Wei Ling Tang*.
5. For cases with over fatigue and tiredness: combine with *Xiao Chai Hu Tang*.

## Administration:
Take with warm or room-temp water, after meals.

Source: *Pi Wei Lun* (脾胃論)

# Qing Wei San 清胃散

Coptis and Rehmannia Formula
Clear the Stomach Powde

## Indications:

Used in the treatment of disorders where heat accumulation in the stomach is present.

May be used in the treatment of toothaches, especially those that extend and radiate to the head, and cheek, and which are accompanied by fever. Treats toothaches that are averse to heat and prefer cold; other symptoms include gum ulceration; gum bleeding; swelling and pain in the lips, tongue, and cheeks; and persistent bad breath or dry mouth.

**Tongue**:  red, yellow coating
**Pulse**:  slippery and rapid

## Clinical Applications:

1. This formula is commonly used for toothaches with swollen gums and bleeding of the gums due to stomach heat or blood heat with fire accumulation.
2. Currently used for stomatitis, periodontal disease, trigeminal neuralgia, glossitis, idiopathic halitosis, congestive inflammation, and gingivitis.

## Ingredients:

1. huang lian     3.6
2. sheng di      3.6
3. mu dan pi     6.0
4. dang gui      3.6
5. sheng ma     12.0

## Functions:

Clears stomach heat, cools the blood heat, relieves heat toxins and nourishes the *yin*.

## Modifications:

1. For cases with constipation due to intestines dryness: add *da huang.*
2. For cases with thirst or desire to drink cold beverages: increase the dosage of *shi gao.*
3. For summer heat with toothache: add *Bai Hu Tang.*
4. For gum swollen ulcers: add *Gan Lu Yin.*
5. For mouth and tongue ulcers: add *jin yin hua* and *lian qiao.*

## Cautions and Contraindications:

Not to be used for the treatment of toothaches due to wind-cold or tooth and gum problems due to kidney deficiency.

## Administration:

Take with warm water, as needed.

Source: *Lan Shi Mi Cang* (蘭室秘藏)

# Qing Wen Bai Du San 清瘟敗毒散
## Clear Epidemics and Overcome Toxicity Decoction

## Indications:
Used in the treatment of blazing fire toxicity in the *qi* and blood levels of epidemic febrile disease.

Symptoms may include intense fever, strong thirst, severe and splitting headache, dry heaves, extreme irritability; in severe cases, delirium, unconsciousness, blurred vision, or maculae and erythema, vomiting of blood, nosebleeds, or convulsions may occur.

**Tongue:**    deep red and scorched lips
**Pulse:**    deep, thready and rapid  or superficial, large and rapid pulse

## Clinical Applications:
1. This formula is especially useful for treating severe fire in the *qi* and blood level. Intense fever and strong thirst are signs of excess heat in the *qi* level. Severe stabbing headaches may be due to fire toxin rising to the head.
2. Currently used for encephalitis and meningitis due to toxic heat.

## Ingredients:
1. shi gao — 50
2. zhi mu — 10
3. gan cao — 5
4. huang lian — 6
5. huang qin — 10
6. zhi zi — 10
7. xi jiao — 5
8. sheng di — 15
9. chi shao — 10
10. mu dan pi — 10
11. lian qiao — 10
12. xuan shen — 15
13. jie geng — 10
14. dan zhu ye — 10

## Functions:
Clears fire heat, relieves toxins, cools the blood and drains fire.

## Cautions and Contraindications:
*Yang* deficiency or weakness of spleen and stomach.

## Administration:
Take with warm water, as needed.

Source: *Yi Zhen Yi De* (疫疹一得)

# Qing Xin Li Ge Tang 清心利膈湯
### Arctium Combination
### Clear the Heart and Enable the Diaphragm Decoction 887

## Indications:
Heart and spleen smoldering heat.

Swollen pain in throat, cheek and tongue, and constipation.

**Tongue**:     red tongue with yellow coating
**Pulse**:      large, flooded, and rapid

## Clinical Applications:
1. This formula is for treating accumulated heat in the lungs and stomach.
2. The key symptoms are red, swollen, and painful throat with pain that extends to the lower edge of the ear.
3. Currently used in treating difficulty swallowing, small pustules on the tonsils, high fever, thirst, mouth odor, spitting up of thick yellow phlegm, abdominal distention, constipation, and short, dark urination.

## Ingredients:
| | | | | | |
|---|---|---|---|---|---|
| 1. | fang fen | 2.6 | 8. | lian *qi*ao | 1.3 |
| 2. | jing jie | 2.6 | 9. | xuan shen | 1.3 |
| 3. | lian *qi*ao | 2.6 | 10. | da huang | 1.3 |
| 4. | jie geng | 2.6 | 11. | niu pang zi | 1.3 |
| 5. | huang *qi*n | 2.6 | 12. | gan cao | 1.3 |
| 6. | huang lian | 2.6 | 13. | mang xiao | 0.6 |
| 7. | zhi zi | 1.3 | | | |

## Functions:
Clear heat, expel the wind, resolve toxin, and disinhibit the throat.

## Modifications:
1. For cases with swollen sore throat: add *shan dou gen* and *she gan.*
2. For cases with phlegm fluid and thirsty: add *tian hua fen* and *zhu ru.*
3. For cases with irritability and cold drink: add *shi gao* and *zhi mu.*

## Cautions and Contraindications:
Caution with pregnancy.

## Administration:
Take with warm water, after meals.

Source: *Zhong Guo Yi Xue Da Ci Dian* (中國醫學大辭典)

# Qing Xin Lian Zi Yin 清心蓮子飲
Lotus Seed Combination
Clear the Heart Drink with Lotus Seed

## Indications:
Damp-heat "*lin*" syndrome.

Excess above and deficiency below, heart fire blazing upward with dry mouth and tongue.

Heart fire pouring into the lower burner and vaginal discharge.

## Clinical Applications:
1. This formula is for treating upper body heat with lower body deficiency.
2. The key symptoms are bitter taste, dry throat, damp-heat bladder, nocturnal emission and turbid "*lin*"; seminal efflux, vaginal discharge, exacerbation of symptoms on exertion, restlessness and sleep disturbances, tired limbs, five center-heat.
3. Currently used in treating kidney tuberculosis, chronic gonorrhea, chronic cystitis, chronic pyelitis, leukorrhea and other diseases; can also be applied to sexual neurasthenia, diabetes, intraoral inflammation. And when the surface of urine has oily substance.

## Ingredients:
1. shi lian rou    4.5
2. fu ling         4.5
3. huang qi        4.5
4. ren shen        4.5
5. huang qin       3.0
6. mai men dong    3.0
7. di gu pi        3.0
8. che qian zi     3.0
9. zhi gan cao     3.0

## Functions:
Clear heat, disinhibit damp, supplement *qi*, and transform stagnation.

## Modifications:
For cases with feverishness: add *chai hu* and *bo he.*

## Administration:
Take with warm water, as needed.

Source: *Tai Ping Hui Min He Ji Ju Fang* (太平惠民和劑局方)

# Qing Yan Li Ge Tang 清咽利膈湯
### Arctium and Cimicifuga Formula
### Clear the Throat and Enable the Diaphragm Decoction

## Indications:
Lung and spleen heat accumulation.

Throat, cheek and tongue swollen pain.

## Clinical Applications:
1. This formula is for treating accumulated heat in the heart and spleen.
2. The key symptoms are canker sore, sore throat, and gum ulcer pain.
3. Currently used in treating intraoral inflammation, sore throat, gum ulcers, and tonsillitis.

## Ingredients:
1. niu bang zi        3.0
2. sheng ma          3.0
3. bai shao          3.0
4. gan cao           3.0
5. xuan shen         3.0
6. fang fen          3.0
7. jie geng          3.0
8. fu ling           3.0
9. huang qin         3.0
10. huang lian       3.0

## Functions:
Clear heat, expel the wind, resolve toxin, and smooth the *qi*, release toxin.

## Modifications:
1. For cases with swollen sore throat: add *shan dou gen* and *she gan*.
2. For cases with phlegm fluid and thirsty: add *tian hua fen* and *zhu ru*.
3. For cases with irritability and cold drink: add *shi gao* and *zhi mu*.

## Administration:
Take with warm water, after meals.

Source: *Zheng Zhi Zhun Sheng* (證治準繩)

# Qing Ying Tang 清營湯
## Clear the Nutritive Level Decoction

## Indications:

This formulation addresses heat evil entering the *ying* level from warm-febrile disease (*wen bing*).

Symptoms may include high fever that worsens at night, irritability and restlessness, sometimes delirium, indistinct maculae rash and erythema.

**Tongue:**   scarlet, dry coating
**Pulse:**    thin, rapid

## Clinical Applications:

1. This formula can be used for patients exhibiting faint and indistinct erythema and purpura.
2. Currently used for pneumonia, encephalitis, meningitis, septicemia, and leukemic crisis.

## Ingredients:

1. shui niu jiao    30.0 - 120.0 (xi jiao 9.0)
2. sheng di         15.0
3. xuan shen         9.0
4. mai men dong      9.0
5. jin yin hua       9.0
6. lian qiao         6.0
7. huang lian        5.0
8. dan zhu ye        3.0
9. dan shen          6.0

## Functions:

Clears *ying* level, vents the heat, relieves fire toxin and nourishes the *yin*.

## Modifications:

1. For severe depletion of *yin* and fluid: omit *huang lian*, add *sha shen* and *gou qi zi*.
2. For severe *qi*-level fire: add *shi gao*.

## Cautions and Contraindications:

Not to be used for cases with white and slippery tongue coating.

## Administration:

Take with warm water, after meals.

Source: *Wen Bing Tiao Bian* (溫病條辨)

# Qing Zao Jiu Fei Tang 清燥救肺湯
Erioblrya and Ophiopogon Combination
Eliminate Dryness and Rescue the Lungs Decoction

## Indications:
This formula is used for the treatment of disorders where external warm-dryness does injury to the lungs.

Symptoms may include coughing without sputum, or sputum that is difficult to expectorate, nausea or vomit; in severe cases, there may also be difficulty breathing, thirst and irritability.

**Tongue:**    red, dry coating
**Pulse:**    rapid and deficiency surging

## Clinical Applications:
1. This formula treats damage to the *yin* and fluid of lungs, regardless of whether the damage comes from internal disharmony or from external warm-dry attacks.
2. The key symptoms are thirst and dry cough, cough with less phlegm, and thirst with sore throat.
3. Currently used in treating dry cough, dryness pneumonia, bronchitis, and pulmonary tuberculosis.

## Ingredients:
| | | |
|---|---|---|
| 1. sang ye | 7.5 | |
| 2. shi gao | 6.5 | |
| 3. mai men dong | 3.0 | |
| 4. gan cao | 2.5 | |
| 5. hu ma ren | 2.5 | |
| 6. pi pa ye | 2.0 | |
| 7. e jiao | 2.0 | |
| 8. xing ren | 2.0 | |
| 9. ren shen | 2.0 | |

## Functions:
Clears dryness and moistens lungs.

## Modifications:
1. For dry throat: add *zhi mu* and *jie geng.*
2. For cough without phlegm: *add di gu pi* and *bei mu.*

## Cautions and Contraindications:
Not to be used for patients experiencing cough with excess phlegm.

## Administration:
Take with warm water, after meals.

Source: *Yi Zong Jin Jian*（醫宗金鑑）

# Ren Shen Bai Du San 人參敗毒散
Ginseng and Mint Formula
Ginseng Powder to Overcome Pathogenic Influences

## Indications:
This formula is used for the treatment of exterior wind-cold damp disorder with *qi* deficiency syndrome.

Symptoms may include high fever and severe chills with shivering, no sweating, painful and stiff head and neck, soreness and pain of the extremities, fullness and distention of the chest, nasal congestion with especially loud breathing and productive cough.

| **Tongue:** | greasy, white coating |
| **Pulse:** | floating, soggy |

## Clinical Applications:
1. This formula was originally used for children; later the application of this formula was expanded to include all cases of wind-cold dampness in patients with underlying qi deficiency, including the elderly, postpartum women, and those recovering from debilitating illnesses.
2. Currently used for the early stages of flu season, irritability with chest and epigastric fullness, flu, headache, stuffy nose, and cough; early-stage hives, allergic dermatitis, urticaria and eczema.

## Ingredients:

| | | | | | | | |
|---|---|---|---|---|---|---|---|
| 1. | qiang huo | 3.0 | 5. | jie geng | 3.0 | 9. gan cao | 1.5 |
| 2. | du huo | 3.0 | 6. | zhi ke | 3.0 | 10. ren shen | 3.0 |
| 3. | chuan xiong | 3.0 | 7. | qian hu | 3.0 | 11. sheng jiang | 3.0 |
| 4. | chai hu | 3.0 | 8. | fu ling | 3.0 | 12. bo he | 0.5 |

## Functions:
Disperses cold, dispels wind and dampness, releases the exterior and augments the *qi*.

## Modifications:
1. For wind-cold fever: add *fang feng* and *jing jie*.
2. For dry mouth: add *huang qin*.
3. For beriberi: add *da huang* and *cang zhu*.
4. For early-stage sores with exterior symptoms: omit *ren shen* and replace with *jin yin hua* and *lian qiao*.
5. For wind rashes, urticaria: add *Xiao Feng San*.
6. For wind-cold fever: add *Sheng Ma Ge Gen Tang*.

## Cautions and Contraindications:
Not to be used for cases with heat.

## Administration:
Take with water, as needed, cold type with warm water, heat type with cold water.

Source: *Tai Ping Hui Min He Ji Ju Fang* (太平惠民和劑局方)

0070

# Ren Shen Dang Shao San 人參當芍散
### Ginseng and Tangkuei Formula

**Indications:**
Blood loss and anemia.

Anemia, pain in the lower abdomen, menstrual difficulties, leukorrhea, headache, and dizziness.

**Clinical Applications:**
1. This formula is for treating postpartum women who suffer from mild pain and cramping. when these are due to *qi* and blood deficiency.
2. The key symptoms are pain in the lower abdomen, menstrual difficulties, leukorrhea, headache, and dizziness.
3. Currently used in treating people who are usually overly fatigued, lose blood, and have weak internal organs due to chronic illness.

**Ingredients:**
1. dang gui      1.5
2. bai shao      1.5
3. fu ling       1.5
4. bai zhu       1.5
5. chuan xiong   1.0
6. ren shen      1.5
7. ze xie        1.5
8. rou gui       0.5
9. gan cao       0.5

**Functions:**
Nourish blood, boost *qi*, disinhibit damp, and quiet the fetus.

**Modifications:**
1. For cases with restless fetus due to heat: add *huang qin.*
2. For cases with severe blood deficiency: add *sang ji sheng.*

**Note:**
This formula is a modification of *Dang Gui Shao Yao San* by adding *dang gui, ren shen,* and *gan cao.*

**Administration:**
Take with warm water, before meals.

Source: *Yan Fang* （驗方）

126

# Ren Shen Ge Jie San 人參蛤蚧散
Ginseng and Gecko Combination
Ginseng and Gecko Powder

## Indications:
Lung and kidney *qi* deficiency with heat in the lungs.

Chronic coughing and wheezing, thick and yellow sputum, expectoration of pus and blood, a sensation of heat and irritability in the chest and/or facial edema.

**Tongue:**       thin, white or greasy, thin yellow coating.
**Pulse:**        floating and deficient.

## Clinical Applications:
1. This formula is for treating chronic asthma and bronchitis lung disorders due to both lung and kidney deficiency.
2. The key symptoms are chronic coughing and wheezing, thick and yellow sputum, expectoration of pus and blood, a sensation of heat and irritability in the chest, facial edema, and gradual emaciation.
3. Currently used in treating emphysema, pulmonary heart disease, chronic illness, cough, wheezing, and thick yellow phlegm.

## Ingredients:
1. ren shen        2.0
2. ge jie          2.0
3. xing ren        5.0
4. zhi gan cao     3.0
5. fu ling         2.0
6. sang bai pi     2.0
7. chuan bei mu    2.0
8. zhi mu          2.0

## Functions:
Tonify *qi*, clear the lung, alleviate cough, and stabilize asthmatic breathing.

## Cautions and Contraindications:
Any condition with external pathogenic flu.

## Administration:
Take with warm water, before meals.

Source: *Wei Sheng Bao Jian* (衛生寶鑒)

# Ren Shen Xie Fei Tang 人参瀉肺湯
Ginseng and Scute Combination
Ginseng Decoction to Drain the Lungs

## Indications:
Accumulated heat in the lungs and phlegm.

Heat accumulation in the lung meridian, wheezing, fullness of the chest and diaphragm, excessive phlegm, and constipation.

## Clinical Applications:
1. This formula is for treating heat in the diaphragm and chest ascending to scorch the fluids and raising the phlegm-heat in the lungs.
2. The key symptoms are wheezing, distention and fullness in the chest and diaphragm with copious sticky phlegm and constipation.
3. Currently used in treating pneumonia, pharyngitis, tonsillitis, bronchitis, and tuberculosis. Swelling, cough, wheezing, loss of voice, and excessive thirst for water.

## Ingredients:

| | | | | | |
|---|---|---|---|---|---|
| 1. | ren shen | 2.0 | 7. | xing ren | 2.0 |
| 2. | huang qin | 2.0 | 8. | sang bai pi | 2.0 |
| 3. | zhi zi | 2.0 | 9. | jie geng | 2.0 |
| 4. | zhi ke | 2.0 | 10. | gan cao | 0.8 |
| 5. | bo he | 2.0 | 11. | da huang | 1.2 |
| 6. | lian qiao | 2.0 | | | |

## Functions:
Purging the lung heat, eliminate phlegm and regulate the *qi*.

## Modifications:
1. For cases with cold and heat attack to lungs: add *chai hu* and *di gu pi*.
2. For cases with excess phlegm cough: add *fu ling* and *chen pi*.
3. For cases with fullness and distention in hypochondriac area: add *huang lian* and *hou po*.
4. For cases with recurrent of bronchitis or pneumonia: add *shi gao* and *zhi mu*.
5. For cases with watery phlegm cough: combine with *Er Chen Tang*.
6. For cases with wind-cold cough: combine with *Hua Gai San*.
7. For cases with tuberculosis cough: combine with *Qing Fei Tang*.

## Administration:
Take with room-temp water, after meals.

Source: *Tai Ping Hui Min He Ji Ju Fang* (太平惠民和劑局方)

# Ren Shen Yang Ying (Rong) Tang 人參養營（榮）湯
### Ginseng and Rehmannia Combination
### Ginseng Decoction to Nourish Luxuriance

## Indications:
Heart and spleen *qi* and blood deficiency due to accumulating damage from overexertion. Palpitations, forgetfulness, restlessness at night, feverishness, reduced appetite, fatigue, cough, shortness of breath, dyspnea on exertion, weight loss, dry skin, and a dry mouth and throat. Chronic unhealing sore.

## Clinical Applications:
1. This formula is for treating deficiency of heart and spleen *qi*, insufficiency of blood, lack of taste and tired and weak muscles. As earth fails to nourish metal, the lung *qi* also becomes deficient, leading to shortness of breath, coughing and dyspnea on exertion.
2. The key symptoms are palpitation, forgetfulness, restlessness at night, feverish, reduce appetite, fatigue, shortness of breath, SOB on exertion, weight loss, and dry skin.
3. Currently used in treating weak physique, post-illness weakness, anemia, dry and dull hair and hair loss, low appetite, and fatigue.
4. Trauma causes deficiency over time, and chronic unhealing sores.
5. Stubborn cough that makes it difficult to talk.

## Ingredients:

| | | | | | | |
|---|---|---|---|---|---|---|
| 1. ren shen | 2.5 | 6. rou gui | 2.5 | 11. yuan zhi | 1.5 |
| 2. bai zhu | 2.5 | 7. dang gui | 2.5 | 12. bai shao | 4.0 |
| 3. huang qi | 2.5 | 8. shu di huang | 2.0 | 13. sheng jiang | 3.0 |
| 4. zhi gan cao | 2.5 | 9. wu wei zi | 2.0 | 14. da zao | 1.0 |
| 5. chen pi | 2.5 | 10. fu ling | 2.0 | | |

## Functions:
Tonify *qi*, nourish blood, regulate *ying* and *wei*; nourish the heart, and calm the spirit.

## Modifications:
1. For cases with lung deficiency cough: add *bei mu* and *xing ren.*
2. For cases with poor appetites: add *cang zhu, hou po* and *chen pi.*
3. For cases with spermatorrhea: add *long gu.*
4. For cases with heart deficiency and startle, palpitations: combine with *Yang Xin Tang.*
5. For cases with fatigue and spleen deficiency: combine with *Gui Pi Tang.*

## Cautions and Contraindications:
This formula is not indicated for *qi* and blood deficiency with excess cold.

## Administration:
Take with warm water, before meals.

Source: *Tai Ping Hui Min He Ji Ju Fang*(太平惠民和劑局方)

# Run Chang Wan 潤腸丸
### Hemp Seed and Rhubarb Formula
### Moisten the Intestines Pill

## Indications:
This formula is used for the treatment of constipation due to blood and *yin* deficiency syndrome.

Symptoms may include constipation or dry stool caused by intemperate diet that has damaged the *yin* and *qi* of the spleen and stomach. Constipation with difficult defecation or lack of desire to eat, dry mouth with an unquenchable thirst.

**Tongue:**   dry coating
**Pulse:**    thin

## Clinical Applications:
1. This formula treats constipation due to lack of fluid and lazy bowel movements.
2. Currently used for habitual constipation, or constipation caused by hypertension, arteriosclerosis, or nephritis.

## Ingredients:
| | | | | | |
|---|---|---|---|---|---|
| 1. | huo ma ren | 6.0 | 4. | qiang huo | 3.0 |
| 2. | tao ren | 6.0 | 5. | da huang | 3.0 |
| 3. | dang gui wei | 3.0 | | | |

## Functions:
Moistens the intestines and unblocks the bowels, benefiting *qi* and nourishing the blood.

## Modifications:
This formula has another version called *Run Chang Wan* (Moisten the Intestines Pill from Master Shen's Book).

The ingredients are:
| | | | | | |
|---|---|---|---|---|---|
| 1. | huo ma ren | 6.0 | 4. | sheng di huang | 3.0 |
| 2. | tao ren | 6.0 | 5. | zhi ke | 3.0 |
| 3. | dang gui | 3.0 | | | |

This formula treats constipation due to desiccated intestines, a common condition among the elderly and debilitated. It is also frequently seen after childbirth when the loss of blood injures the *yin* and depletes the fluids.
1. For no appetite: add *cang zhu and chen pi.*
2. For common cold constipation: add *fang feng and qiang huo.*
3. For postpartum digestion issues: add *chuan xiong and hong hua.*

## Administration:
Take with warm water, before meals.

Source: *Li Dong Yuan Fang* (李東垣方)

# San Bi Tang 三痺湯
## Tuhuo and Astragalus Combination
### Three Painful Obstruction Decoction

## Indications:

Wind-cold-damp *Bi.*

*Qi* and blood coagulation and stagnation, tremor and spasm in limbs, wind-cold damp *Bi* pain.

## Clinical Applications:

1. This formula is for treating wind-cold-damp *Bi.*
2. The key symptoms are chronic joint pain (bi) with *qi* deficiency and cold.
3. Currently used in treating chronic nerve palsy, motor palsy, cerebral hemorrhage palsy, stubborn numbness all over the body, numbness of hands and feet, and joint pain.

## Ingredients:

| | | | | | |
|---|---|---|---|---|---|
| 1. | ren shen | 1.5 | 10. | niu xi | 1.5 |
| 2. | huang qi | 1.5 | 11. | xu duan | 1.5 |
| 3. | fu ling | 1.5 | 12. | rou gui | 1.5 |
| 4. | gan cao | 1.5 | 13. | xi xin | 1.5 |
| 5. | dang gui | 1.5 | 14. | qin jiao | 1.5 |
| 6. | chuan xiong | 1.5 | 15. | du huo | 1.5 |
| 7. | bai shao | 1.5 | 16. | fang fen | 1.5 |
| 8. | sheng di huang | 1.5 | 17. | sheng jiang | 1.5 |
| 9. | du zhong | 1.5 | 18. | da zao | 1.5 |

## Functions:

Tonify *qi* and blood, dispel wind-cold-damp *Bi*, soothe sinews and stop *Bi* pain.

## Modifications:

1. For cases with wind-*Bi* pain: add *qiang huo* and *gui zhi.*
2. For cases with cold-*Bi* pain: add ma *huang* and *fu zi.*
3. For cases with damp-*Bi* pain: add *cang zhu*, and *yin chen hao.*

## Cautions and Contraindications:

It is not suitable for patients who exhibit signs of *yin* deficiency or heat.

## Note:

This formula is *Du Huo Ji Sheng Tang (Tuhuo* and Loranthus Combination) with *sang ji sheng* (loranthus) removed and *xu duan* (dipsacus) and *huang qi* (astragalus) added.

## Administration:

Take with warm water, after meals.

Source: *Fu Ren Liang Fang* (婦人良方)

# San Huang Shi Gao Tang 三黃石膏湯
### Gypsum, Coptis, and Scute Combination
### Three-Yellow and Gypsum Decoction

## Indications:
External contractions with signs of interior heat.

Typhoid fever, warm toxin, external and internal heat, irritability, insomnia, red face, dry nose, dry tongue and thirst, delirium or nose bleeding.

Summer-heat damage that manifests with severe fever due to heat and toxin spreading throughout the triple burner.

## Clinical Applications:
1. This formula is for treating external contractions that have strong heat.
2. The key symptoms are fever, red eyes, constipation, thirst, and irritability.
3. Currently used in treating acute fever, fever and thirst, hemorrhagic rash, macular delirium, jaundice heat, and thirst for cold water.
4. Heat-toxin patterns that present with bleeding or popular eruptions. Measles that present with bleeding and nosebleeds during high fevers.

## Ingredients:

| | | | | | |
|---|---|---|---|---|---|
| 1. | huang lian | 3.5 | 5. | dan dou chi | 2.8 |
| 2. | huang qin | 3.5 | 6. | zhi zi | 4.2 |
| 3. | huang bai | 3.5 | 7. | cong bai | 2.1 |
| 4. | ma huang | 3.5 | 8. | shi gao | 7.0 |

## Functions:
Disperse the exterior and clear interior heat; purge the fire and resolve the toxin.

## Modifications:
1. For case with cold injured and warm toxin: add *jin yin hua* and *lian qiao.*
2. For case with rashes and measles: add *tu fu ling* and *xuan shen.*
3. For case with irritability and thirst: add *zhi mu* and *can cao.*
4. For case with macula toxin: combine with *Yin Qiao San.*
5. For case with summer-heat irritable heat: combine with *Gan Lu Yin.*

## Cautions and Contraindications:
Any deficiency heats.

## Note:
This formula is *Huang Lian Jie Du Tang* (Coptis and Scute Combination) with added *ma huang* (ephedra), *shi gao* (gypsum), *dan dou chi, zhi zi,* and *cong bai.*

## Administration:
Take with warm water, after meals; take with room-temp water if patient has heat thirst.

Source: *Tao Hua Fang* (陶華方)

# San Huang Xie Xin Tang 三黃瀉心湯
## Coptis and Rhubarb Combination

### Indications:
Heart fire and upper body heat.

Damp-heat repletion with heat in the epigastrium.

### Clinical Applications:
1. This formula is for treating intense upper body heat signs and irritability accompanied with constipation.
2. The key symptoms are fever, irritability, restlessness, flushed face, red eyes, dark urine, and constipation. Also treats jaundice, diarrhea, dysentery, vomiting of blood, nosebleed, red or swollen eyes or ears, ulcers of the mouth and tongue, and toxic sores.
3. Currently used in treating post several days of onset of cerebral congestion and cerebral hemorrhage; also used for restlessness caused by arteriosclerosis and hypertension, as well as insomnia, dermatitis, eye diseases, neurasthenia, neurosis, schizophrenia, epilepsy and gynecological uprising diseases.

### Ingredients:
1. huang lian       4.5
2. da huang        9.0
3. huang qin       4.5

### Functions:
Purge fire and dissolve heat toxin.

### Modifications:
1. For cases with any bleeding syndromes: add *dang gui* and *sheng di huang*.
2. For cases with thirsty, irritable heat: add *shi gao* and *zhi mu*.
3. For cases with constipation: add *zhi shi* and *hou po*.

### Cautions and Contraindications:
Deficiency heat.

### Note:
*Da Huang Huang lian Xie Xin Tang* is the base formula of the *Xie Xin Tang* (Heart-Draining Decoction).

*Huang Lian Jie Du Tang* (Coptis and Scute Combination), which replaces *da huang* (rhubarb) with *zhi zi* (gardenia) and *huang bai* (phellodendron bark).

### Administration:
Take with room-temp water to stop bleeding.

Source: *Jin Gui Yao Lue* (金匱要略)

133

# San Miao San 三妙丸
## Atractylodes and Phellodendron Formula
### Three-Marvel Pill

## Indications:
Damp-heat lodged in the lower burner.

Numbness or burning pain in the feet, also weakness in the lower back and limbs.

## Clinical Applications:
1. This formula is for treating damp-heat in the lower *jiao* with numbness or burning pain in the legs or feet.
2. The key symptoms are weakness in the lower back or extremities, rashes or joint pain in the lower body, vaginal discharge, or genital sores.
3. Currently used in treating atrophy, paralysis, beriberi, sores, rheumatoid arthritis, eczema, pelvic inflammatory disease, cervicitis.

## Ingredients:
1. huang bai (jiu chao)      3.35
2. cang zhu (mi gan jin)     5.00
3. niu xi                    1.65

## Functions:
Clear heat and dry damp.

## Modifications:
1. For case with severe red, swollen, heat pain joints: add *fang ji*, *sang zhi*, and *can sha*.
2. For case with difficulty urination: add *yi yi ren*

## Note:
*San Miao San* is *Er Miao San* adding *niu xi.*

## Administration:
Take with warm water, after meals, on an empty stomach with ginger juice or salted water.

Source: *Dan Xi Xin Fa* （丹溪心法）

# San Ren Tang 三仁湯
Triple Nut Combination
Three-Seed Decoction

## Indications:
Early stage of damp-warm or summer-heat warm febrile disease (*Qi* stage).

Headache, chills, afternoon fever, heaviness or pain in the body, pale yellow complexion, fullness in the chest, loss of appetite, and no thirst.

**Tongue:**    white coating
**Pulse:**    wiry, thin and soggy

## Clinical Applications:
1. This formula is commonly used for early stage of damp-warm febrile disease. The symptoms are headache, chills, afternoon tidal fever, heaviness or pain in the body, pale yellow complexion, fullness in the chest, and no thirst.
2. Currently used for treating enteric fever, pyelonephritis, undulant fever, flu, arthritis, gastritis, colitis, and bacillary dysentery and edema due to damp heat with dampness being the predominate factor.
3. It also can use for arthritis, morning sickness, fever of unknown origin, chronic bronchitis, diabetes, and biliary ascariasis.

## Ingredients:
| | | | | |
|---|---|---|---|---|
| 1. yi yi ren | 6.0 | | 5. hou po | 2.0 |
| 2. hua shi | 6.0 | | 6. bai dou kou | 2.0 |
| 3. xing ren | 5.0 | | 7. tong cao | 2.0 |
| 4. ban xia | 3.0 | | 8. dan zhu ye | 2.0 |

## Functions:
Clears damp-heat, facilitates the *qi* and separates turbidity.

## Modifications:
1. 1. For cases with alternative chills and fever, add *qing huo,* and *cao guo.*
2. For cases with *wei* stage symptoms, add *huo xiang* and *xiang ru.*
3. For cases with severe fever, dark urine, a red tongue, add *yin chen hao, zhi zi,* and *huang qin.*

## Cautions and Contraindications:
More heat less damp.

## Administration:
Take with warm water, before meals.

Source: *Tai Ping Hui Min He Ji Ju Fang* (太平惠民和劑局方)

# San Wu Xiang Ru Yin 三物香薷飲

Elsholtzia Three Combination

a.k.a. Mosla Powder 香薷散

## Indications:

Exterior cold with interior dampness constrained in the summer (summer *yin* evil syndrome).

Aversion to cold and fever without sweating, sensation of heaviness in the head, headache, abdominal pain, vomiting, diarrhea and stifling sensation in the chest and general body ache.

**Tongue:**     white greasy coating
**Pulse:**     floating (superficial)

## Clinical Applications:

1. This is a formula used for damp cold contracted during the summertime; this type of disorder occurs most often during the warm weather.
2. The key symptoms are headache, fever, aversion to cold, vexation and agitation, thirst, pain in the epigastrium and abdomen, vomiting, and diarrhea.
3. Currently used for upper respiratory tract infection, summer cold, acute gastroenteritis due to summer-damp with exterior wind-cold.

## Ingredients:

1. xiang ru     10.0
2. hou po     5.0
3. bai bian dou     7.5

## Functions:

Releases the exterior, scatters cold, transforms dampness, and harmonizes the MJ.

## Modifications:

1. For case with vomit and diarrhea: add *fu ling* and *gan cao.*
2. For case with spontaneous sweating and fatigued limbs: add *ren shen* and *huang qi.*

## Cautions and Contraindications:

Exterior deficiency with sweating, sunstroke with fever, or summer heat.

## Note:

This formula is also called *Xiang Ru San* (Mosla Powder).

## Administration:

Take with room-temp water, as needed (note: it will cause diarrhea if taken with hot water).

Source: *Tai Ping Hui Min He Ji Ju Fang* (太平惠民和劑局方)

# San Zhong Kui Jian Tang 散腫潰堅湯
### Forsythia and Laminaria Combination
### Decoction to Disperse Swelling and Ulcerate What is Hard

## Indications:

Scrofula (*luo li*) or saber sores (*ma dao li*, lit "horse-knife sores").

Knotted and hard lumps, as hard as stones. These may be located on the neck or shoulders and down to the armpit. It also addresses scrofula, goiter and other tumors.

## Clinical Applications:

1. This formula is for treating hot and toxic accumulations of blood and phlegm that are generally in the neck and head.
2. The key symptoms are hard, stone-like swellings such as saber and pearl-string lumps (scrofula), enlarged thyroid, and deep-tissue or submaxillary cellulitis.
3. Currently used in treating neck lymphadenoma, goiter, cellulitis, and leprosy.
4. It is also for acute inflammation and suppurative sores that are swollen and hard, and for those that are still hard after ulceration.

## Ingredients:

| | | | | | | | |
|---|---|---|---|---|---|---|---|
| 1. huang qin | 4.0 | 7. kun bu | 2.5 | 13. e zhu | 1.5 |
| 2. zhi mu | 2.5 | 8. chai hu | 2.5 | 14. ge gen | 1.5 |
| 3. huang bai | 4.0 | 9. sheng ma | 0.5 | 15. dang gui wei | 1.0 |
| 4. long dan cao | 2.5 | 10. lian qiao | 1.5 | 16. bai shao | 1.0 |
| 5. gua lou gen | 2.5 | 11. zhi gan cao | 1.5 | 17. huang lian | 1.0 |
| 6. jie geng | 2.5 | 12. san leng | 1.5 | | |

## Functions:

Clears heat, resolves toxicity, reduces swelling, induces ulceration, moves the blood, and dispels stasis.

## Modifications:

1. For cases with unformed swollen pus: add *jin yin hua* and *zhi shi*.
2. For cases with formed pus erupted: add *huang qi* and *bai zhi*.
3. For cases with hot swelling pain: add *shi gao* and *zhi zi*.
4. For cases with sore swelling pain: combine with *Zhen Ren Huo Ming Yin*.
5. For cases with carbuncle, gangrene swelling pain: combine with *Tuo Li Xiao Du Yin*.
6. For cases with goiter, tumor swelling pain: combine with *Pai Nong San*.

## Cautions and Contraindications:

Weakness of righteous *qi*.

## Administration:

Take with warm water, after meals.

Source: *Lan Shi Mi Cang* (蘭室秘藏)

# San Zi Yang Qin Tang 三子養親湯
## Three-Seed Decoction to Nourish One's Parents

## Indications:
This formula is used for the treatment of phlegm and food accumulation, in conjunction with *qi* stagnation syndromes.

Symptoms may include coughing and wheezing, copious sputum, focal distention in the chest, loss of appetite, and digestive difficulties.

**Tongue:**    white, greasy coating
**Pulse:**    slippery

## Clinical Applications:
1. This formula is used for excess phlegm-food-*qi* accumulation.
2. This is phlegm clogging the lungs with *qi* stagnation or food stagnation, often occurring in the elderly, whose digestive systems are becoming weaker.
3. Currently used in treating acute and chronic bronchitis, bronchial asthma, emphysema, pediatric asthma, spasms of the diaphragm.

## Ingredients:
1. bai jie zi    6.0
2. zi su zi    9.0
3. lai fu zi    9.0

## Functions:
Pushes down the rebellious *qi*, relaxes the diaphragm, transforms phlegm, and reduces food stagnation.

## Modifications:
1. For hard and firm stool: add honey to the strained decoction.
2. For winter cold: add *sheng jiang*.

## Cautions and Contraindications:
Formula shouldn't be taken long-term.

## Administration:
Take with warm water, as needed.

Source: *Han Shi Yi Tong* (韓氏醫通)

# Sang Ju Yin 桑菊飲
### Morus and Chrysanthemum Combination

## Indications:
Early stage of wind-warm febrile illness (*wen bing tiao bian*): coughing, slight fever, and slight thirst.

**Tongue:**      thin, white coating
**Pulse:**      floating or superficial and rapid

## Clinical Applications:
1. This formula is the standard mild, pungent, and cool formula. It is used for early stage warm-febrile disease and for other wind-heat exterior disorders in which coughing is the dominant symptom.
2. It is also used for eye disorders due to wind-heat and hacking cough due to exterior dryness.
3. Currently used for upper respiratory tract infection, flu, acute bronchitis, and acute conjunctivitis.

## Ingredients:
1. sang ye      7.5
2. ju hua      3.0
3. xing ren      6.0
4. jie geng      6.0
5. lian qiao      5.0
6. bo he      2.5
7. lu gen      6.0
8. gan cao      2.5

## Functions:
Disperses wind, clears heat, ventilates the lung, and stops cough.

## Modifications:
1. For *qi* level heat, or labored breathing or slight wheezing, add *shi gao* and *zhi mu*.
2. For severe thirst, add *tian hua fen*.
3. For coughing with blood, add *bai mao gen*, *ou jie*, and *mu dan pi*.
4. For fever with thirst, add *shi gao* and *zhi mu*.
5. For wind-warm common cold, add *jin yin hua* and *dan zhu ye*.
6. For irritable dry cough, add *mai men dong* and *wu wei zi*.

## Administration:
Swallow with warm water, after meals.

Source: *Wen Bing Tiao Bian* (溫病條辨)

# Sang Piao Xiao San 桑螵蛸散
### Mantis Cocoon Formula
### Mantis Egg-Case Powder

## Indications:
This formula is used for the treatment of heart and kidney deficiency syndrome.

Symptoms may include frequent urination, turbid urination (the color of rice water – gray and cloudy), or incontinence, spermatorrhea, disorientation, and forgetfulness.

**Tongue**:     pale, white coating
**Pulse**:     thin, slow, and frail

## Clinical Applications:
1. This formula is used for the problem between *shen* (heart) and *zhi* (kidney) deficiency; the key symptoms are frequent urination, or enuresis (incontinence), or spermatorrhea. Also suitable for childhood enuresis.
2. Currently used for diabetes, neurosis, and postpartum incontinence; also turbid urine from chronic nephritis or cystitis. Not suitable for turbid *lin* syndrome.

## Ingredients:
1. sang piao xiao      3.0
2. long gu      3.0
3. gui ban (su zhi)      3.0
4. ren shen      3.0
5. fu shen      3.0
6. shi chang pu      3.0
7. yuan zhi      3.0
8. dang gui      3.0

## Functions:
Regulates and tonifies the heart and kidney, stabilizes the essence, and stops leakage.

## Modifications:
1. For frequent urination: add *bai zhu* and *gan cao*.
2. For thick urination: add *shan yao* and *qian shi*.
3. For incontinence: add *lu jiao shuang* and *mu li*.
4. For severe kidney *yang* deficiency with cold: add *fu zi* and *rou gui*.

## Cautions and Contraindications:
Not to be used for patients with damp-heat in the lower burner (*jiao*).

## Administration:
Take with warm water, before meals.

Source: *Ben Cao Yan Yi* (本草衍義)

# Sang Xing Tang 桑杏湯
## Mulberry Leaf and Apricot Kernel Decoction

## Indications:
This formula is used for the treatment of disorders caused by external warm dryness attacks.

Symptoms may include headache, moderate fever, dry cough with no sputum or sticky and scanty sputum, thirst and dry throat.

**Tongue:**    red; thin, dry and white coating
**Pulse:**    superficial and rapid

## Clinical Applications:
1. This formula is used for treating mild warm dryness and evil attacking the lung with dry cough. This warm-dryness injures the lung *qi* at the superficial level. This condition occurs most often in the early autumn when the summer warm *qi* has still not been dispersed, but the autumn dryness is already prevalent.
2. Currently used for treating the common cold, acute bronchitis, bronchiectasis with hemoptysis, pertussis due to damage of the lung fluids by warm dryness.

## Ingredients:
1. sang ye          3.0
2. dan dou chi      3.0
3. xing ren         4.5
4. sha shen         6.0
5. zhe bei mu       3.0
6. li pi            3.0
7. zhi zi           3.0

## Functions:
Gently disperses warm dryness, moistens lungs and stops coughing.

## Modifications:
1. For cases with nosebleed, omit *dou chi* and add *bai mao gen* and *sheng di* or increase *zhi zi* and add *dan pi* and *qing hao*.
2. For severe sore throat: add *niu bang zi* and *xuan shen*.
3. For coughing with thick, yellow sputum: add *gua lou pi* and *ma dou ling*.

## Cautions and Contraindications:
Not to be used for patients with current *yin* deficiency.

## Administration:
Take with warm water, as needed.

Source: *Wen Bing Tiao Bian* (溫病條辨)

# Sha Shen Mai Men Dong Tang 沙參麥冬湯
Glehnia and Ophiopogon Combination
Glehnia and Ophiopogonis Decoction

## Indications:
Lung and stomach *yin* damaged by dryness and fluid depletion.
Dry throat, thirst, fever, and a hacking cough with scanty sputum.

**Tongue**: red tongue with little coating
**Pulse**: rapid and thin

## Clinical Applications:
1. This formula is for treating *yin*-deficient patients who contract external cool-dryness during the autumn.
2. The key symptoms are dry throat, thirst, hacking cough with scant sputum, dry nasal passages, and a dry, red tongue with scant coating.
3. Currently used in treating chronic bronchitis, bronchiectasis, chronic pharyngitis, chronic glossitis, chronic gastritis, atrophic gastritis, diabetes mellitus, fever convalescence, those with deficiency of lung and stomach *yin* after surgery, dryness bronchitis, or dry-heat attacks on the lungs.
4. Pulmonary tuberculosis, diabetes-like disorders, and stomach-*yin* deficiency stomach pain or mouth sores.

## Ingredients:
1. sha shen       5.4
2. mai men dong   5.4
3. gua lou gen    2.7
4. ga cao         1.8
5. sang ye        2.7
6. bai bian dou   2.7

## Functions:
Clears and nourishes the lungs and stomach, generates fluids, and moistens dryness.

## Modifications:
1. For cases with deficiency heat: add *sheng di* and *di gu pi.*
2. For cases with blood in sputum: add *bai ji, xian he cao*, and *bai mao gen.*
3. For cases with difficulty expectorating: add *kuan dong hua, guo lou ren*, and *bei mu.*
4. For cases with abdominal dull pain: add *bai shao* and *chen pi.*

## Administration:
Take with warm water, before meals.

Source: *Wen Bing Tiao Bian* (溫病條辨)

# Shang Zhong Xia Tong Yong Tong Feng Wan 上中下通用痛風丸
### Cinnamon and Angelica Formula
### Pill to Treat Painful Wind Anywhere

## Indications:
Wind-cold-damp *Bi* pain.

Whole body wind-pain anywhere; *Bi* pain that moves around or is in both the upper and lower body.

## Clinical Applications:
1. This formula is for treating wind-cold dampness, phlegm-heat, poor blood vessels, and joint pain.
2. The key symptoms are chronic or acute joint pain, including arthritis, gout, and migratory *Bi* patterns.
3. Currently used in treating acute and chronic arthritis, rheumatism, uric acid joint pain, low back pain, hand and foot paralysis, beriberi, bone pain and rheumatism pain.

## Ingredients:

| | | | | | | | | |
|---|---|---|---|---|---|---|---|---|
| 1. | cang zhu | 4.0 | 6. | tao ren | 2.0 | 11. | wei ling xian | 1.0 |
| 2. | huang bai | 4.0 | 7. | long dan cao | 2.0 | 12. | gui zhi | 1.0 |
| 3. | tian nan xing | 4.0 | 8. | fang ji | 2.0 | 13. | hong hua | 0.5 |
| 4. | shen qu | 2.0 | 9. | bai zhi | 2.0 | | | |
| 5. | chuan xiong | 2.0 | 10. | qiand huo | 1.0 | | | |

## Functions:
Dispel the wind and expel the phlegm, clears heat, dries dampness, invigorates blood, and stop pain.

## Modifications:
1. For cases with wind-damp-*Bi* pain: add *fang fen* and *du huo.*
2. For cases with blood deficiency *Bi* pain: add *dang gui* and *bai shao.*
3. For cases with *qi* deficiency sore and pain: add *ren shen* and *huang qi.*
4. For cases with wind-cold pain: combine with *Ma Huang Tang.*
5. For cases with phlegm damp pain: combine with *Er Chen Tang.*

## Note:
*Shang Zhong Xia Tong Yong Tong Feng Wan* (Cinnamon and Angelica Formula) and *Shu Jing Huo Xue Tang* (Clematis and Stephania Combination) both treat migratory *Bi* pain. The former is more drying and less nourishing to the blood than the latter.

## Administration:
Take with warm water, as needed.

Source: *Dan Xi Xin Fa* (丹溪心法)

# Shao Fu Zhu Yu Tang 少腹逐瘀湯
Fennel Seed and Corydalis Combination
Drive Out Blood Stasis in the Lower Abdomen Decoction

## Indications:
This formula is used for the treatment of blood stasis, resulting in painful or irregular periods in women.

Symptoms may include lower abdominal masses, possibly causing pain, and sometimes without clots, lower abdominal distention, lower back pain caused by irregular menstruations, dark or purple color of blood, menorrhagia, and infertility.

## Clinical Applications:
Symptoms include irregular periods, painful periods, amenorrhea, menorrhagia, infertility, habitual miscarriages, uterine fibroids, ovarian cysts, blood clots and sharp pain during periods.

## Ingredients:
1. dang gui      5.40
2. chi shao      3.60
3. chuan xiong   1.80
4. wu ling zhi   3.60
5. pu huang      5.40
6. mo yao        1.80
7. xiao hui xing 0.04
8. yan hu suo    1.80
9. gan jiang     0.36
10. rou gui      1.80

## Functions:
Invigorates the blood, dispels blood stasis, warms the menses, and alleviates pain.

## Modifications:
1. For painful periods with cold damp: add *cang zhu, fu ling* and *yi yi ren.*
2. For painful periods with deficiency-cold accumulation: add *ba ji tian* and *xian mao.*
3. For pain from breast distention: add *yu jin* and *chuan lian zi.*
4. For soreness and weakness of lower back during menstruation: add *xu duan, niu xi, du zhong* and *san ji sheng.*
5. For *qi* and blood deficiency: add *Dang Gui Bu Xue Tang.*
6. For infertility: add *shan yao* and *zi he che.*
7. For delayed period: add *gou qi yin.*
8. For irritability with constipation: add *Tao He Cheng Qi Tang.*
9. For habitual miscarriages: add *Dang Gu Shao Yao San.*
10. For ovarian cysts: add *Zi Cao Gen Mu Li Tang.*

## Cautions and Contraindications:
Not to be used during pregnancy.

## Administration:
Take with warm water, before or between meals.

Source: *Yi Lin Gai Cuo* (醫林改錯)

# Shao Yao Gan Cao Tang 芍藥甘草湯
### Peony and Licorice Combination
### Peony and Licorice Decoction

## Indications:
This formula is used for the treatment of muscle spasmodic pain due to liver blood and *yin* deficiency.

Symptoms may include irritability, slight chills, spasms of the calf muscles, and also cramps in the hands and pains in the abdomen.

**Tongue:**    No visible coating

## Clinical Applications:
1. This formula is very popular for treating a wide variety of pain syndromes, especially the spasmodic calf muscle pain or cramping pain accompanied by diarrhea, associated with disharmony between the liver and spleen. Abdominal spasms, weakness of legs, foot pain, and pediatric abdominal pain are all treatable.
2. Currently used for intercostal neuralgia, sciatica, trigeminal neuralgia, chronic pelvic inflammatory disease (P.I.D.), and primary dysmenorrhea; frozen shoulder, gallstones or kidney stone pain.

## Ingredients:
1. bai shao        11.0
2. zhi gan cao    11.0

## Functions:
Tonifies *qi* and blood, clears heat and harmonizes the middle *jiao*, moderates painful spasms, and alleviates pain.

## Modifications:
1. For *yin* deficiency with blood stagnation: substitute *chi shao* for *bai shao*.
2. For limbs cramping pain: add *xi xin* and *gan jiang*.
3. For lower abdominal pain: *chen pi* and *wu yao*.
4. For difficulty with urination: add *bai zhu* and *fu ling*.
5. For four-limb cold fidget: add *Si Ni Tang*.
6. For four-limb heat fidget: add *Si Ni San*.
7. For kidney stones: add *Zhu Ling Tang,* which can reduce the pain and help to expel the stone and increase the urine volume.

## Administration:
Take with warm water, before meals.

Source: *Shang Han Lun* (傷寒論)

# Shao Yao Tang 芍藥湯
### Peony Decoction

## Indications:
This formula is used for the treatment of damp-heat dysentery with *qi* and blood stagnation.

Symptoms may include abdominal pain, tenesmus, difficult defecation, pus and bloody diarrhea, burning sensation around the anus, dark and scanty urine.

**Tongue:**   greasy and slightly yellow coating
**Pulse:**   wiry, rapid

## Clinical Applications:
1. This formula is commonly used for damp-heat dysentery. This is damp-heat lodged in the intestines where it caused *qi* and blood stagnation.
2. Key symptoms include pus and bloody diarrhea, abdominal pain, tenesmus, and dysentery.
3. Currently used in treating bacillary or amebic dysentery, acute enteritis, ulcerative colitis, Crohn's disease, and pediatric acute enteritis.

## Ingredients:
1. bai shao        6.0
2. huang lian     3.0
3. huang qin      3.0
4. da huang       1.8
5. dang gui        3.0
6. zhi gan cao    1.2
7. mu xiang       1.2
8. bing lang       1.2
9. rou gui          0.9

## Functions:
Clears heat and drains damp, relieves stagnation and toxicity, regulates and harmonizes *qi* and blood.

## Modifications:
1. For severe sticky pus and blood: add *chuan xiong* and *sheng di huang.*
2. For severe diarrhea with pus and blood: add *bai zhu* and *fu ling.*
3. For severe tenesmus: add *zhi shi* and *hou po.*

## Cautions and Contraindications:
Not to be used for the early stages of dysentery with exterior symptoms, or chronic dysentery due to deficient cold.

## Administration:
Take with warm water, before meals.

Source: *Bing Ji Qi Yi Bao Ming Ji* (病機氣宜保命集)

# Shen Fu Tang 參附湯

Ginseng and Aconite Accessory Root Decoction

## Indications:

For the treatment of *yang qi* collapse syndrome.

May be used for patients experiencing extremely cold extremities, sweating, weak breathing and or shortness of breath, dizziness and extremely pale complexion.

**Tongue**: pale tongue
**Pulse**: faint

## Clinical Applications:

1. This formula can be used for emergency due to sudden *yang qi* collapse.
2. Currently used for cardiac failure, myocardial infarction, cardiogenic shock, postpartum hemorrhage, uterine bleeding, and other causes of hypovolemic shock.

## Ingredients:

1. ren shen       6.0
2. fu zi          9.0
3. gan jiang      6.0
4. zhi gan cao    6.0

## Functions:

Rescues the *yang* and stabilizes the *yang qi* system after collapse.

## Modifications:

For shock or cardiac failure, add *long gu, mu li, bai shao,* and *zhi gan cao.*

## Administration:

Take with warm water, anytime.

Source: *Fu Ren Da Quan Liang Fang* (婦人大全良方)

# Shen Ling Bai Zhu San 參苓白朮散
Ginseng and Atractylodes Formula

## Indications:
Spleen and stomach *qi* deficiency with dampness: reduced appetite, loose stools or diarrhea or vomiting, weakness in the limbs, emaciation, withered complexion, and distention and a stifling sensation in the chest and epigastrium.

**Tongue:**  pale tongue with white coating
**Pulse:**  thin and moderate or deficient and moderate

## Clinical Applications:
1. This formula is good for the transportation and transformation function of the spleen in regulating both ascending *qi* and descending *qi*.
2. This formula tonifies and strengthens the spleen *qi* and harmonizes the stomach, leaches out dampness, and unblocks the flow of lung *qi*.
3. Currently used for chronic gastritis, anemia, chronic bronchitis, chronic nephritis, diabetes mellitus, and leukorrhea due to spleen deficiency with dampness.

## Ingredients:
| | | | | |
|---|---|---|---|---|
| 1. | ren shen | 6.0 | 7. yi yi ren | 3.0 |
| 2. | bai zhu | 6.0 | 8. lian zi rou | 3.0 |
| 3. | fu ling | 6.0 | 9. sha ren | 3.0 |
| 4. | zhi gan cao | 6.0 | 10. jie geng | 3.0 |
| 5. | shan yao | 6.0 | 11. da zao | 3.0 |
| 6. | bai bian dou | 6.0 | | |

## Functions:
Benefits *qi*, strengthens spleen, leaches out dampness, and treats diarrhea.

## Modifications:
1. For poor digestion, add *shan zha* and *shen qu*.
2. For vomiting clear fluid, add *chen pi* and *ban xia*.
3. For constant diarrhea, add *mu xiang* and *qian shi*.
4. For food stagnation, vomiting, and diarrhea, combine with *Pi Wei San*.

## Cautions and Contraindications:
Should not be used when patient has *yin* deficiency heat. Patients should avoid raw food, cold food, greasy food, and any food that is hard to digest.

## Administration:
Swallow with warm water, as needed.

Source: *Tai Ping Hui Min He Ji Ju Fang* (太平惠民合劑局方)

# Shen Mi Tang 神秘湯
Ephedra and Magnolia Combination
Mysterious Decoction

## Indications:
Bronchitis or bronchial asthma.

Asthmatic breathing and cough that have a component of binding depression of liver *qi*.

Suffering from *qi* cough for a long time, gasping for breath, cannot breathe sitting or lying down, and making a squeak in the throat (the sound of gasping in the throat).

**Tongue:** thin, white coating
**Pulse:** wiry

## Clinical Applications:
1. This formula is for treating breathing difficulties.
2. The key symptoms are worsening with anger or stress, bitter fullness in the chest, bitter taste, flank pain, wiry pulse, and scant phlegm; asthmatic condition is one that worsens when the patient lies down.
3. Currently used in treating bronchial wheezing, emphysema, and infantile wheezing with less phlegm, stagnant *qi* and neurological symptoms.

## Ingredients:
1. ma huang    6.0
2. xing ren    4.8
3. hou po      3.6
4. chen pi     3.0
5. gan cao     2.4
6. chai hu     2.4
7. zi su ye    1.8

## Functions:
Disperses wind-cold, directs *qi* downward, and releases asthma.

## Modifications:
1. For cases with severe shortness of breath: add *su zi* and *qian hu.*
2. For cases with excess phlegm: add *ban xia, bai jie zi,* and *dan na xing.*
3. For cases with severe stifling sensation in chest: add *zhi ke, jie geng,* and *zi su geng.*
4. For cases with internal heat and thirsty: add *shi gao* and *zhi mu.*

## Cautions and Contraindications:
1. Spontaneous sweating or *yin*, *yang*, *qi* and blood deficiency.
2. Raw, cold and greasy food.

## Administration:
Take with warm water, after meals.

Source: *Wai Tai Mi Yao* (外台秘要)

# Shen Su *Yin* 參蘇飲

Ginseng and Perilla Combination
Ginseng and Perilla Leaf Drink

## Indications:
External wind-cold attack with internal *qi* deficient.

Fever and chills, headache, nasal congestion, productive cough with thin phlegm, stifling sensation in the chest.

| | |
|---|---|
| **Tongue:** | white coating |
| **Pulse:** | frail |

## Clinical Applications:
1. This formula is for treating external wind-cold with internal phlegm-damp.
2. The key symptoms are aversion to cold, fever, headache, a stuffy nose, a cough with copious phlegm, fullness and oppression in the chest and diaphragm, a white tongue coating, and a weak pulse.
3. Currently used in treating postpartum cold and cough, also for colds among the weak and the elderly. Also deficiency patient without the heat sign.

## Ingredients:

| | | | | | |
|---|---|---|---|---|---|
| 1. | ren shen | 3.0 | 8. | chen pi | 2.0 |
| 2. | zi su ye | 3.0 | 9. | jie geng | 2.0 |
| 3. | ge gen | 3.0 | 10. | gan cao | 2.0 |
| 4. | qian hu | 3.0 | 11. | sheng jiang | 2.0 |
| 5. | ban xia | 3.0 | 12. | da zao | 1.0 |
| 6. | fu ling | 3.0 | 13. | mu xiang | 2.0 |
| 7. | zhi ke | 2.0 | | | |

## Functions:
Augments the *qi*, releases the exterior, ventilates lung, and transforms phlegm.

## Modifications:
1. For cases with dizziness and headache: add *chai hu* and *chuan xiong*.
2. For cases in which patients cough up the phlegm: add sang *bai* pi and *di gu pi*.
3. For cases with abdominal pain and diarrhea: add *huo xiang* and *sha ren*.

## Cautions and Contraindications:
Yellow phlegm, high fever and sore throat.

## Administration:
Take with warm water, as needed.

Source: *Tai Ping Hui Min He Ji Ju Fang* (太平惠民和劑局方)

# Shen Tong Zhu Yu Tang 身痛逐瘀湯
### Ligusticum and Motopterygium Combinations
### Drive Out Blood Stasis from a Painful Body Decoction

## Indications:
For the treatment of *bi* syndromes due to *qi* and blood obstruction in the channels and collaterals, resulting in shoulder pain, arm pain, lower back pain, leg pain or other chronic aches and pains of the body.

**Tongue:**     dark purple with spots; color may extend to lips
**Pulse:**     deep and wiry or deep and choppy

## Clinical Applications:
1. Formula used to treat nerve and joint pain with *qi* and blood stagnation.
2. Treats soreness of limbs, especially including numbness or pain, scapula and lower back soreness, multiple peripheral neuritis, sciatica, stroke sequelae of limb paralysis, rheumatoid arthritis, soft tissue disease, neuropathic migraine, trigeminal neuralgia and/or gout.

## Ingredients:
| | | | | |
|---|---|---|---|---|
| 1. qi jiao | 1 | 7. mo yao | 2 |
| 2. chuan xiong | 2 | 8. dang gui | 3 |
| 3. tao ren | 3 | 9. wu ling zhi | 2 |
| 4. hong hua | 3 | 10. xiang fu | 1 |
| 5. gan cao | 2 | 11. niu xi | 3 |
| 6. qiang huo | 1 | 12. di long | 2 |

## Functions:
Invigorates the blood, dispels blood stasis; expel the wind to eliminate dampness; opens the collaterals, unblocks obstruction to alleviate pain.

## Modifications:
1. For more pain in upper limbs: add *fang feng, san leng,* and *er zhu.*
2. For more pain in lower limbs: add *mu gua, du huo,* and *wei ling xian.*
3. For more blood stagnation: add *qi li san.*
4. For more cold pain: add *gui zhi,* and *xi xin.*
5. For more damp and slight swelling: *fang ji, yi yi ren,* and *cang zhu.*
6. For paralysis of limbs: add *xiao xu ming tang* and *jiang can,* and *quan xie.*
7. For chest contusion: add *Fu Yuan Hou Xue Tang.*
8. For psoriasis: add *cang zhu, ji xue teng,* and *xuan shen.*

## Administration:
Take with warm water, before/between meals.

Source: *Yi Lin Gai Cuo* (醫林改錯)

# Shen Zhuo Tang 腎著湯
Poria, Atractylodes, and Ginger Combination
(Gan Cao Gan Jiang Fu Ling Bai Zhu Tang 甘草乾薑茯苓白朮湯)
(Licorice, Ginger, Poria and White Atractylodes Decoction)

## Indications:
For a heavy sensation in the body, cold and pain in the lower back, pressure in the lower back as if carrying a heavy weight, normal appetite and absence of thirst, and copious urine.

## Clinical Applications:
1. This formula is used to fix kidney disorder (腎著 *Shen Zhao*), a type of painful obstruction of the waist and lower back due to cold-dampness.
2. The key symptoms are "cold in the low back, as though one is sitting in water."
3. Currently used in treating low back cold and pain, sciatica, enuresis, vaginal discharge, pregnancy, lower extremity edema, labia swollen, inability to urinate, bladder sphincter paralysis in the elderly and nocturia in children.
4. Pregnancy edema and enuresis, for cold feeling below the waist, cold and heavy feeling up to the waist or feet, cold pain, physical fatigue.

## Ingredients:
1. pao jiang       6.0
2. fu ling         6.0
3. zhi gan cao     3.0
4. chao bai zhu    3.0

## Functions:
Warms the spleen, overcomes dampness, and stops pain.

## Modifications:
1. For case with severe cold: add *fu zi.*
2. For case with frequent urination: add *shan zhu yu* and *yi zhi ren.*
3. For case with vaginal discharge: add *chun gen pi.*
4. For case with severe dampness, add *cang zhu, ze xie,* and *yi yi ren.*

## Cautions and Contraindications:
Heaviness of the body and backache due to damp-heat.

## Note:
It is also named *Gan Cao Gan Jiang Fu Ling Bai Zhu Tang.*

## Administration:
Take with warm water, before meals.

Source: *Jin Gui Yao Lue* (金匱要略)

# Sheng Hua Tang 生化湯
Tangkuei and Ginger Combination
Generation and Transformation Decoction

## Indications:
For the treatment of postpartum abdominal pain due to blood stagnation syndrome.

Also used to treat retention of the lochia with cold and pain in the lower abdomen.

**Tongue:** pale-purple with purple spots
**Pulse:** thin, submerged, and choppy

## Clinical Applications:
1. This is a common formula used to take during postpartum period.
2. Currently used for retention of placental fragments within the uterus, lochioschesis, painful postpartum uterine contractions, and chronic endometritis.

## Ingredients:
1. dang gui     16.0
2. chuan xiong   6.0
3. tao ren       3.0
4. pao jiang     1.0
5. zhi gan cao   1.0

## Functions:
Invigorates and dispels blood stasis, generates new blood, warms the collaterals, and disperses the cold.

## Modifications:
1. For abdominal cramps and pain due to blood stagnation, add *hong hua* and *shao yao*.
2. For abdominal pain due to excess cold, add *rou gui*.
3. For retention of blood, add *zhi shi* and *cang zhu*.
4. For occipital pain, add *niu xi* and *du zhong*.

## Cautions and Contraindications:
Not to be taken during pregnancy; contraindicated for blood stasis due to heat.

## Administration:
Take with warm water, before meals.

Source: *Fu Qing Zhu Nu Ke* (傅青主女科)

# Sheng Jiang Xie Xin Tang 生薑瀉心湯
## Pinellia and Ginger Combination
### Fresh Ginger Decoction to Drain the Epigastrium

## Indications:
Water and heat mutually binding.

After sweating from a cold pathogen attack is resolved, there is disharmony in the stomach, a focal distention under the heart, dry belching, water sound under the diaphragm, and rumbling diarrhea in the abdomen.

| | |
|---|---|
| **Tongue:** | white coating |
| **Pulse:** | wiry and slippery |

## Clinical Applications:
1. This formula is for treating all manner of stomach ailments that present as coldness bound with heat.
2. The key symptoms are hard glomus below the heart, belching with a foul odor, thunderous rumbling in the abdomen, and diarrhea.
3. Currently used in treating acute and chronic gastroenteritis, gastrointestinal ulcers, nausea and dry belching, abdominal pain and borborygmus and diarrhea.

## Ingredients:

| | | | | | |
|---|---|---|---|---|---|
| 1. | sheng jiang | 4.8 | 5. | huang qin | 3.6 |
| 2. | gan cao | 3.6 | 6. | ban xia | 4.8 |
| 3. | da zao | 3.6 | 7. | huang lian | 1.2 |
| 4. | gan jiang | 1.2 | 8. | da zao | 1.8 |

## Functions:
Clear heat, expel cold, strengthen the spleen, and harmonize the stomach.

## Modifications:
1. For cases with vomiting of food retention: *zhi shi* and *hou po.*
2. For cases with thirst and desire water: add *fu ling* and *ze xie.*
3. For cases with abdominal pain diarrhea: add *shao yao* and *chen pi.*
4. For cases with indigestion of food retention: combine with *Ping Wei San.*
5. For cases with water retention and belching: combine with *Wu Ling San.*
6. For cases with disharmony of post-illness: combine with *Xiao Chai Hu Tang.*

## Note:
This formula is similar to *Ban Xia Xie Xin Tang*, but with a reduced dose of *gan jiang* (dried ginger) and an added large dose of *sheng jiang* (fresh ginger).

## Administration:
Take with warm water, before meals.

Source: *Shang Han Lun* (傷寒論)

# Sheng Ma Ge Gen Tang 升麻葛根湯
### Cimicifuga and Pueraria Combination
### Cimicifuga and Kudzu Decoction

## Indications:
For the treatment of early-stage measles, and for other rash syndromes.

May also be used for patients with measles or rashes that do not surface evenly, accompanied by fever and aversion to wind, headache, cough, generalized body aches, sneezing, red eyes, excessive tearing of the eyes and thirst.

**Tongue:**   red and dry coating
**Pulse:**   floating, rapid

## Clinical Applications:
1. This formula ensures a smooth resolution of early-stage measles and similar rashes, especially when the rash does not develop smoothly. It can release heat and toxin and strong penetration force.
2. For cases that have heat constraint without sweating, headache and aversion to cold or measles or rashes that do not express easily.
3. Currently used for measles, herpes simplex, varicella and scarlet fever.

## Ingredients:
1. sheng ma   7.5
2. ge gen   5.0

3. bai shao   5.0
4. gan cao   2.5
5. sheng jiang   2.5

## Functions:
Releases the muscle layer and vents rashes, resolves toxins, allowing papules to express.

## Modifications:
1. For more pronounced exterior heat, add *bo he, chan tui, niu bang zi,* and *jin yin hua.*
2. For headache and dizziness, add *chuan xiong* and *bai zhi.*
3. For stiff back and body ache, add *fang feng* and *qiang huo.*
4. For swollen and sore throat, add *jie geng* and *huang qin.*
5. If the rash is dark red, add *zi cao* and *mu dan pi.*

## Cautions and Contraindications:
Not for pediatric use. Not to be used for rashes with evenly expressed surface, or when measles toxins go internally. Contraindicated for patients with sweating, shortness of breath, cough and wheezing.

## Administration:
Take with warm water, as needed.

Source: *Yi Fang Ji Jie* (醫方集解)

# Sheng Mai Yin 生脈飲
Ginseng and Ophiopogon Formula
# (Sheng Mai San 生脈散)
(Generate the Pulse Powder)

**Indication:**
Summer heat causes profuse sweating, exhausting *qi*, and injuring fluids: shortness of breath, dry mouth, thirsty and fatigue.

Chronic lung deficiency cough, *qi* and *yin* injured: chronic cough with sparse sputum that is difficult to expectorate, shortness of breath, spontaneous sweating, and dry mouth and tongue.

**Tongue:**     pale red tongue; dry, thin coating
**Pulse:**     deficient, rapid, or deficient, thin

**Clinical Applications:**
1. This formula is well-balanced: tonifies, nourishes and clears, and astringes.
2. Currently used for *Lu* TB, chronic bronchitis, arrhythmias, rheumatic heart disease, coronary artery disease (CAD), cardiogenic shock, toxic shock and hemorrhagic shock.
3. Arrhythmia, heart failure, pulmonary heart disease and cardiovascular regulation, dyspnea, chronic bronchitis, tuberculosis, neurasthenia, yin deficiency diabetes.
4. It can promote the transformation of lymphocytes and increase immunity.

**Ingredients:**
1. ren shen       10.0
2. mai men dong    6.0
3. wu wei zi       4.0

**Functions:**
Benefits *qi*, generates fluids, preserves the *yin*, and stops excessive sweating.

**Modifications:**
1. For profuse sweating with dark, scanty, and difficult urination, add *huang qi* and *dang gui*.
2. For irritability with relatively severe insomnia, add *suan zao ren* and *he huan pi*.
3. For myocardial infarction, add *Si Ni San*.
4. For palpitation with tight chest, add *dan shen, he shou wu*, and *da zao*.
5. For limb fatigue, add *huang qi, gan cao*, and *dang gui*.
6. For deficiency heat and night sweat, add *gui ban, bie jiao*, and *long gu*.
7. For body fluid exhaustion, add *tian hua fen, bei mu*, and *sha shen*.
8. For kidney yin deficiency, combine with *Liu Wei Di Huang Wan*.
9. For dizziness and shortness of breath: combine with *Er Chen Tang* and add *huang qi* and *bai bu*.
10. For irritability and insomnia: combine with *Gan Mai Da Zao Tang* and add *suan zao ren* and *fu shen*.

**Cautions and Contraindications**:
High fever without *qi* and *yin* deficiency; external pathogenic influence.

**Note:**
1. *Sheng Mai Yin*, also *Sheng Mai San* – from [醫學啟源 *Yi Xue Qi Yuan*] – *Jin, Yuan* dynasty.
2. *Sheng Mai San*, also *Sheng Mai Yin* – from [內外傷辨惑論 *Nei Wai Sheng Bian Huo Lun*].
3. *Sheng Mai San* is also known as *Sheng Mai Yin* and *Sheng Mai Tang*.

**Administration:**
Take with warm water, any time.

Source: *Yi Lu Fang* (醫錄方)

# Sheng Yang San Huo Tang 升陽散火湯
Bupleurum and Ginseng Combination
Raise the Yang and Disperse Fire Decoction

## Indications:
Over-consumption of cold foods leading to stomach deficiency and *yang* channels restrained the *yang qi*.

Deficiency spleen *yin* blood, *qi* weakness in stomach, *shao-yang qi* stagnation and internal heat in between muscle and bone.

## Clinical Applications:
1. This formula is for treating underlying blood and stomach deficiency, or lingering coolness after spring, or heat fire in stomach and intestine.
2. The key symptoms are steaming bone heat that is warm to the touch when these are belonging to damp-heat and suppressed fire in the stomach channel. Also eating too much cold food or other dietary issues, restrain the *yang qi* within the spleen earth.
3. Currently used in treating limbs fatigue and five-center heat.

## Ingredients:

| | | | | | |
|---|---|---|---|---|---|
| 1. | sheng ma | 3.0 | 6. | ren shen | 3.0 |
| 2. | ge gen | 3.0 | 7. | zhi gan cao | 1.8 |
| 3. | du huo | 2.0 | 8. | chai hu | 1.8 |
| 4. | qiang huo | 3.0 | 9. | fang fen | 1.2 |
| 5. | bai shao | 3.0 | 10. | gan cao | 1.2 |

## Functions:
Raises the *yang*, disperses fire, benefits the *qi*, and expels damp-heat.

## Modifications:
For case with severe steaming bone heat, add *yin chai hu.*

## Cautions and Contraindications:
Raw and cold food.

## Note:
This formula is known as *Chai Hu Sheng Ma Tang.*

## Administration:
Take with warm water, as needed.

Source: *Yi Zong Jin Jian* (醫宗金鑑)

# Sheng Yu Tang 聖愈湯
Tangkuei Four Plus Combination
Sage-Like Healing Decoction

## Indications:
Blood loss and *yin* deficiency.

Irritability, difficulty sleeping, anemia, and malnutrition.

| | |
|---|---|
| **Tongue:** | pale tongue with a thin coating |
| **Pulse:** | weak, fine |

## Clinical Applications:
1. This formula is for treating *qi* and blood deficiency.
2. The key symptoms are vexation heat, thirst, and disturbed sleep, or constant ache in the lower abdomen that occurs either during or just after menstruation and responds favorably to pressure.
3. Currently used in treating sores that bleed profusely and cause irritability and insomnia, and postpartum deficiency.

## Ingredients:
1. shu di huang      2.4
2. bai shao          2.4
3. chuan xiong       2.4
4. ren shen          2.4
5. dang gui          8.0
6. huang qi          8.0

## Functions:
Tonify *qi*, nourish blood.

## Note:
*Sheng Yu Tang* is from *Si Wu Tang* with the addition of *huang qi* and *ren shen*.

## Administration:
Take with warm water, before meals.

Source: *Yi Zong Jin Jian* (醫宗金鑑)

# Shi Hui San 十灰散
## Ten Partially Charred Substance Powder

**Indications:**

For the treatment of upper and middle *jiao* bleeding due to blood-heat-runs-reckless syndrome.

May also be used for patients with acute bleeding, including vomiting, spitting, or coughing up blood, or nosebleeds.

| | |
|---|---|
| **Tongue**: | red |
| **Pulse**: | rapid |

**Clinical Applications:**

1. This formula treats fire blazing in the upper and middle *jiao*; the symptoms are acute bleeding from upper orifices with bright red blood, red tongue and rapid pulse.
2. Currently used for acute hemorrhagic esophagitis or gastritis, bleeding peptic ulcers, pulmonary TB, or bronchiectasis, causing hemoptysis.

**Ingredients:**

| | | | | | |
|---|---|---|---|---|---|
| 1. | da ji | 1.0 | 6. | he ye | 1.0 |
| 2. | xiao ji | 1.0 | 7. | zong lu pi | 1.0 |
| 3. | qian cao gen | 1.0 | 8. | zhi zi | 1.0 |
| 4. | ce bai ye | 1.0 | 9. | da huang | 1.0 |
| 5. | bai mao gen | 1.0 | 10. | mu dan pi (daikon juice) | 1.0 |

Note: an aliquot portion of herbs is charred, then ground and mixed into a fine powder.

**Functions:**

Cools the blood and stops bleeding.

**Modifications:**

For severe bleeding due to rebellious *qi* and fire blazing upward, change powder to decoction, increase *da huang, zhi zi* to higher dosage and add *niu xi* and *dai zhe shi*.

**Cautions and Contraindications:**

Not to be used for bleeding due to deficient cold.

**Administration:**

Take with cool water or daikon radish juice, as needed.

Source: *Lao Zheng Shi Yao Shen Shu* (勞症十藥神書)

# Shi Liu Wei Liu Qi Yin 十六味流氣飲
Tangkuei Sixteen Herbs Combination
Sixteen-Ingredient Drink for *Qi* Flow

### Indications:
Breast abscesses or for the toxic abscesses and tumors of pox disorders.

This is a combination of external and internal disharmonies; the primary internal deficiency, and the external either dermal or deeper, appear as excess in the form of heat and/or stagnation of *qi* and blood.

### Clinical Applications:
1. This formula is for treating hard swellings in the breast that after an extended period develop into open sores.
2. The key symptoms are excess worry that generates *qi* stagnation appear as excess in the form of heat and/or stagnation of *qi* and blood in deeper or dermal abscesses.
3. Currently used in treating mastitis, breast tumor, goiter, and cervical lymphadenopathy.
4. Unknown malignant sores, carbuncles and tumors, or breast cancer, and lumps due to stagnation of *qi*, and stubborn ulcers of unknown disease.

### Ingredients:

| | | | | | |
|---|---|---|---|---|---|
| 1. | dang gui | 1.5 | 9. | mu xiang | 1.0 |
| 2. | chuan xiong | 1.5 | 10. | wu yao | 1.0 |
| 3. | bai shao | 1.5 | 11. | hou po | 1.0 |
| 4. | gui zhi | 1.5 | 12. | zhi ke | 1.0 |
| 5. | ren shen | 1.5 | 13. | bing lang | 1.0 |
| 6. | jie geng | 1.5 | 14. | zi su ye | 1.0 |
| 7. | bai zhi | 1.0 | 15. | fang fen | 1.0 |
| 8. | huang qi | 1.0 | 16. | gan cao | 1.0 |

### Functions:
Tonify the *qi*, nourish the blood; thrust pus out and dissipate swelling.

### Modifications:
1. For cases with breast abscesses, add *wang bu liu xing* and *pu gong ying*.
2. For cases with swollen lymph nodes, add *xia ku cao*, *xuan shen*, and *huang qin*.
3. For cases with enlarged thyroid, add *xia ku cao*, *xuan shen*, *zhe bei mu* and *kun bu*.
4. For cases with swellings that are slow to come to a head and burst, add *zao jia ci*.

### Administration:
Take with room-temp water, after meals.

Source: *Zheng Zhi Zhung Shang* (證治準繩)

# Shi Pi Yin 實脾飲

Bolster the Spleen Decoction

## Indications:

For the treatment of *yin* edema due to *yang* deficiency.

May also be used for generalized edema that is more severe below the waist, cold extremities, chest and abdominal fullness and distention, a heavy sensation in the body, loss of appetite, no thirst, scanty urine, and semiliquid or unformed stools.

| | |
|---|---|
| **Tongue:** | pale, thick, greasy coating |
| **Pulse:** | submerged and slow or submerged and thin |

## Clinical Applications:

1. The key symptoms are severe edema in the lower body, distention and fullness in the chest and abdomen caused by *yang* deficiency; *qi* fails to transform water, leading to internal accumulation of water and dampness.
2. Currently used in treating chronic nephritis, cardiac edema, ascites or other chronic hepatic disorders.

## Ingredients:

| | | |
|---|---|---|
| 1. | zhi fu zi | 6.0 |
| 2. | gan jiang (pao jiang) | 6.0 |
| 3. | fu ling | 6.0 |
| 4. | bai zhu | 6.0 |
| 5. | mu gua | 6.0 |
| 6. | hou po | 6.0 |
| 7. | mu xiang | 6.0 |
| 8. | da fu pi | 6.0 |
| 9. | cao guo | 6.0 |
| 10. | zhi gan cao | 3.0 |
| 11. | sheng jiang | 5 pcs |
| 12. | da zao | 1 pc |

## Functions:

Strengthens the spleen, warms the kidney *yang*, and promotes urination to reduce edema.

## Modifications:

1. For urinary difficulty, add *zhu ling* and *ze xie.*
2. For constipation, add *qian niu zi.*

## Administration:

Take with warm water, after meals.

Source: *Ji Sheng Fang* (濟生方)

# Shi Quan Da Bu Tang 十全大補湯
### Ginseng and Tangkuei Ten Combination

## Indications:
Used in the treatment of *qi* and blood deficiency with cold patterns: pallid or sallow complexion, poor appetite, spermatorrhea, weakness of the lower extremities, nonhealing sores, or continuous spotting from uterine bleeding.

## Clinical Applications:
1. This is a commonly used formula for *qi* and blood deficiency with a predominance of *qi* deficiency that tends toward cold.
2. Currently used for anemia, nervous exhaustion, nonhealing ulcers, and postoperative recovery enhancement.

## Ingredients:

| | | | | |
|---|---|---|---|---|
| 1. | ren shen | 3.0 | 7. shu di | 3.0 |
| 2. | bai zhu | 3.0 | 8. chuan xiong | 3.0 |
| 3. | fu ling | 3.0 | 9. rou gui | 3.0 |
| 4. | zhi gan cao | 3.0 | 10. huang qi | 3.0 |
| 5. | dang gui | 3.0 | 11. sheng jiang | 3.0 |
| 6. | bai shao | 3.0 | 12. da zao | 2.0 |

## Functions:
Warms and tonifies *qi* and blood.

## Modifications:
1. For emaciation, add *shan yao* and *qian shi*.
2. For *bi* pain of the joints, add *niu xi* and *xu duan*.
3. For *qi* and blood deficiency ulceration with unformed pus, add *zhi ke*, *xiang fu*, and *lian qiao*.
4. For extreme fatigue and depletion, combine with *xiao jian zhong tang*.
5. For heart deficiency palpitation, combine with *Yang Xin Tang*.
6. For spleen deficiency fatigue, combine with *Gui Pi Tang*.

## Administration:
Swallow with warm water, after meals.

Note: This formula is *Ba Zhen Tang* — which is *Si Wu Tang* (tonifies blood deficiency and invigorates the heart and liver) combined with *Si Jun Zi Tang* (tonifies *qi* deficiency and invigorates the spleen and stomach) — with the additions of *huang qi* and *rou gui*. It tonifies *qi* and blood, *yin* and *yang*, internally and externally.

Source: *Tai Ping Hui Min He Ji Ju Fang* (太平惠民合劑局方)

# Shi Wei Bai Du Tang 十味敗毒湯
## Bupleurum and Schizonepeta Formula

### Indications:
Carbuncles, boils, eczema, or hives.

This is for toxic sores in their initial stage, that is, swellings that have not yet suppurated.

### Clinical Applications:
1. This formula is for treating purulent diseases and improving allergic constitution.
2. The key symptoms are carbuncles, boils, eczema or hives.
3. Currently used in treating urticaria, athlete's foot, eczema, otitis media, empyema, and various other skin diseases.

### Ingredients:
| 1. | chai hu | 3.0 | 5. | jie geng | 3.0 | 9. | gan cao | 1.0 |
|---|---|---|---|---|---|---|---|---|
| 2. | du huo | 3.0 | 6. | chuan xiong | 3.0 | 10. | sheng jiang | 1.0 |
| 3. | jin ying pi | 3.0 | 7. | fu ling | 1.0 | | | |
| 4. | fang fen | 3.0 | 8. | jing jie | 1.0 | | | |

### Functions:
Dispel wind, transform damp, clear heat, and resolve toxin.

### Modifications:
1. For case with wind-cold-damp toxin: add *jin yin hua* and *tu fu ling.*
2. For case with carbuncle, boil, sores: add *huang qi* and *dang gui.*
3. For case with measles, eczema: combine with *Sheng Ma Ge Gen Tang.*
4. For case with swelling-hot carbuncle: combine with *Huang Lian Jie Du Tang.*
5. For case with swelling pain sore, ulcer: combine with *Tuo Li Xiao Du Yin.*

### Cautions and Contraindications:
The sores have already burst.

### Note:
1. This formula is a modification of *Jing Fang Bai Du San* (Schizonepeta and Siler Powder to Overcome Pathogenic Influences) from which *qiang huo* and *qian hu* are omitted. It is for resolving the exterior, and thus its strength is in mitigating symptoms such as chills and fever that often accompany the outbreak of toxic sores.
2. It should be used at the onset of carbuncles and boils, when symptoms are redness, swelling and pain, and it is appropriate to use it within a few days after the onset of the disease.
3. Those with mild symptoms will recover within four or five days after taking this formula.
4. It should be followed with *Tou Li Xiao Du Yin* (Support the Interior and Eliminate Toxin).
5. For chronic conditions, take *Shi Quan Da Bu Tang.*

### Administration:
Take with warm water, before meals or on an empty stomach.

Source: *Hua Gang Qing Zhou* (華岡青洲)

# Shi Wei Xiang Ru Yin 十味香薷飲
Elsholtzia Ten Combination
Ten-Ingredient Drink with Mosla

## Indications:
Externally contracted damp-cold during the summertime.

Characterized by mild fever and chills and relatively profuse sweating, headache, in patients with preexisting spleen deficiency and dampness who then contract a summer-heat disorder.

**Tongue:**     thick coating

## Clinical Applications:
1. This formula is for treating externally contracted summer-heat with cold disorders that most frequently occur in the summer and are characterized by signs of both heat and damp.
2. The key symptoms are steaming hot skin, heaviness and pain in the head, spontaneous sweating, fatigued limbs, vexation, thirst, vomiting, and diarrhea.
3. Currently used in treating summertime flu-like, heavy-headedness and body fatigue, fever and thirst, loss of appetite, cloudy spirit, general malaise, fever, and indigestion, gastrointestinal discomfort (diarrhea and vomiting).

## Ingredients:

| | | | | | |
|---|---|---|---|---|---|
| 1. | xiang ru | 4.0 | 6. | bai bian dou | 2.0 |
| 2. | ren shen | 2.0 | 7. | huang qi | 2.0 |
| 3. | chen pi | 2.0 | 8. | mu gua | 2.0 |
| 4. | bai zhu | 2.0 | 9. | hou po | 2.0 |
| 5. | fu ling | 2.0 | 10. | gan cao | 2.0 |

## Functions:
Expel summer-heat and release extremal, transform interior dampness; regulate *qi* and strengthen the spleen.

## Modifications:
1. For cases with tiredness and fatigue: add *mai men dong* and *wu wei zi*.
2. For cases with dry throat and thirst: add *shi gao* and *zhi mu*.

## Cautions and Contraindications:
Summer-heat with damage of *qi* and body fluid.

## Administration:
Take with warm water, after meals; take with room-temp water if the patient has a fever.

Source: *Zhou Huo Bai Yi Fang* （肘後百一方）

# Shi Xiao San 失笑散
## Sudden Smile Powder

## Indications:
For the treatment of blood-stasis-obstruction syndrome.

May also be used for patients with irregular menstruation, dysmenorrhea, retention of the lochia, postpartum abdominal pain, acute, colicky pain in the lower abdomen, severe pain in the middle abdomen, or epigastric pain.

## Clinical Applications:
1. This formula is used for pain due to blood stagnation, especially used for blood stasis obstructing in the *liver* channels.
2. Currently used for dysmenorrhea, chronic gastritis, endometriosis, and angina pectoris.

## Ingredients:
1. pu huang      6.0
2. wu ling zhi   6.0

## Functions:
Invigorates the blood, dispels blood stasis, disperses accumulation in liver channels, and alleviates pain.

## Modifications:
1. For cases with severe *qi* stagnation, combine with *jin ling zi san*.
2. For cases with severe cold, add *xiao hui xiang* and *pao jiang*.
3. For irregular menstruation due to blood stasis and blood deficiency, take with *si wu tang*.

## Cautions and Contraindications:
Not to be taken during pregnancy (*pu huang*); not for the treatment of stomach deficiency (*wu ling zhi*).

## Administration:
Take with warm water, as needed.

Source: *Tai Ping Hui Min He Ji Ju Fang* (太平惠民和劑局方)

# Shou Tai Wan 壽胎丸
Fetus Longevity Pill

## Indications:
For the treatment of kidney *qi* deficiency with unstable fetus syndrome.

May also be used for patients with soreness and distention of the lower abdomen and vaginal bleeding during pregnancy. Other symptoms include dizziness, tinnitus, weakness of the legs, and frequent urination to the point of incontinence.

**Tongue**: pale; white, slippery coating
**Pulse**: submerged, frail at *chi* position

## Clinical Applications:
1. This formula is used for pregnancies with a risk of miscarriage, or for women with a history of miscarriage. It calms and stabilizes the fetus.
2. It was designed to prevent problems during pregnancy in women who are kidney *qi* deficient, or who have suffered miscarriages in the past.
3. Additionally used for infertility and hypertension.

## Ingredients:
1. tu si zi          120.0
2. sang ji sheng     60.0
3. xu duan           60.0
4. e jiao            60.0

## Functions:
Stabilizes the kidneys and calms the fetus.

## Modifications:
For severe *qi* deficiency, add *ren shen*.

## Cautions and Contraindications:
Contraindicated if the threat of miscarriage is due to heat or stagnation.

## Administration:
Take with warm water, as needed.

Source: *Yi Xue Zhong Shen Xi Lu* (醫學中參西錄)

# Shu Gan Tang 舒肝湯
Bupleurum and Evodia Combination
Dredge the Liver Decoction

## Indications:
Pain in liver channel from stagnation of *qi* and blood.

Pain beneath the left side of the ribcage, liver *qi* and blood stagnation, it could be brought on by internal damage from the emotions, such as anger, or could be the result of trauma.

## Clinical Applications:
1. This formula is for treating pain in the liver channel, the stagnation of which could be brought on by internal damage from anger or could be bruised or broken ribs.
2. The key symptoms are abdominal pain in left flank, intercostal neuralgia, chest and flank pain, liver *qi* stagnation, alternative chills and fever, or traumatic injury.
3. Currently used in treating left hypochondriac abdominal pain, intercostal neuralgia, flank pain from falls, and pancreatitis.

## Ingredients:

| 1. chai hu | 2.7 | 6. chuan xiong | 1.4 |
|---|---|---|---|
| 2. dang gui | 2.7 | 7. zhi ke | 1.8 |
| 3. tao ren | 1.8 | 8. huang lian | 2.7 |
| 4. bai shao | 1.4 | 9. hong hua | 0.9 |
| 5. qing pi | 1.8 | 10. wu zhu yu | 0.9 |

## Functions:
Dredge the liver, regulate the *qi*, move the stagnation and relieve the pain; activate blood and clear the heat.

## Modifications:
1. For case with severe pain, add *yan hu suo.*
2. For case with severe intercostal neuralgia, add *chuan lian zi.*

## Cautions and Contraindications:
Trauma with Internal bleeding.

## Note:
It is also known as *Shu Gan San* (Powder to Dredge the Liver).

## Administration:
Take with warm water, before meals.

Source: *Wan Bing Hui Chun* (萬病回春)

# Shu Jing Huo Xue Tang 疏經活血湯
## Clematis and Stephania Combination
### Relax the Channels and Invigorate the Blood Decoction

## Indications:
Wind-damp invasion of the channels and blood stasis.

Painful wind-cold-damp *Bi* patterns that worsen at night; joint pain, low back pain, muscle pain, and pain all over the body.

## Clinical Applications:
1. This formula is for treating painful wind-cold-damp *Bi* patterns and pain all over the body.
2. The key symptoms are migratory stabbing pain in the bones and joints of the whole body, muscle aches, joint pain, and radiating pain or numbness in the leg.
3. Currently used in treating sciatic pain, lumbar pain, arthritis, non-sciatic numbness and pain in the lower extremities, and sprains and strains of the knees, legs, or lower back pain.
4. Knee joint fluid arthritis, low back pain, lower limb numbness, beriberi, edema, hemiplegia, high blood pressure, postpartum thrombotic pain.

## Ingredients:

| | | | | | | | | |
|---|---|---|---|---|---|---|---|---|
| 1. | dang gui | 2.0 | 7. | bai shao | 2.5 | 13. | long dan cao | 1.0 |
| 2. | sheng di huang | 2.0 | 8. | niu xi | 2.0 | 14. | sheng jiang | 3.0 |
| 3. | cang zhu | 2.0 | 9. | wei ling xiang | 2.0 | 15. | chen pi | 2.0 |
| 4. | chuan xiong | 1.0 | 10. | fang ji | 1.0 | 16. | bai zhi | 1.0 |
| 5. | tao ren | 2.0 | 11. | qiand huo | 1.0 | 17. | gan cao | 1.0 |
| 6. | fu ling | 1.0 | 12. | fang fen | 1.0 | | | |

## Functions:
Unblock and relax the channels, activate blood, expel the wind.

## Modifications:
1. For cases with weakness of muscle: add *gui zhi* and *ma huang*.
2. For cases with pain of tendon and bone: add *huang qi* and *bai zhu*.
3. For cases with pain in the lower back and legs: add *xu duan* and *hong hua*.
4. For cases with severe pain or difficulty walking: add *mu gua, mu tong, huang bai*, and *yi yi ren*.

## Cautions and Contraindications:
This formula nourishes blood but not *qi* and thus should not be used long-term unless amended with supplementing herbs.

## Note:
1. This formula has more blood-nourishing and blood-moving ingredients than *Juan Bi Tang* (Notopterygium and Turmeric Combination) but is less able to tonify *qi*.
2. *Shang Zhong Xia Tong Yong Tong Feng Wan* (Cinnamon and Angelica Formula) and *Shu Jing Huo Xue Tang* (Clematis and Stephania Combination) both treat migratory *Bi* pain. The former is more drying and less nourishing to the blood than the latter.

## Administration:
Take with warm water, before meals.

Source: *Wan Bing Hui Chun* (萬病回春)

# Shuang Jie Tong Sheng San 雙解通聖散
### Siler and Platycodon Formula (Minus Rhubarb)
### Double Releasing Powder that Sagely Unblocks

## Indications:
Excess wind-heat in internal and external three *jiao*.

Strong fever and aversion to cold, dizziness, headache, red eyes and pain, tinnitus and nasal congestion, dry mouth and tongue, poor throat, sticky nasal discharge, cough.

**Tongue:**  yellow, greasy coating
**Pulse:**  flooding and rapid or wiry and slippery

## Clinical Applications:
1. This formula is for treating excess wind-heat in internal, external and three *jiao*, aversion to cold and excess heat.
2. The key symptoms are dizziness, sore, red eyes, difficulty swallowing, nasal congestion with thick and sticky discharge, a bitter taste in the mouth, dry mouth, glomus and oppression in the chest and diaphragm, and dark, rough urination.
3. Currently used in treating wind-heat dryness and irritability, difficulty and hesitant urination, chronic nephritis, cardiac asthma, alcoholism, hemorrhoids, empyema, hypertension and stroke prevention.

## Ingredients:

| | | | | | | | |
|---|---|---|---|---|---|---|---|
| 1. fang fen | 1.0 | 6. bai zhu | 1.0 | 11. huang qin | 2.0 |
| 2. jing jie | 1.0 | 7. chuan xiong | 1.0 | 12. jie geng | 2.0 |
| 3. dang gui | 1.0 | 8. bo he | 1.0 | 13. gan cao | 4.0 |
| 4. bai shao | 1.0 | 9. ma huang | 1.0 | 14. shi gao | 2.0 |
| 5. lian qiao | 1.0 | 10. zhi zi | 1.0 | 15. hua shi | 6.0 |

## Functions:
Expel wind and clear heat; tonify *qi* and nourish blood.

## Modifications:
1. For case with *qi* deficiency fatigue: add *ren shen* and *huang qi*.
2. For case with blood deficiency and tired weak: add *sheng di* and *shu di huang*.
3. For case with deficiency physique tired and sleepiness: add *mai men dong* and *wu wei zi*.

## Note:
This formula is the same as *Fang Fen Tong Sheng San* (Siler and Platycodon Formula) but has removed *da huang* (rhubarb) and *mang xiao* (mirabilitum).

## Administration:
Take with warm water, before meals.

Source: *Yi Zong Jin Jian* (醫宗金鑑)

# Si Jun Zi Tang 四君子湯
## Major Four Combination

### Indications:

Spleen and stomach *qi* deficiency: pallid complexion, low and soft voice, poor appetite, loose stools, and weakness in the limbs.

**Tongue**:      pale tongue body
**Pulse**:      thin and/or frail

### Clinical Applications:

1. This is a commonly used formula for tonifying *qi*. It is distinguished by its relatively harmonious and moderate nature.
2. It treats the classic presentation of deficient spleen *qi*, usually caused by improper eating habits, excessive thinking, or overworking.
3. Currently used for common neurasthenia, chronic gastritis, stomach ulcer, peptic ulcer, irritable bowel syndrome (IBS), diabetes mellitus, and uterine fibroids.

### Ingredients:

| | | | | | |
|---|---|---|---|---|---|
| 1. | ren shen | 6.0 | 4. | zhi gan cao | 3.0 |
| 2. | bai zhu | 6.0 | 5. | sheng jiang | 3.0 |
| 3. | fu ling | 6.0 | 6. | da zao | 2.0 |

### Functions:

Benefits *qi* and strengthens the spleen.

### Modifications:

1. For poor digestion in children with spleen deficiency cough, add *chen pi*.
2. For lung deficiency phlegm accumulation, add *chen pi* and *ban xia*.
3. For cold stomach vomit and diarrhea, add *mu xiang* and *sha ren*.
4. For spleen deficiency tidal fever, add *chai hu* and *sha ren*.
5. For *qi* and blood deficiency, combine with *Si Wu Tang*.
6. For deficiency cold diarrhea, combine with *Li Zhong Wan*.
7. For abdominal distention with heat and vomiting, combine with *San Huang Xie Xin Tang*.

### Cautions and Contraindications:

This formula should not be used without modifications for patients with high fever, heat from deficiency, or a combination of irritability, thirst, and constipation. Overuse of this formula may result in a dry mouth, thirst, and irritability.

### Administration:

Swallow with warm water, after meals.

Source: *Yi Fang Ji Jie* (醫方集解)

# Si Ni San 四逆散
Bupleurum and Aurantium Immaturus Formula
Frigid Extremities Powder

## Indications:

For the treatment of *shao yang* frigid extremities syndrome (*yang jue – yang* or hot-type collapse), or generally for cold hands and feet, sometimes accompanied by slight body fever, cough, heart palpitations, urinary difficulty, abdominal pain, or diarrhea.

May also be used for patients with liver and spleen disharmony, including distention and stifling sensation in hypochondrium and pain in epigastrium and abdomen.

**Tongue**:     red, yellow coating
**Pulse**:       wiry

## Clinical Applications:

1.  This formula may be used for spreading the liver *qi* and regulating the spleen; often used for treating frigid extremities due to liver and/or gallbladder *qi* stagnation, or pain in epigastrium and abdomen.
2.  Currently used for cholecystitis, chronic hepatitis, gastritis pain, peptic ulcers, gallstones, acid regurgitation, pyelonephritis, fallopian tube obstruction, and acute mastitis.
3.  Also may be used for serious pain in the digestive system or abdominal pain due to diarrhea and tenesmus.

## Ingredients:

1.  chai hu          5.5
2.  bai shao         5.5
3.  zhi shi          5.5
4.  zhi gan cao      5.5

## Functions:

Spreads the liver *qi* and regulates the spleen, expels the evil, releases constrained *qi*.

## Modifications:

1.  For coughing, add *wu wei zi* and *gan jiang.*
2.  For palpitations, add *gui zhi* and *dang gui.*
3.  For abdominal pain and diarrhea, add *bai zhu* and *fu ling.*
4.  For urinary difficulty, add *Wu Ling San.*
5.  For abdominal pain, add *huang lian tang.*
6.  For severe *qi* stagnation, add *xiang fu* and *yu jin.*

## Cautions and Contraindications:

Caution: this formula is different from *Si Ni Tang (see next entry),* which treats cold or frigid four limbs; this formula is used for treating frigid limbs due to neurological dysfunction.

## Administration:

Take with warm water, as needed.

Source: *Shang Han Lun* (傷寒論)

# Si Ni Tang 四逆湯
Aconite, Ginger, and Licorice Combination
Frigid Extremities Decoction

## Indications:

For the treatment of *shao yin*-stage syndrome, as well as *tai yang*-stage *yang* collapse syndrome. May also be used for patients with excessive *yin* and deficiencies in *yang*, four limbs frigid cold, and general body weakness. Extremely cold extremities, aversion to cold, sleeping with the knees drawn up, lethargic state with a constant desire to sleep, vomiting, lack of thirst, abdominal pain and cold and diarrhea with undigested food are all symptoms.

**Tongue**:     pale, white and slippery coating
**Pulse**:     submerged, thin or submerged, faint

## Clinical Applications:

1. This formula can be used for tonifying kidney *yang* in non-emergency situations. It is used to wake up the systems when the metabolic function has become extremely weak.
2. For excessive sweating or induced sweat by mistake, and/or diarrhea, vomiting, cholera, food poisoning, trauma or excessive blood loss due to surgery; may be taken after heart failure with the feeble pulse, and when the hands and feet are cold and frigid.
3. Currently used for first aid formula occurring from acute myocardial infarction, cardiac insufficiency, vomiting and diarrhea from acute and chronic gastroenteritis, hypopituitarism, hypothyroidism, and adrenal insufficiency.

## Ingredients:

1. pao fu zi     2.0
2. gan jiang     4.0
3. zhi gan cao     6.0

## Functions:

Rescues devastated *yang* and warm the channels.

## Modifications:

1. For vomit with sore throat, add *sheng jiang* and *jie geng*.
2. For red face with irritability, add *ren shen* and *cong bai*.
3. For treating four limbs frigid and cold, add *xi xin* and *gui zhi*.
4. For diarrhea with undigested food, add *Li Zhong Tang*.
5. For *qi* deficiency body pain, add *Si Jun Zi Tang*.
6. For blood-deficiency abdominal pain, add *Si Wu Tang*.

## Cautions and Contraindications:

Not used to treat true heat false cold syndrome.

## Administration:

Take with warm water, as needed.

Source: *Shang Han Lun* (傷寒論)

# Si Shen Wan 四神丸

Four-Miracle Pill

## Indications:

For the treatment of early-morning diarrhea syndrome (*wu geng xie* – cock-crow diarrhea). This diarrhea occurs daily just before sunrise, or chronic diarrhea with no appetites, undigested food, abdominal pain, and generally for cold extremities, and fatigue and lethargy.

**Tongue:** pale; thin, white coating
**Pulse:** submerged, slow, and forceless

## Clinical Applications:

1. This formula is used for daybreak diarrhea due to waning *ming men* fire that is unable to warm the earth. The key symptom is diarrhea occurring daily just before sunrise.
2. Currently also used for chronic colitis, allergic colitis, and intestinal TB.

## Ingredients:

1. bu gu zhi    12.0
2. rou dou kou   6.0
3. wu wei zi    6.0
4. wu zhu yu    3.0
5. sheng jiang  24.0
6. da zao     10 pcs

## Functions:

Warms and tonifies spleen and kidney, binds up the intestines, and stops diarrhea.

## Cautions and Contraindications:

Contraindicated when there is damp-heat in the lower *jiao.*

## Administration:

Take with warm, salted water, before meals.

Source: *Zheng Zhi Zhun Sheng* (證治準繩)

# Si Sheng Wan 四生丸
### Rehmannia Four Formula
### Four-Fresh Pill

## Indications:
Upper *jiao* bleeding due to blood heat runs recklessness syndrome.

Coughing, spitting or vomiting of blood or nosebleed particularly of fresh-red blood accompanied by dry mouth and throat.

**Tongue**:   red or deep red
**Pulse**:   wiry, rapid, or forceful, wiry and rapid

## Clinical Applications:
1  This formula treats bleeding in the upper *jiao* due to blood heat running recklessness.
2  Currently used for acute hemorrhagic esophagitis or gastritis, bleeding peptic ulcer, pulmonary TB, or bronchiectasis causing hemoptysis, gingivitis.
3  Nose bleeding, hemorrhoid bleeding, rectal bleeding, uterine bleeding embolism.

## Ingredients:
1.  sheng di huang   6.0
2.  sheng ce bai ye   6.0
3.  sheng he ye   6.0
4.  sheng ai ye   6.0

## Functions:
Cool blood and stop bleeding.

## Modifications:
For more bleeding, add *xiao ji, bai mao gen, ou jie* and *xian he cao*.

## Cautions and Contraindications:
It should be discontinued once the bleeding has stopped; prolonged use increases the chances of developing blood stasis.

## Administration:
Take with warm water, after meals.

Source: *Yi Zong Jin Jian* (醫宗金鑑)

# Si Wu Tang 四物湯
## Tangkuei Four Combination

## Indications:
Used to promote eficiency of the *chong* and *ren* channels or to treat blood deficiency with stagnation: irregular menstruation with scant flow or amenorrhea, lower abdominal pain, dizziness, blurred vision, also used for hard abdominal masses with recurrent pain, restless fetus disorder, and lochioschesis with a firm and painful abdomen and sporadic fever and chills.

**Tongue**:   pale tongue
**Pulse**:    thin and wiry or thin and choppy

## Clinical Applications:
1. This is the standard formula for tonifying blood and regulating menstruation.
2. Currently used for dysmenorrhea, irregular menstruation, anemia of various etiologies, threatened miscarriage, postpartum weakness, and neurogenic headache. Also used for men with anemia or dry skin from loss of blood.

## Ingredients:
| | | | | | |
|---|---|---|---|---|---|
| 1. | shu di huang | 7.5 | 3. | bai shao | 7.5 |
| 2. | dang gui | 7.5 | 4. | chuan xiong | 7.5 |

## Functions:
Nourishes blood and regulates liver blood.

## Modifications:
1. For blood deficiency and cold in the womb, add *ai ye* and *xiang fu*.
2. For female blood stagnation, add *tao ren* and *hong hua*.
3. For blood deficiency and fatigue with deficiency heat, add *ren shen* and *huang qi*.
4. For nosebleed or bleeding stomach, add *ce bai ye*, *qian cao*, and *niu xi*.
5. For obesity with phlegm, add *chen pi* and *ban xia*.
6. For emaciation with phlegm, add *zhi zi* (*tan*), *zhi mu*, and *huang bai*.
7. For *qi* stagnation, add *xiang fu* and *yu jin*.
8. For *qi* excess, add *zhi shi* and *hou pu*.
9. For lung and heart depletion, combine with *Si Jun Zi Tang*.
10. For post-illness deficiency depletion, combine with *Xiao Chai Hu Tang*.
11. For postpartum deficiency heat, combine with *Si Ni Tang*.

## Cautions and Contraindications:
High fever with *yin* deficiency, or acute profuse bleeding that causes sudden *qi* collapse.

## Administration:
Swallow with warm water, after meals.

Source: *Tai Ping Hui Min He Ji Ju Fang* (太平惠民合劑局方)

# Su Zi Jiang Qi Tang 蘇子降氣湯
Perilla Seed Combination
Perilla Fruit Decoction for Directing *Qi* Downward

## Indications:
For the treatment of wheezing due to excessive cold-phlegm-obstruction syndrome.

May also be used for patients with coughing and wheezing with watery, copious sputum, a stifling sensation in the chest and diaphragm, and shortness of breath. Also may be used to treat pain and weakness of the lower back and legs, edema of the extremities, and/or fatigue.

**Tongue**: white, slippery or greasy coating
**Pulse**: wiry, slippery pulse

## Clinical Applications:
1. This formula is used for wheezing and coughing due to excessive-above, deficient-below syndrome, which is excessive pathogenic *qi* obstruction of the downward directing functions of the lung and a *qi* deficiency which is disabling the grasping *qi* functions of the kidney.
2. Currently used for chronic bronchitis, emphysema, bronchial asthma and cardiac asthma.

## Ingredients:

| | | | | | |
|---|---|---|---|---|---|
| 1. | zi su zi | 5.0 | 6. | rou gui | 3.0 |
| 2. | ban xia | 5.0 | 7. | dang gui | 2.0 |
| 3. | hou po | 2.0 | 8. | gan cao | 2.0 |
| 4. | chen pi | 3.0 | 9. | sheng jiang | 2.0 |
| 5. | qian hu | 2.0 | 10. | da zao | 1.0 |

## Functions:
Pushes down the rebelling *qi*, calms the asthma, warm to transform damp-phlegm, and stops coughing.

## Modifications:
1. For cases with cough and asthma, add *bei mu* and *xing ren*.
2. For cases with vomit phlegm damp, add *fu ling* and *jie geng*.
3. For fullness and distention in the hypochondriac area, add *huang qin* and *chai hu*.
4. For wind-cold cough, add *Ding Chuan Tang*.
5. For phlegmatic cough: add *Er Chen Tang*.

## Cautions and Contraindications:
Phlegm-heat in the lung or kidney *yin* deficiency.

## Administration:
Take with warm water, after meals.

Source: *Tai Ping Hui Min He Ji Ju Fang* (太平惠民和劑局方)

# Suan Zao Ren Tang 酸棗仁湯
Zizyphus Combination

### Indications:
Used to treat liver blood deficiency insomnia: deficiency fatigue, palpitations, insomnia, irritability, inability to sleep, night sweats, dizziness, vertigo, and dry throat and mouth.

**Tongue:**   dry and red
**Pulse:**   wiry or thin and rapid

### Clinical Applications:
1. This formula treats insomnia with restlessness and irritability caused by liver blood deficiency with deficiency fire.
2. Currently used for neurosis, menopausal syndrome, insomnia, nervous exhaustion, and depression.

### Ingredients:
1. suan zao ren   10.0
2. fu ling   4.0
3. zhi mu   2.0
4. chuan xiong   4.0
5. gan cao   2.0

### Functions:
Regulates the blood and calms the spirit, nourishes the *yin*, clears heat, and eliminates irritability.

### Modifications:
1. For irritability, heat, and night sweats, add *ren shen* and *huang qi*.
2. For irritability, thirst, and insomnia, add *mai men dong* and *wu wei zi*.
3. For unsettled palpitations, add *yuan zhi* and *shi chang pu*.
4. For insomnia with irritability and restlessness, combine with *Wen Dan Tang*.
5. For insomnia with palpitations, combine with *Yi Gan San*.

### Cautions and Contraindications:
Should not be used when patient has loose stool.

### Administration:
Swallow with warm water, after meals.

Source: *Jin Gui Yao Lüe* (金匱要略)

# Tai Shan Pan Shi San 泰山磐石丸
## Powder that Gives the Stability of Mount Tai

**Indications:**

For the treatment of pregnant women with *qi* and blood deficiency syndrome.

May also be used for patients with restless fetus, risk of miscarriage, or habitual miscarriage accompanied with pale face, fatigue and loss of appetite.

| | |
|---|---|
| **Tongue:** | pale, thin, slippery coating |
| **Pulse:** | slippery, forceless, submerged, frail |

**Clinical Applications:**

This formula is also used for women with *qi* and blood deficiency, as well as pregnant women with a history of miscarriage.

**Ingredients:**

1. ren shen        3.0-5.0
2. huang qi        3.0-5.0
3. bai zhu         6.0-9.0
4. zhi gan cao     1.0-2.0
5. dang gui        3.0-5.0
6. bai shao        2.0-3.0
7. shu di          2.0-3.0
8. chuan xiong     2.0-3.0
9. xu duan         3.0-5.0
10. huang qin      3.0-5.0
11. sha ren        1.0-2.0
12. nuo mi         15.0-20

**Functions:**

Augments the *qi*, nourishes the blood, strengthens the kidney and spleen, calms the fetus.

**Modifications:**

For prevention of miscarriage, take this formula once a week from 2ⁿᵈ to the 4ᵗʰ or 5ᵗʰ month of pregnancy.

**Administration:**

Take with warm water, as needed.

Source: *Jin Yue Quan Shu* (景岳全書)

# Tao Ren Cheng Qi Tang 桃仁承氣湯
## Persica and Rhubarb Combination

## Indications:
Used to treat blood buildup in the lower *jiao*: acute lower abdominal pain, urinary incontinence, night fevers, delirious speech, irritability, restlessness, and thirst. In more severe cases there may be manic behavior and female patients may have dysmenorrhea or amenorrhea.

**Pulse:** submerged, full, or choppy

## Clinical Applications:
1. This formula treats accumulation of blood stasis and heat in the lower *jiao* with lower abdominal tension and urinary incontinence.
2. Currently used for acute endometritis, retained placenta, pelvic inflammatory disease, intestinal obstruction, ectopic pregnancy, benign prostatic hypertrophy, epilepsy, cystitis, and ulcerative colitis.

## Ingredients:
1. tao ren           5.0
2. da huang        10.0
3. gui zhi           5.0
4. mang xiao       5.0
5. zhi gan cao     5.0

## Functions:
Eliminates stasis and clears heat, relieves the exterior and moistens dryness, drains bowels and breaks up blood stasis.

## Modifications:
1. For severe fire and blood stasis in the upper *jiao* with headache, red eyes and face, and nosebleed, add *sheng di huang*, *mu dan pi*, and *niu xi*.
2. For trauma, add *chi shao*, *dang gui wei*, *hong hua*, and *su mu*.
3. For excess patterns of irregular menstruation and amenorrhea, add *dang gui* and *hong hua*.
4. For irritability and thirst, add *huang qin* and *huang lian*.
5. For difficult urination, add *mu tong* and *sheng di*.
6. For constipation, add *zhi shi* and *hou pu*.

## Cautions and Contraindications:
Should not be used during pregnancy or when patient has exterior symptoms.

## Administration:
Swallow with warm or cold water, before meals.

Source: *Shang Han Lun* (傷寒論)

# Tao Hong Si Wu Tang 桃紅四物湯
## Tangkuei Four, Persica, and Carthamus Combination
## Four-Substance Decoction with Safflower and Peach Pit

## Indications:
Blood deficiency and blood stagnations
1. Female patients who tend to have blood deficiency and blood stasis. For concurrent blood deficiency and blood stasis leading to a shortened menstrual cycle with copious bleeding of dark-purple, sticky blood, with or without clots.
2. Second-stage trauma injuries where stasis is frequent.

**Tongue:**  purple spots
**Pulse:**  rough and fine or rough and wiry

## Clinical Applications:
1. This formula is for treating women with blood stasis in the lower abdomen who present with abdominal pain that is worse with pressure.
2. The key symptoms are irregular menstruation, dysmenorrhea, and poor menstrual flow with blood clots.
3. Currently used in treating chronic pelvic inflammatory disease, sequelae of cerebral hemorrhage, hypertension, hyperlipidemia, angioneurotic headache, and migraine.

## Ingredients:
1. tao ren          5.0
2. hong hua         2.5
3. shu di huang     5.0
4. dang gui         5.0
5. bai shao         5.0
6. chuan xiong      2.5

## Functions:
Tonify and invigorate the blood and regulate menstruation.

## Cautions and Contraindications:
Pregnancy.

Caution with virginal bleeding.

## Administration:
Take with warm water, before meals.

Source: *Yi Zong Jin Jian* (醫宗金鑑 )

# Tian Ma Gou Teng Yin 天麻鈎藤飲
Gastrodia and Gambir Combination
Gastrodia and Uncaria Decoction

## Indications:
For the treatment of liver *yang* rising and liver wind rising syndromes. May be used generally for patients with headache, dizziness, tinnitus, blurred vision, a sensation of heat rushing to the head, deviation on eyes and mouth, stiff tongue, aphasia, palpitations, insomnia with dream-disturbed sleep; in severe cases, there may also be numbness, twitching, and spasms in the extremities, prickly sensation on the skin, or hemiplegia.

**Tongue:**   red tongue with yellow coating
**Pulse:**    wiry and rapid

## Clinical Applications:
1.  This formula is commonly used for hypertension caused by liver *yang* rising. This is ascendant liver *yang* accompanied by internal movement of liver wind. The liver can extinguish the wind, quiet the heart, and calm *shen*, therefore, it can also calm chronic rheumatoid arthritis.
2.  Currently used for treating essential hypertension, transitory ischemic attacks, renal hypertension, aphasia, epilepsy, and neurosis.
3.  Other symptoms include hypertensive headache, pregnancy hypertension, cerebral hemorrhage, arteriosclerosis symptoms, irritability, insomnia, eye pain, and bitter taste in the mouth.

## Ingredients:
| | | | | | | |
|---|---|---|---|---|---|---|
| 1. | tian ma | 1.0 | 5. | huang *qin* | 1.0 | 9. sang ji sheng  2.6 |
| 2. | gou teng | 1.6 | 6. | yi mu cao | 1.6 | 10. ye jiao teng  3.2 |
| 3. | shi jue ming | 3.2 | 7. | zhi zi | 1.0 | 11. fu shen  1.6 |
| 4. | chuan niu xi | 1.3 | 8. | du zhong | 1.6 | |

## Functions:
Calms the liver, suppresses yang; relives spasm, extinguishes wind, nourishes *yin*, clears heat.

## Modifications:
1.  For thirst with phlegm retention, add *bei mu* and *zhu ru.*
2.  For dizziness and headache, add *huai hua, lian qiao* and *hai zao.*
3.  For wind from excess heat, add *sang ye, ju hua,* and *long dan cao.*
4.  For liver *yang* rising, add *dai zhe shi, long gu* and *mu li.*
5.  For symptoms of blurred vision, dry eyes, weakness of lower back and extremities, combine with *Qi Ju Di Huang Wan.*
6.  For severe cases, combine with *Ling Jiao Gou Teng Tang.*

## Cautions and Contraindications:
Contraindicated for patients with *yin* deficiency.

## Administration:
Take with warm water, before meals.

Source: *Za Bing Zheng Zhi Xin Yi* (雜病證治新義)

# Tian Tai Wu Yao San 天台烏藥散
Top-quality Lindera Powder

## Indications:
For the treatment of small intestine hernia, especially caused by cold and *qi* stagnation syndrome.

May also be used for patients suffering from lower abdominal pain radiating to the testicles, which may feel pendent and swollen.

**Tongue:**     pale, white coating
**Pulse:**      submerged and slow or wiry

## Clinical Applications:
This formula is used for hernia due to cold coagulation and *qi* stagnation in the area traversed by the liver channel, which passes around and connects with the external genitalia.
Currently used for orchitis, epididymitis, peptic ulcers, dysmenorrhea and chronic gastritis.

## Ingredients:
1. wu yao          12.0
2. qing pi          6.0
3. mu xiang         6.0
4. xiao hui xiang   6.0
5. gao liang jiang  9.0
6. bing lang        9.0
7. chuan lian zi   12.0
8. ba dou          12.0

## Functions:
Moves the *qi*, spreads liver *qi*, disperses cold, and alleviates pain.

## Modifications:
For severe swelling and pain, add *li zhi he* and *ju he*.
For excessive cold, add *rou gui* and *wu zhu yu*.

## Cautions and Contraindications:
Not to be administered for patients with damp-heat in the lower *jiao*.

## Administration:
Take with warm wine, as needed.

Source: *Unknown (Bu Xiang 不詳)*

# Tian Wang Bu Xin Dan 天王補心丹
### Ginseng and Zizyphus Formula

## Indications:
Used to treat *yin* and blood deficiency of the heart and kidney with deficient fire: palpitations, insomnia, irritability, fatigue, nocturnal emissions, forgetfulness, heat sensation in the palms and soles, low-grade fever, night sweats, dry stools, and sores and/or ulcers of the mouth and tongue.

**Tongue:**   red tongue with scant coating
**Pulse:**   thin and rapid

## Clinical Applications:
1. This formula treats *yin* and blood deficiency leading to restlessness, which is viewed as heart and kidney failing to communicate.
2. Currently used for neurosis, dementia praecox, cardiac diseases, and hyperthyroidism.

## Ingredients:

| | | | | | |
|---|---|---|---|---|---|
| 1. sheng di | 12.0 | 7. ren shen | 12.0 | 13. zhu sha | 12.0 |
| 2. tian men dong | 12.0 | 8. fu ling | 12.0 | 14. jie geng | 12.0 |
| 3. mai men dong | 12.0 | 9. bai zi ren | 12.0 | 15. shi chang pu | 12.0 |
| 4. xuan shen | 12.0 | 10. yuan zhi | 12.0 | 16. bai bu | 12.0 |
| 5. dan shen | 12.0 | 11. wu wei zi | 12.0 | 17. du zhong | 12.0 |
| 6. dang gui | 12.0 | 12. suan zao ren | 12.0 | 18. fu shen | 12.0 |

## Functions:
Enriches the *yin*, nourishes the blood, tonifies the heart, calms the spirit, and clears heat.

## Modifications:
1. For severe insomnia, add *long gu* and *ci shi*.
2. For ulcerations of the mouth and tongue, add *huang lian* and *mu dan pi*.
3. For constipation, add *zhi shi* and *hou pu*.
4. For blurry vision and dizziness, add *chuan xiong* and *bai zhi*.
5. For excessive worry, combine with *xiao yao san*.
6. For unsettled heart and spirit, combine with *suan zao ren tang*.
7. For canker sores and toothache, combine with *qing wei san*.

## Cautions and Contraindications:
Should not be used for long periods of time or by patients with spleen or stomach deficiency.

## Administration:
Swallow with warm water or salty warm water, after meals.

Source: *Shi Yi De Jiu Fang* (世醫得救方)

# Tiao Jing Wan 調經丸
Cyperus and Tangkuei Formula

## Indications:
Anemia with a painful period.

Irregular menstrual cycle, dysmenorrhea and lower abdominal pain caused by postpartum blood stasis.

## Clinical Applications:
1. This formula is for treating women with irregular menstruation, painful period, and postpartum blood stasis with lower abdomen pain.
2. The key symptoms are anemia, weak constitution, irregular menstruation, dysmenorrhea, and menstruation pain.
3. Currently used in treating any gynecological diseases caused by anemia and weak constitutions, such as discharge, dysmenorrhea, lower back pain and constipation.
4. Infertility, endometriosis, chronic endometritis, oophoritis, and vaginal discharge.

## Ingredients:

| | | | | | |
|---|---|---|---|---|---|
| 1. dang gui | 2.0 | 6. rou cong rong | 2.0 | 11. yan hu suo | 2.0 |
| 2. bai shao | 2.0 | 7. xiang fu | 4.0 | 12. wu yao | 2.0 |
| 3. chuan xiong | 2.0 | 8. chen pi | 2.0 | 13. hai piao xiao | 2.0 |
| 4. sheng di huang | 2.0 | 9. qing pi | 2.0 | 14. huang qin | 2.0 |
| 5. du zhong | 4.0 | 10. xiao hui xiang | 2.0 | | |

## Functions:
Invigorate the blood and regulate menstruation; move the *qi* and stop the pain.

## Modifications:
1. For pale complexion with light color blood: add *shu di huang, e jiao,* and *dan shen.*
2. For abdominal cold pain with light flow dark color blood: add *rou gui* and *gan jiang.*
3. For aversion to cold, soreness of lower back and feet: add *xu duan, tu si zi,* and *fu zi;* or combine with *Ba Wei Di Huang Wan.*

## Cautions and Contraindications:
Pregnancy or excess virginal bleeding

## Note:
This formula is a modification of *Si Wu Tang,* combined with *du zhong* and *rou cong rong* to tonify kidney and strengthen tendon and bone; *xiang fu, chen pi,* and *qing pi* to move *qi,* soothe the liver, and regulate menses; *wu yao, yan hu sou,* and *xiao hui xiang* to move *qi* and blood, warm channel and stop pain; *hai piao xio* to astringe to stop bleeding; and *huang qi* to clear heat and stop bleeding.

## Administration:
Take with warm water, after meals.

Source: *Nu Ke Zheng Zhi Zhun Sheng* (女科證治準繩)

# Tiao Wei Cheng Qi Tang 調胃承氣湯
### Rhubarb and Mirabilitum Combination
### Regulate the Stomach and Order the *Qi* Decoction

## Indications:
For the treatment of *yang ming fu* disease, with organ, stomach, and large intestine heat.

May be used for the treatment of patients in *shanghan yangmin* stage, but with aversion to heat.

Also used for the treatment of constipation, thirst, irritability, delirium; patients with middle *jiao* experiencing fullness and dryness; abdominal fullness and distention after vomiting, or irritability; excessive hunger and urination in *xiao ke* syndrome.

| | |
|---|---|
| **Tongue:** | yellow coating |
| **Pulse:** | slippery and rapid |

## Clinical Applications:
1. This formula treats for *yang ming fu* organ disease characterized by obvious dryness and excess heat, with slight distention and fullness; delirium caused by febrile disease constipation.
2. Currently used for nosebleed, gum bleeding, vomiting with blood, toothaches, sore throat, and macular eruption due to heat in the stomach and intestines.
3. Symptoms may also include sore throat, mouth sores, constipation heat traveling upward, swollen gums, bad breath, red eyes, headache, and elderly constipation.

## Ingredients:
1. da huang     8.0
2. gan cao      4.0
3. mang xiao    8.0

## Functions:
Regulates the middle, clears heat; eliminates stagnation, alleviates dryness.

## Modifications:
For distention in the middle, fullness, and irritability: add *zhi shi* and *hou po.*

## Cautions and Contraindications:
Use only when necessary; for weak patients add tonic herbs. Not to be taken during pregnancy.

## Administration:
Take with warm water, after meals.

Source: *Shang Han Lun* (傷寒論)

# Tong Qiao Huo Xue Tang 通竅活血湯
Persica and Ligusticum Combination
Unblock the Orifices and Invigorate the Blood Decoction

## Indications:
Blood stasis and obstruction in the head, face, or outer body.

Headache, dizziness, hearing loss, hair loss, vitiligo, dry-blood stasis in women, and children's "gan" patterns that present with distended abdomen, weight loss, and tidal fevers.

## Clinical Applications:
1. This formula is for treating blood stasis patterns according to a system of three locations: the upper and outer body, the blood mansion (chest), and the abdomen (below the diaphragm).
2. The key symptoms are hair loss, red or painful eyes, drinker's nose, chronic hearing loss, white patch wind (vitiligo), infantile gan, and blood-dryness menstrual block.
3. Currently used in treating deafness, rosacea, "brandy" nose, purpura and internal injury stasis. Also sudden deafness and post-concussion headaches.

## Ingredients:
1. chi shao        2.0
2. chuan xiong     2.0
3. tao ren         6.0
4. hong hua        6.0
5. cong bai        2.0
6. sheng jiang     6.0
7. da zao          5.0

## Functions:
Invigorates the blood, dispels blood stasis, and opens up the orifices.

## Modifications:
Taking this formula with a small glass of warm rice wine will increase its blood-quickening and help guide the herbs to the upper *jiao*.

## Note:
The original formula contained *she xiang* (musk), but it is not in most of the concentrated herb formulae.

## Administration:
Take with warm water, before bedtime or after meals.

Source: *Yi Lin Gai Cuo* (醫林改錯)

# Tong Xie Yao Fang 痛瀉藥方
Important Formula for Painful Diarrhea

## Indications:
For the treatment of painful diarrhea due to liver and spleen disharmony.

May also be used to treat patients with recurrent borborygmus, abdominal pain or diarrhea with pain which starts with the urge to defecate and subsides afterward.

**Tongue**: thin, white coating
**Pulse**: wiry, moderate or wiry, thin

## Clinical Applications:
1. This formula is often used for painful diarrhea due to earth deficiency, especially with overactive wood element, and general disorder of the ascending and descending function.
2. Currently used for chronic colitis, acute enteritis, and irritable bowel syndrome (IBS).

## Ingredients:
1. bai zhu    18.0
2. bai shao   12.0
3. chen pi     9.0
4. fang feng   6.0

## Functions:
Spreads the liver *qi* and tonifies the spleen.

## Modifications:
1. For chronic diarrhea, add *sheng ma*.
2. For blood and pus in the stool, add *bai tou weng* and *huang lian*.
3. For severe abdominal pain, add *yan hu suo* and *chuan lian zi*.
4. For cases with severe dampness, watery diarrhea and white, greasy tongue, add *che qian zi* and *fu ling*.

## Administration:
Take with warm water, as needed.

Source: *Liu Cao Chuang Fang* (劉草窗方)

# Tuo Li Xiao Du Yin 托裏消毒飲
Gleditsia Combination
Support the Interior and Eliminate Toxin Drink

## Indications:
Swelling abscesses and flat abscesses with *qi* and blood deficiency.

It dissipates sores that have not yet formed pus and upthrusts pus from those that already have.

Boils, abscesses (including breast abscesses), inflamed lymph nodes, and other toxic swellings.

| **Tongue:** | pale |
|---|---|
| **Pulse:** | rapid and weak |

## Clinical Applications:
1. This formula is for treating toxic swellings, and swellings in patients who suffer from *qi* and blood deficiency.
2. The key symptoms are sores that refuse to come to a head or, after bursting, are slow to heal and continue to leak thin pus.
3. Currently used in treating carbuncle, suppurative lymphadenitis, polymyositis, perianal inflammation, subcutaneous ulcer, and mastitis.

## Ingredients:

| | | | | | | | |
|---|---|---|---|---|---|---|---|
| 1. zao jiao ci | 1.2 | 5. bai zhi | 1.2 | 9. bai shao | 2.4 |
| 2. jin yin hua | 2.4 | 6. chuan xiong | 2.4 | 10. ren shen | 2.4 |
| 3. gan cao | 1.2 | 7. huang qi | 2.4 | 11. fu ling | 2.4 |
| 4. jie geng | 1.2 | 8. dang gui | 2.4 | 12. bai zhu | 2.4 |

## Functions:
Tonifies the *qi* and blood, expels pus from the interior, and draws out toxicity.

## Modifications:
1. For cases with the sore swelling but cannot burst, add *sheng ma* and *chuan shan jia*.
2. For cases with the sore after bursting cannot heal, add *ge ge* and, *huang lian*.
3. For cases with severe pain, add *ru xiang* and *mo yao*.
4. For cases with the sore swellings pain, combine with *San Huang Xie Xin Tang*.
5. For cases with the sore is hot and swollen pain, combine with *Huang Lian Jie Du Tang*.

## Cautions and Contraindications:
During pregnancy because of *zao jiao ci*.

## Administration:
Take with warm or cold water, after meals.

Source: *Wai Ke Zheng Zong* (外科正宗)

# Wan Dai Tang 完帶湯
## Atractylodes and Discorea Combination
### End Discharge Decoction

**Indications:**
For the treatment of leukorrhea due to spleen deficiency and liver constraint with turbid cold-dampness syndrome.

May also be used for patients with profuse vaginal discharge that is white or pale yellow in color, and clear and thin in consistency, with no foul smell. Other symptoms include fatigue, lethargy, shiny or pale complexion, and loose stools.

| | |
|---|---|
| **Tongue:** | Pale, white coating |
| **Pulse:** | Soggy and frail or moderate |

**Clinical Applications:**
1. This formula is used for vaginal discharge due to spleen deficiency of the cold/damp type. For females after a period having poor appetite and indigestion.
2. Currently used for genital itching, vaginitis, or cervical erosion due to disharmony between the liver and spleen with turbid damp discharge.

**Ingredients:**

| | | | | | | | | |
|---|---|---|---|---|---|---|---|---|
| 1. | bai zhu | 10.0 | 5. | chen qian zi | 3.0 | 9. | jing jie tan | 0.5 |
| 2. | shan yao | 10.0 | 6. | cang zhu | 3.0 | 10. | chai hu | 0.6 |
| 3. | ren shen | 2.0 | 7. | gan cao | 1.0 | | | |
| 4. | bai shao | 5.0 | 8. | chen pi | 0.5 | | | |

**Functions:**
Strengthens the spleen to dry dampness, soothes the liver to regulate *qi*, and transforms dampness to stop vaginal discharge.

**Modifications:**
1. For severe damp-heat, add *huang bai* and *long dan cao*.
2. For severe damp-cold with abdominal pain, add *pao jiang* and *xiao hui xiang*.
3. For chronic discharge, add *long gu, mu li*.
4. For wind-damp discharge: add *bai zhi* and *hai piao xiao*.
5. For heat deficiency, add *dang gui* and *mu li*.
6. For cold deficiency, add *gan jiang* and *long gu*.
7. For severe cold-damp, add *Li Zhong Tang*.
8. For severe fire heat, add *Huang Lian Jie Du Tang*.

**Cautions and Contraindications:**
Contraindicated for damp-heat in the lower *jiao*.

**Administration:**
Take with warm water, before meals.

Source: *Fu Qing Zhu Nu Ke* (傅青主女科)

# Wei Jing Tang 葦莖湯
## Reed Decoction

## Indications:
For the treatment of toxin-heat lung abscess syndrome.

May also be used to treat patients with chronic cough, accompanied by foul-smelling sputum that may be streaked with blood. Other symptoms include slight fever, mild chest pain, and dry scaly skin.

**Tongue:**  red, yellow, greasy
**Pulse:**  slippery, rapid

## Clinical Applications:
1. This formula is used to treat toxin heat obstructing the lungs, accompanied by phlegm and blood stasis.
2. Currently used in treating bronchitis, bronchiectasis, pneumonia, pertussis, asthmatic bronchitis.

## Ingredients:
1. lu gen          40.0
2. dong gua ren    20.0
3. yi yi ren       30.0
4. tao ren          9.0

## Functions:
Clears heat, transforms phlegm, breaks blood stagnation, discharges pus.

## Modifications:
1. For heat in the lungs without the presence of pus, add *jin yin hua* and *yu xing cao.*
2. For pus in the sputum, add *jie geng, can cao,* and *chuan bei mu.*

## Cautions and Contraindications:
Not to be used during pregnancy.

## Administration:
Take with warm water, as needed.

Source: *Bei Ji Qian Jin Yao Fang* (備急千金要方)

# Wei Ling Tang 胃苓湯
Magnolia and Poria Combination
Calm the Stomach and Poria Decoction

## Indications:
Spleen and stomach *qi* damage during summer-heat or summer stroke.
Cold-dampness in the spleen with accumulation of fluids.

Frequent watery diarrhea, focal distention in the epigastrium and abdomen, reduced appetite, and semi-liquid stools; heaviness of the extremities.

## Clinical Applications:
1. This formula is for treating digestive disorders due to the spleen-stomach damage, and water metabolism dysfunction that reflects the spleen's failure to transform and transport fluids.
2. The key symptoms are watery diarrhea, edema, abdominal pain, nausea and vomiting, and heaviness of the extremities.
3. Currently used in treating acute and chronic nephritis, acute gastroenteritis, gastritis, enteritis, edema, and stomach flu, thirst and abdominal pain, dysuria, beriberi, restlessness and insomnia, diabetes, nocturia, etc.

## Ingredients:

| 1. | cang zhu | 3.0 | 7. | zhu ling | 2.0 |
|----|----------|-----|-----|----------|-----|
| 2. | hou po | 3.0 | 8. | gan cao | 1.2 |
| 3. | chen pi | 3.0 | 9. | rou gui | 1.0 |
| 4. | bai zhu | 3.0 | 10. | sheng jiang | 1.0 |
| 5. | fu ling | 3.0 | 11. | da zao | 1.0 |
| 6. | ze xie | 2.0 | | | |

## Functions:
Dry damp, strengthen the spleen, transform *qi*, disinhibit water, move *qi*, and climate stagnation.

## Modifications:
1. For cases with wind-cold, chills and fever, add *shao yao* and *chai hu*.
2. For cases with vomiting water fluid, add *ban xia* and *jie geng*.
3. For cases with diarrhea and abdominal pain, add *xiang fu* and *sha ren*.

## Note:
This formula is a combination of *Ping Wei San* (Magnolia and Ginger Formula) and *Wu Ling San* (Poria Five Herb Formula), using *rou gui* instead of *gui zhi*.

## Administration:
Take with warm water, after meals.

Source: *Zhong Guo Yi Xue Da Ci Dian* (中國醫學大辭典)

# Wen Dan Tang 溫膽湯
Poria and Bamboo Combination
Warm the Gallbladder Decoction

## Indications:
For the treatment of gallbladder and stomach disharmony, with phlegm heat obstructing the *qi*. Other symptoms that may be treated using this decoction include irritability, anxiety, nervousness or being easily frightened, insomnia, excessive dreams, dizziness, vertigo, nausea, especially vomiting copious fluid, palpitations, bitter taste in the mouth, oppressed sensation in the chest, indeterminate gnawing hunger, or epilepsy accompanied by copious sputum.

**Tongue:** greasy, yellow coating
**Pulse:** rapid, slippery or wiry

## Clinical Applications:
1. This formula is used for phlegm-heat obstructing the *qi,* caused by gallbladder and stomach disharmony.
2. These patterns are due to constrained internal heat from *qi*, characterized by irritability, body not feeling hot to the touch, dry throat with no desire to drink, and insomnia without feeling hot. Neurological symptoms may include palpitations and insomnia.
3. Also currently used in treating cardiovascular disease, chronic gastritis, peptic ulcers, chronic hepatitis, early stages of schizophrenia, Meniere's disease, or general psychosis.

## Ingredients:
| | | | | | |
|---|---|---|---|---|---|
| 1. | *ban xia* | 3.3 | 5. | *fu ling* | 2.3 |
| 2. | *zhu ru* | 3.3 | 6. | *gan cao* | 1.3 |
| 3. | *zhi shi* | 3.3 | 7. | *sheng jiang* | 1.3 |
| 4. | *chen pi* | 5.0 | 8. | *da zao* | 1.0 |

## Functions:
Regulates the *qi*, transforms phlegm, stops nausea, warms gallbladder, and harmonizes the stomach.

## Modifications:
1. For severe irritability, add *huang lian* and *mai men dong.*
2. For epilepsy, add *dan nan xing, gou teng,* and *quan xie.*
3. For heart deficiency anxiety, add *ren shen* and *suan zao ren.*
4. For gallbladder deficiency irritable heat, add *mai men dong* and *huang lian.*
5. For severe thirst and dry throat, add *wu wei zi* and *tian hua fen.*
6. For overthinking insomnia, add *Xiao Yao San.*
7. For depression insomnia, add *yu ju tang.*

## Cautions and Contraindications:
Not to be used during pregnancy.

## Administration:
Take with warm water, after meals.

Source: *Zhong Gou Yi Xue Da Ci Dian* (中國醫學大辭典)

# Wen Jing Tang 溫經湯
Tangkuei and Evodia Combination
Warm the Menses Decoction

## Indications:
For the treatment of *chong* and *ren* channel deficiency-cold, especially with blood stasis obstruction.

May also be used to treat patients with mild, persistent uterine bleeding, irregular menstruation either early or late, for patient experiencing their period twice a month, or periods which have stopped, infertility, pain, distention and cold in the lower abdomen, dry lips and mouth with low-grade fever at dusk and warm five palms.

## Clinical Applications:
1. This formula is used for *chong* and *ren* deficiency and cold due to blood stagnation; it can regulate menstruation for patients having irregular or prolonged periods, and/or metrorrhagia.
2. Currently used for functional uterine bleeding, chronic pelvic inflammation, and infertility. Females with menopausal uterine bleeding or cold waist and uterine infertility.

## Ingredients:

| | | | | | |
|---|---|---|---|---|---|
| 1. wu zhu yu | 2.4 | 5. chuan xiong | 1.6 | 9. ren shen | 1.6 |
| 2. gui zhi | 1.6 | 6. mu dan pi | 1.6 | 10. gan cao | 1.6 |
| 3. dang gui | 1.6 | 7. e jiao | 1.6 | 11. sheng jiang | 2.4 |
| 4. bai shao | 1.6 | 8. mai men dong | 3.2 | 12. ban xia | 3.2 |

## Functions:
Warms the channels, disperses the cold, actives and nourishes the blood.

## Modifications:
1. For dry mouth and irritable heat, add *wu wei zi* and *sheng di huang*.
2. For lower back and abdominal pain, add *xiang fu* and *ai ye*.
3. For headache and dizziness, add *huang qi* and *bai zi ren*.
4. For severe cold pain in the lower abdomen, omit *mu dan pi* and *mai men dong* and add *ai ye*.
5. For cases with *qi* stagnation, add *xiang fu* and *wu yao*; for persistent uterine bleeding with pale color, omit *mu dan pi*, add *ai ye* and *shu di huang*.

## Cautions and Contraindications:
Contraindicated for cases with abdominal masses due to blood stasis from excess.

## Administration:
Take with warm water, before meals.

Source: *Jin Gui Yao Lue* (金櫃要略)

# Wen Qing Yin 溫清飲
## Tangkuei and Gardenia Combination
## Warming and Clearing Drink

## Indications:
Blood deficiency combined with blood heat.

Female patients suffering from metrorrhagia, abdominal pain and fever, irritability and thirst, thin body and yellow complexion.

**Tongue:**     dry, red tip, thin white coating
**Pulse:**      submerge and rapid

## Clinical Applications:
1. This formula is for treating blood deficiency with blood heat, uterine bleeding, and skin heat disorders.
2. The key symptoms are blood flooding and spotting, abdominal pain, dry, itching skin, vaginal discharge, heat toxic swellings, and inflammation of the bladder, urinary tract, uterus, or ovaries.
3. Currently used in treating women with acute and chronic metritis, oophoritis, urethritis, cystitis. or liver spots, purpura, or skin swollen toxin heat.

## Ingredients:

| 1. shu di huang | 2.5 | 6. huang lian | 2.5 |
|---|---|---|---|
| 2. bai shao | 2.5 | 7. huang bai | 2.5 |
| 3. dang gui | 2.5 | 8. zhi zi | 2.5 |
| 4. chuan xiong | 2.5 | 9. sheng di hung | 2.5 |
| 5. huang qin | 2.5 | | |

## Functions:
Warm channels, nourish blood, cool blood, clear heat, and resolve toxin.

## Modifications:
1. For severe uterine bleeding and spotting, add *e jiao* and *ai ye.*
2. For painful menstruation, add *chen pi* and *xiang fu.*
3. For virginal discharge and itching, add *jin yin hua, lian qiao,* and *che qian zi.*

## Note:
This formula is a combination of *Si Wu Tang* (Tangkuei Four Combination) and *Huang Lian Jie Du Tang* (Coptis and Scute Combination). It is also known as *"Jie Du Si Wu Tang".*

## Administration:
Take with warm water, before meals.

Source: *Yi Xue Ru Men*(醫學人門)

195

# Wu Ji San 五積散

Tangkuei and Magnolia Five Formula
Five-Accumulation Powder

**Indications:**
Externally contracted wind-cold combined with internal cold damage.

Fever and chills without sweating, headache, body aches, stiff neck and back, a sensation of fullness in the chest and abdomen, nausea and aversion to food, vomiting, abdominal pain and cold, and diarrhea with borborygmus.

| | |
|---|---|
| **Tongue:** | white, greasy coating |
| **Pulse:** | submerged and wiry or floating and slow |

**Clinical Applications:**
1. This formula is for treating disorders associated with the five types of accumulation: cold, dampness, *qi*, blood, and phlegm.
2. The key symptoms are fever with no sweating, head and body aches, neck and back stiffness, thoracic fullness, aversion to food, nausea, vomiting, and abdominal pain.
3. Currently used in treating acute and chronic gastroenteritis, gastric ulcer, duodenal ulcer, hyperacidity, gastro-spasm hernia (enteric neuralgia), low back pain, sciatica, various neuralgia, and rheumatic pain. It can also be used to treat beriberi, leukorrhea, menstrual pain, irregular menstruation, and deficiency cold symptoms.

**Ingredients:**

| | | | | | | | | |
|---|---|---|---|---|---|---|---|---|
| 1. | cang zhu | 8.0 | 7. | pao gan jiang | 1.5 | 13. | bai shao | 1.0 |
| 2. | jie geng | 4.0 | 8. | ban xia | 1.0 | 14. | chuan xiong | 1.0 |
| 3. | ma huang | 2.0 | 9. | fu ling | 1.0 | 15. | rou gui | 1.0 |
| 4. | zhi ke | 2.0 | 10. | zhi gan cao | 1.0 | 16. | sheng jiang | 2.0 |
| 5. | chen pi | 2.0 | 11. | bai zhi | 1.0 | | | |
| 6. | hou po | 1.5 | 12. | dang gui | 1.0 | | | |

**Functions:**
Release the exterior, warm the center, transform phlegm, move the blood, and reduce accumulation.

**Modifications:**
1. For wind-cold headache, add *sheng ma* and *ge gen*.
2. For abdominal pain from food, add *shan zha*, *mai ya* and *shen qu*.
3. For painful period, add *xiang fu* and *ai ye*.

**Cautions and Contraindications:**
Damp-heat or *yin* deficiency.

**Administration:**
Take with warm water, as needed.

Source: *Tai Ping Hui Min He Ji Ju Fang*（太平惠民和劑局方）

# Wu Lin San 五淋散

Gardenia and Poria Formula
Powder for Five Types of Painful Urinary Dribbling

## Indications:

*Lin* syndrome with damp-heat bloody painful dribbling urination.

Rough, painful urination that is red or the color of red bean juice, or with multiple tiny stones. Urinary symptoms may be accompanied by acute lower abdominal pain.

**Tongue:**    white coating
**Pulse:**      floating

## Clinical Applications:

1. This formula is for treating damp-heat bloody painful dribbling urination.
2. The key symptoms are burning urination, thirst, fever, absence of a thick tongue fur, and blood in the urine. Or overindulgence in spicy, sweet, or rich foods, or overconsumption of alcohol. It may also be caused by the penetration of damp-heat from the exterior into the lower burner.
3. Currently used in treating cystitis, urethritis, bladder stones, kidney stones, gonorrhea; difficulty urinating, and painful urination.

## Ingredients:

| | | | | | |
|---|---|---|---|---|---|
| 1. | chi fu ling | 6.0 | 4. | dang gui | 4.8 |
| 2. | chi shao | 4.0 | 5. | gan cao | 4.8 |
| 3. | zhi zi | 4.0 | 6. | deng xin cao | 2.0 |

## Functions:

Clears heat, cools the blood, dispel damp, drain heat, promotes urination.

## Modifications:

1. For fire heat and thirsty, add *hua shi* and *shi gao*.
2. For stagnation jaundice, add *yin chen hao* and *huang qi*n.
3. For difficulty urination, add *mu tong* and *fang ji*.
4. For fire heat in urinary bladder: combine with *Dao Chi San*.
5. For inhibited urination: combine with *Wu Ling San*.

## Cautions and Contraindications:

Chronic condition or deficiency cold.

## Administration:

Take with warm water, before meals.

Source: *Tai Ping Hui Min He Ji Ju Fang* (太平惠民和劑局方)

0700

# Wu Ling San 五苓散
Poria Five Herb Formula
Five-Ingredient Powder with Poria

## Indications:
1. For the treatment of *tai yang fu* organ water buildup (*xu shui*) syndromes: Headache, fever, irritability, strong thirst but with vomiting immediately after drinking and difficult. or scanty urination.
2. Also used to treat edema: interior water-damp accumulation without exterior syndrome, a generalized sensation of heaviness, diarrhea, difficult and scanty urination, or sudden turmoil disorder with vomiting and diarrhea.
3. May be used to treat congested fluids syndrome: Throbbing sensation just below the navel, vomiting, frothy saliva, vertigo, possible shortness of breath and coughing.

**Tongue:** white coating
**Pulse:** floating, superficial, or moderate

## Clinical Applications:
1. This formula is used for severe accumulation of water in the bladder and inability of the *qi* to transform fluids, and failure of spleen to transport water, manifested as urinary difficulty or edema.
2. The key symptoms are water retention with scanty and difficult urination.
3. Currently used in treating edema due to acute or chronic nephritis, ascites from liver cirrhosis, chronic renal failure, congestive heart failure and acute enteritis (vomiting, diarrhea, thirst with difficulty urinating). Gastric dilatation, flaccid gastric disorder, water retention syndrome or acute cystitis.

## Ingredients:
1. ze xie    7.5
2. fu ling    4.5
3. zhu ling    4.5
4. bai zhu    4.5
5. gui zhi    3.0

## Functions:
Promotes urination, drains dampness, strengthens the spleen, warms the *yang* and promotes the transforming functions: of *qi*.

## Modifications:
1. For edema with excessive water retention, combine with *Wu Pi Yin.*
2. For excess damp-heat diarrhea, omit *gui zhi* add *che qian zi* and *mu tong.*
3. For edema with exterior signs, combine with *Yue Bi Tang.*
4. For upper *jiao* irritability, add *yin chen hao* and *zhi zi.*
5. For middle *jiao* water retention and thirst, add *shi gao* and *zhi mu.*
6. For lower *jiao* water retention, add *mu tong* and *sheng di.*
7. For scrotal edema, add *che qian zi* and *mu tong.*
8. For small intestine hernia, add *mu dan pi* and *fang feng.*

9. For tongue soreness, add *huang lian* and *shi gao*.
10. For phlegmy cough, irritability, and insomnia, add *e jiao*.
11. For summer heat thirst retention, add *Bai Hu Tang*.
12. For improper appetite, vomiting, and diarrhea: add *Ping Wei San*.
13. For water retention around the navel, add *Ji Sheng Shen Qi Wan*.

## Cautions and Contraindications:
Contraindicated for difficulty with urination due to *yin* deficiency or spleen and kidney *qi* deficiency.

## Administration:
Take with warm or cool water, as needed.

Source: Shang Han Lun (傷寒論)

# Wu Mei Wan 烏梅丸
Mume Formula
Mume Pill

## Indications:
Collapse from roundworm (*Hui Jue*) syndromes.

Intermittent attacks of abdominal pain, a stifling sensation, irritability, cold hands and feet, and possibly vomiting of roundworms.

Unquenchable thirst, *qi* rushing upward toward the heart, pain and heat in the stomach, hunger with no desire to eat or vomiting immediately after eating and cold extremities.

## Clinical Applications:
1. This formula is used for *Hui Jue* syndromes with upper stomach heat and intestine cold.
2. Currently used in treating roundworm in the bile duct and ascariasis.
3. Chronic disorder with a mixing of cold and hot symptoms, such as chronic conjunctivitis, cold menstrual pain, enlarged prostate, chronic gastritis, and duodenal ulcers.

## Ingredients:

| | | | | |
|---|---|---|---|---|
| 1. | wu mei | 3.0 | 6. pao fu zi | 2.0 |
| 2. | xi xin | 2.0 | 7. chuan jiao | 1.5 |
| 3. | gan jiang | 3.0 | 8. gui zhi | 2.0 |
| 4. | huang lian | 5.0 | 9. ren shen | 2.0 |
| 5. | dang gui | 1.5 | 10. huang bai | 2.0 |

## Functions:
Warm the organs, drain heat, clear the liver and calm roundworms.

## Modifications:
1. For roundworms in the bile duct, add *shi jun zi, ku lian gen pi, fei zi*, and *bing lang*.
2. For severe heat, omit *fu zi* and *gan jiang*.
3. For cases without deficiency, omit *ren shen* and *dang gui*.

## Cautions and Contraindications:
Explosive diarrhea or damp-heat dysentery

## Administration:
Take with warm water, before meals.

Source: *Shang Han Lun* （傷寒論）

# Wu Pi Yin 五皮飲
## Poria and Areca Combination
### Five-Peel Drink

## Indications:
For the treatment of skin edema (*pi shui*) due to spleen *qi* deficiency with excess dampness.

May also be used to treat generalized edema with sensation of heaviness, distention and fullness in the epigastrium and abdomen, labored and heavy breathing and urinary difficulties.

| **Tongue:** | white, greasy coating |
| **Pulse:** | submerged and moderate |

## Clinical Applications:
1. This formula is used for skin edema. The focus of this formula is on leaching out dampness and promoting urination.
2. The key symptoms are generalized edema with a sensation of heaviness, distention and fullness in the face, epigastrium and abdomen, with urinary difficulty.
3. Currently used in treating edema during pregnancy, nephritis, menopausal edema, and congestive heart failure.

## Ingredients:
1. wu jia pi          6.0
2. di gu pi           6.0
3. fu ling pi         6.0
4. da fu pi           6.0
5. sheng jiang pi     6.0

## Functions:
Strengthens the spleen and transforms the damp, regulates the *qi* and promotes urination to reduce edema.

## Modifications:
1. For facial edema, add *chen pi* and *sang bai pi*.
2. For waist and abdominal edema, add *bai zhu* and *cang zhu*.
3. For lower-leg edema, add *zhi mu* and *huang bai*.
4. For edema with severe spleen *qi* deficiency, add *huang qi, bai zhu,* and *dang shen*.
5. For edema above the waist due to external wind attack, add *fang feng* and *qiang huo*.

## Cautions and Contraindications:
Not to be used for severe spleen deficiency.

## Administration:
Take with warm water, as needed.

Source: *Tai Ping Hui Min He Ji Ju Fang* (太平惠民和劑局方)

# Wu Wei Xiao Du *Yin* 五味消毒飲

Dandelion and Wild Chrysanthemum Combination
Five-Ingredient Decoction to Eliminate Toxin

## Indications:

For the treatment of early-stage boils, sores and carbuncles.

May also be used to treat any kind of localized redness, swelling, and hot, painful skin lesions, especially those with small size and a hard, deep root, accompanied by chills and fever.

**Tongue:**　red with yellow coating
**Pulse:**　rapid

## Clinical Applications:

1. This formula is used for any type of boil or carbuncle, with localized erythema, superficial and purulent infections.
2. For symptoms caused by the fire toxin, which can arise from a variety of causes: external warm pathogen attacks, overindulgence in rich or spicy foods, or heat accumulated through internal organ disharmony.
3. Currently used in treating mastitis, erysipelas, multiple furuncles, conjunctivitis, and urinary tract infections.

## Ingredients:

1. jin yin hua　　　　11.25
2. zi hua di ding　　　4.50
3. zi bei tian kui zi　　4.50
4. pu gong ying　　　　4.50
5. ju hua　　　　　　　4.50

## Functions:

Clears heat, relieves toxins, reduces and dissipates swelling of furuncles or boils.

## Cautions and Contraindications:

*Yin*-type boils or spleen *qi* deficiency.

## Administration:

Take with warm wine, as needed; the patient may be covered to induce sweat.

Source: *Yi Zong Jin Jian* (醫宗金鑑)

# Wu Yao Shun Qi San 烏藥順氣散
Lindera Formula
Lindera Powder to Smooth the Flow of *Qi*

## Indications:
Wind attacking the extremities.

Joint pain or numbness, weakness in the knees and lower back, Bell's palsy, headache, and dizziness. In severe cases, there may be hemiplegia or difficulty in walking, aphasia, and spasms.

**Pulse:** deep, thin

## Clinical Applications:
1. This formula is for treating wind attacking the extremities or cold attacking the chest and armpit in the elderly.
2. The key symptoms are joint pain or numbness, weakness in the knees and lower back, stabbing pain in the flanks, distention in the epigastrium and abdomen, vomiting, diarrhea, and borborygmus.
3. Currently used in the role of hyperactive motor function, in addition to arthralgia and paralysis. It can stimulant the nerve paralysis caused by external pathogen attack.

## Ingredients:
| | | | | | | | |
|---|---|---|---|---|---|---|---|
| 1. wu yao | 4.0 | 5. bai zhi | 2.0 | 9. gan jiang | 1.0 |
| 2. chen pi | 4.0 | 6. jie geng | 2.0 | 10. gan cao | 2.0 |
| 3. ma huang | 4.0 | 7. zhi ke | 2.0 | 11. sheng jiang | 3.0 |
| 4. chuan xiong | 2.0 | 8. bai jiang can | 2.0 | 12. da zao | 1.0 |

## Functions:
Disperse wind, open up the channels, move the *qi* and transform phlegm.

## Modifications:
1. For phlegm in throat, cough: add *ban xia* and *fu ling*.
2. For difficulty in speech: add *shi chang pu* and *yuan zhi*.
3. For skeletal sore and pain: add *niu xi* and *zang ji sheng*.
4. For whole body numbness and pain: combine with *Xiao Xu Ming Tang*.

## Note:
1. For post-stroke: *Wu Yao Shun Qi San* is only moderately focused on moving *qi* and dispelling cold, and *Xiao Huo Luo Dan* (Myrrh and Aconite Formula) treats acute cases where the pathogen is attacking the channel and collateral.
2. For Bi-blocking: *Wu Yao Shun Qi San* only treats acute wind-cold-*Bi* patterns; and *Juan Bi Tang* (Notopterygium and Turmeric Combination) and *San Bi Tang* (Tuhuo and Astragalus Combination) that contain tonifying herbs which treat both root and branch can be given for a longer period of time.

## Administration:
Take with warm water, as needed.

Source: *Tai Ping Hui Min He Ji Ju Fang* (太平惠民和劑局方)

# Wu Zhu Yu Tang 吳茱萸湯
Evodia Combination
Evodia Decoction

## Indications:
For the treatment of stomach deficiency cold syndrome, as indicated by vomiting immediately after eating, acid regurgitation with or without epigastric pain and *cao za* (indeterminate gnawing hunger). Also used for the treatment of *jue yin* headache syndrome, as indicated by dry heaves or spitting out clear fluids with vertex headache.

May also be used to treat patients with *shao yin* vomit and diarrhea, cold hands and feet, unbearable irritability which may make patient want to die.

**Tongue**:     not red, white, slippery coating
**Pulse**:      deep, slow or thin, wiry

## Clinical Applications:
1. This formula may be used for *yang ming, jue yin, shao yin* channel disorders that are all characterized by vomiting due to middle *jiao*-deficient cold and turbid *yin*-fluid rebelling upward.
2. Currently used for chronic or acute gastritis, acute gastroenteritis, cholecystitis, morning sickness, neurogenic headaches, migraine headaches, hypertension, trigeminal neuralgia, and Meniere's disease.

## Ingredients:
1. wu zhu yu      7.5
2. sheng jiang    9.0
3. ren shen       4.5
4. da zao         6.0

## Functions:
Warms the middle, tonifies deficient liver and stomach *qi*; guides rebellious *qi* downward and stops vomit.

## Modifications:
1. For severe vomiting, add *ban xia* and *sha ren.*
2. For belching after food, add *zhi shi* and *bai zhu.*
3. For irritability with cold limbs, add *fu zi* and *xi xin.*
4. For dry heaves or spitting up of fluid, add *gan jiang* and *rou gui.*
5. For deficiency cold headache, add *Li Zhong Tang.*
6. For cold limbs with abdominal pain, add *Si Ni Tang.*

## Cautions and Contraindications:
Not to be used for headache due to liver yang rising, vomit or acid reflux due to heat.

## Administration:
Take with warm water, after meals; take with cool water for severe vomiting.

Source: *Shang Han Lun* (傷寒論)

# Xi Gan Ming Mu San 洗肝明目湯

Gardenia and Vitex Combination
Wash the Liver to Clear the Eyes Powder

### Indications:
Wind-heat headache and red, swollen and painful eyes.

**Pulse:**     rapid and floating

### Clinical Applications:
1. This formula is for treating acute wind-heat patterns with eye pain.
2. The key symptoms are redness and swelling in and around the eyes with a rapid and floating pulse.
3. Currently used in treating conjunctivitis and conjunctivitis-like disorders, styes, orbital herpes infections, iritis, or scleritis.

### Ingredients:

| | | | | |
|---|---|---|---|---|
| 1. | dang gui wei | 0.6 | 9. bai ji li | 0.6 |
| 2. | chuan xiong | 0.6 | 10. cao jue ming | 0.6 |
| 3. | chi shao | 0.6 | 11. shi gao | 0.6 |
| 4. | sheng di huang | 0.6 | 12. lian qiao | 0.6 |
| 5. | huang lian | 0.6 | 13. man jing zi | 0.6 |
| 6. | huang qin | 0.6 | 14. jie geng | 0.6 |
| 7. | zhi zi | 0.6 | 15. gan cao | 0.6 |
| 8. | ju hua | 0.6 | | |

### Functions:
Dispel wind, clear heat, release exterior, alleviate swelling pain, and brighten the eyes.

### Modifications:
1. For severe wind-heat eye swelling pain: add *sheng ma* and *ge gen.*
2. For severe wind-heat blurry eyes: add *xi xin* and *mi meng hua.*
3. For severe wind-heat tearing eyes: add *xiao ku cao* and *xiang fu.*
4. For severe eyes pain: combine with *Fang Feng Tong Sheng San.*

### Cautions and Contraindications:
This is a powerful formula intended for short-term use.

### Administration:
Take with warm water, after meals.

Source: *Wan Bing Hui Chun* (萬病回春)

# Xiang Ru Yin 香薷飲
Elsholtzia Combination
Mosla Powder

## Indications:
Exterior cold with interior dampness constrained in the summer (summer *yin* evil syndrome).

Aversion to cold and fever without sweating, sensation of heaviness in the head, headache, abdominal pain, vomiting, diarrhea, stifling sensation in the chest and general body ache.

**Tongue:**    white greasy coating
**Pulse:**    floating (superficial)

## Clinical Applications:
1. This formula is used for damp cold contracted during the summertime.
2. Currently used for upper respiratory tract infection, summer cold, and acute gastroenteritis due to summer-damp with exterior wind-cold.
3. Acute gastroenteritis, bacillary dysentery, encephalitis B, enteric cholera, and acute tonsilitis.

## Ingredients:
1. xiang ru     12.0
2. hou po       6.0
3. bi bian dou    6.0

## Functions:
Release the exterior, scatter cold, transform dampness, and harmonize the center.

## Modifications:
1. For severe exterior pathogen attacked: add *qing hao*.
2. For severe cold with nasal obstruction: combine with *Cong Chi Tang*.

## Cautions and Contraindications:
Exterior deficiency with sweating, sunstroke with fever, or summer heat.

## Administration:
Take with cool water, as needed.

Source: *Tai Ping Hui Min He Ji Ju Fang* (太平惠民和劑局方)

# Xiang Sha Ping Wei San 香砂平胃散
Cyperus, Amomum, and Atractylodes Formula
Cyperus and Amomum Calm the Stomach Powder

## Indications:
Food stagnation and damaged spleen and stomach.

Abdominal distention and pain, no desire to eat, vomiting of sour fluid, belching, constipation, or diarrhea that does not relieve abdominal pain.

## Clinical Applications:
1. This formula is for treating food stagnation in the center.
2. The key symptoms are belching, vomiting of sour fluid, and irregular stool movements; epigastric and abdominal distention, reduced intake, nausea, and vomiting.
3. Currently used in treating infantile malnutrition, cold food injury, loss of appetite, indigestion, gastrointestinal discomfort, bloating and diarrhea.

## Ingredients:
1. cang zhu      3.6
2. hou po        2.4
3. chen pi       2.4
4. xiang fu      2.4
5. sha ren       2.4
6. zhi ke        2.4
7. mai ya        2.4
8. shen qu       2.4
9. bai shao      2.4
10. gan cao      1.2
11. shan zha     2.4
12. sheng jiang  1.2

## Functions:
Strengthen the spleen, reduce food stagnation, move the *qi,* and alleviate pain.

## Modifications:
1. For internal injury by raw and cold: add *fu ling* and *bai zhu.*
2. For injury by food accumulations: add *bai dou kou* and *rou dou kou.*
3. For common wind-cold flu: add *ge gen, sheng ma.*

## Administration:
Take with warm water, after meals.

Source: *Yi Zong Jin Jian* (醫宗金鑒)

1920

# Xiang Sha Yang Wei Tang 香砂養胃湯
### Cyperus and Cardamon Combination
### Nourish the Stomach Decoction with Aucklandia and Amomum

## Indications:
Disharmony between the spleen and stomach together with dampness.

No appetite, loss of the taste of food, distention, fullness, and pain in the gastric region, lack of appetite, dulling of the palate, nausea, vomiting of sour fluid, and indigestion.

| | |
|---|---|
| **Tongue:** | pale, thick coating |
| **Pulse:** | slippery, weak |

## Clinical Applications:
1. This formula is for treating spleen and stomach deficiency combined with damp and abdominal distention after eating.
2. The key symptoms are reduced appetite, a loss of taste, inability to eat more than a little at a time, bloating after eating, focal distention, discomfort in the epigastrium, and generalized weakness.
3. Currently used in treating chronic gastroenteritis, chronic peritonitis, gastric atony, gastric dilatation, gastroptosis, loss of appetite after illness, gastrointestinal weakness, and dysplasia in children.

## Ingredients:

| | | | | | |
|---|---|---|---|---|---|
| 1. | bai zhu | 3.0 | 8. | ren shen | 2.0 |
| 2. | fu ling | 3.0 | 9. | mu xiang | 1.5 |
| 3. | cang zhu | 2.0 | 10. | sha ren | 1.5 |
| 4. | hou po | 2.0 | 11. | gan cao | 1.5 |
| 5. | chen pi | 2.0 | 12. | da zao | 1.5 |
| 6. | xiang fu | 2.0 | 13. | sheng jiang | 2.0 |
| 7. | bai dou kou | 2.0 | | | |

## Functions:
Strengthens and harmonizes the spleen and stomach and resolves dampness.

## Note:
This formula is *Ping Wei San* combined with *Si Jun Zi Tang* with the addition of *mu xiang*, *sha ren*, *xiang fu* and *bai dou kou*.

## Administration:
Take with warm water, before meals.

Source: *Wan Bing Hui Chun* (萬病回春)

# Xiang Sheng Po Di San 響聲破笛丸
Gasping Formula
Pill for Restoring Sound to a Broken Flute

## Indications:
Hoarseness or loss of voice from overuse.

Overuse of the voice leading to an irritated throat and voice loss.

## Clinical Applications:
1. This formula is for treating loss of voice from overuse.
2. The key symptoms are sore throat, hoarse voice and loss of voice.
3. Currently used in treating loss of voice, dry throat, red cheek and lips, facial swelling, irritability, body heat, or painful mouth and tongue, oral cavity, laryngitis, pharyngitis, esophagitis, and loss of voice from overuse.

## Ingredients:
1. lian qiao      4.0
2. jie geng       3.0
3. gan cao        2.0
4. da huang       1.5
5. sha ren        1.5
6. chuan xiong    4.0
7. he zi          1.5
8. er cha         3.0
9. bo he          6.0

## Functions:
Clear heat, cool the throat, dispel phlegm, and disperse accumulations.

## Modifications:
1. For case with dry mouth and throat: add *mai men dong* and *tian hua fen*.
2. For case with voice loss and hoarse voice: add *jin yin hua* and *she gan*.
3. For case with difficulty speech: add *huang qi*n and *huang lian*.

## Administration:
Take with warm water, morning and night and mixing with egg white or honey, slowly dissolved in the mouth before bedtime.

Source: *Wan Bing Hui Chun* (萬病回春)

# Xiang Su San 香蘇散
Cyperus and Perilla Formula
Cyperus and Perilla Leaf Powder

## Indications:
For the treatment of exterior wind-cold with *qi* constrained in the interior.

May be used for patients experiencing chills and fever without sweating, headache, focal distention and stifling sensation in the chest and epigastrium, poor appetite, *qi* stagnation and excessive belching.

| **Tongue:** | thin, white coating |
| **Pulse:** | floating, superficial |

## Clinical Applications:
1. This formula is used for exterior wind-cold with *qi* constrained in the interior; the body becomes hot internally and cold outside. Other symptoms include headache with no sweat and focal distention.
2. Currently used for upper respiratory tract infection and stomach flu. Seafood poisoning, neuropathic abdominal pain, amenorrhea caused by *qi* stagnations, and allergic rhinitis, accompanied by purulent sputum, loss of sense of smell, and general nasal obstruction.

## Ingredients:
1. xiang fu      8.0
2. zi su ye      8.0
3. chen pi       4.0
4. zhi gan cao   2.0
5. sheng jiang   3.0
6. cong bai      3.0

## Functions:
Regulates *qi* and harmonizes the middle, releases the exterior and disperses the cold.

## Modifications:
1. For severe wind-cold headache, add *chaun xiong* and *bai zhi*.
2. For severe focal distention pain: add *zhi ke* and *jie geng*.
3. For coughing with copious sputum, add *fu ling* and *ban xia*.
4. For hives from seafood poisoning: add *ying pi*.

## Administration:
Take with warm water, as needed.

Source: *Tai Ping Hui Min He Ji Ju Fang* (太平惠民和劑局方)

# Xiang Sha Liu Jun Zi Tang 香砂六君子湯
Valadimiria and Amomum Combination
Six-Gentlemen Decoction with Aucklandia and Amomum

## Indications:
This formula combines the Six-Gentlemen Decoction (*Liu Jun Zi Tang*) with *mu xiang* and *sha ren*. For the treatment of spleen and stomach *qi* deficiency with damp-fluid retention. May be used for patients experiencing nausea or vomiting, localized distention in the chest and epigastrium, accompanied by a persistent urge to belch; coughing accompanied by copious thin white sputum.

Tongue: pale with a white coating
Pulse: soggy and slow

## Clinical Applications:
1. This formula, with its additions, is highly effective for abdominal pain and diarrhea, eliminating distention and bloating.
2. Currently also used for chronic gastritis, chronic diarrhea with undigested food, dull abdominal pain, loss of appetite, gastric ulcers, neuropathic gastrointestinal disease, and flaccid diarrhea.

## Ingredients:
| | | | | | |
|---|---|---|---|---|---|
| 1. | mu xiang | 2.0 | 6. | gan cao | 2.0 |
| 2. | sha ren | 2.0 | 7. | chen pi | 2.0 |
| 3. | ren shen | 2.5 | 8. | ban xia | 2.0 |
| 4. | bai zhu | 5.0 | 9. | sheng jiang | 5.0 |
| 5. | fu ling | 5.0 | | | |

## Functions:
Strengthens the spleen and benefits the stomach.

## Modifications:
1. For severe deficiency cold with abdominal pain: add *xiang fu* and *sha ren*.
2. For severe spleen-deficiency diarrhea: add *shan yao* and *qian shi*.
3. For external-pathogen attacks, add *chai hu* and *shao yao*.
4. For low appetite: add *mai ya* and *shan zha*.
5. For deficiency cold abdominal distention: add *fu zi* and *gan jiang*.
6. For diarrhea with undigested food: combine with *ping wei san*.
7. For vomit and diarrhea due to summer heat: combine with *San Huang Xie Xin Tang*.
8. For vomit and diarrhea due to deficiency cold: combine with *Li Zhong Tang*.
9. For post-illness deficiency: combine with *Xiao Chai Hu Tang*.

## Administration:
Take with warm water, after meals.

Source: *Shan Bu Ming Yi Fang Lun* (刪補名醫方論)

# Xiao Ban Xia Jia Fu Ling Tang 小半夏加茯苓湯
## Minor Pinellia and Poria Combination
## Minor Pinellia plus Poria Decoction

### Indications:
Phlegm and thin mucus accumulated in the epigastric area.

Vomiting, epigastric distention, dizziness and palpitations; sudden vomiting of thin mucus or clear fluids, and absence of thirst.

| | |
|---|---|
| **Tongue:** | white, slippery coating |
| **Pulse:** | wiry |

### Clinical Applications:
1. This formula is for treating thirst and vomiting of clear fluid, fluid retention in the epigastric region.
2. The key symptoms are thirst and a desire to drink a large quantity of fluids but then vomit after drinking; frequently feeling thirsty, even though drinking fluids may then cause vomiting or palpitations and focal distention in the epigastrium.
3. Currently used in treating viral myocarditis, pericarditis, hypertension, morning sickness, gastro-neurosis, and food poisoning. Also acute gastroenteritis, vomiting in children, and dampness of pleurisy, stomach pain, and excess sweating.

### Ingredients:
1. ban xia      10.0
2. sheng jiang   8.0
3. fu ling       4.0

### Functions:
Harmonize the stomach, stop vomiting, alleviate and remove thin mucus and direct rebelliousness downward.

### Modifications:
1. For nausea and vomiting of clear fluid without thirst: add *bai zhu* and *gui zhi.*
2. For nausea and vomiting with thirst: add *zhu ru* and *huang qi*n.
3. For pregnancy morning sickness: add *dang gui* and *chuan xiong.*
4. For nausea and vomiting with clear phlegm, fluid: combine with *Er Chen Tang.*

### Cautions and Contraindications:
This formula is for short-term use only.

### Administration:
Take with warm water, after meals.

Source: *Jin Gui Yao Lue* (金匱要略)

# Xiao Chai Hu Tang 小柴胡湯
Minor Bupleurum Combination
Minor Bupleurum Decoction

## Indications:

1. Used to treat *shang han shao yang* patterns: alternating chills and fever, fullness in the chest and hypochondriac region, poor appetite, irritability, bitter taste in the mouth, dry throat, and dizziness.
2. *Shang han* in women: heat evil entering the blood chamber.
3. Malaria, jaundice, and internal diseases that cause *shao yang* symptoms.

**Tongue:**    thin and white coating
**Pulse:**    wiry

## Clinical Applications:

1. This formula's key symptoms are alternating chills and fever with the sensation of fullness in the chest and hypochondriac region.
2. Currently used for common cold, flu, malaria, chronic hepatitis, cirrhosis, acute or chronic cholecystitis, gallstones, acute pancreatitis, pleurisy, otitis, puerperal endometritis, acute mastitis, orchitis, bile reflux gastritis, and peptic ulcer.

## Ingredients:

| | | | | | |
|---|---|---|---|---|---|
| 1. | chai hu | 24.0 | 5. | ren shen | 9.0 |
| 2. | huang qin | 9.0 | 6. | da zao | 6.0 |
| 3. | ban xia | 15.0 | 7. | zhi gan cao | 9.0 |
| 4. | sheng jiang | 9.0 | | | |

## Functions:

Harmonizes and releases *shao yang* stage disorders.

## Modifications:

1. For thirst, replace *ban xia* with *tian hua fen*.
2. For cases with severe vexation in the chest and with no vomiting, replace *ban xia* and *ren shen* with *gua lou*.
3. For abdominal pain, replace *huang qin* with *bai shao*.
4. For stifling sensation in the hypochondriac region, replace *da zao* with *mu li*.
5. For palpitation with difficult urination, replace *huang qin* with *fu ling*.
6. For cough with excess phlegm, add *zhi ke* and *jie geng*.
7. For distention in the hypochondriac region, add *zhi shi* and *qing pi*.
8. For deficiency irritability with thirst, add *mai meng dong* and *wu wei zi*.
9. For food accumulation, combine with *Ping Wei San*.
10. For cold phlegm dampness, combine with *Wu Ling San*.

## Cautions and Contraindications:

Caution in cases of liver *yang* rising, hypertension, or vomiting of blood due to *yin* deficiency.

## Administration:

Swallow with warm water, as needed.

Source: *Shang Han Lun* (傷寒論)

# Xiao Cheng Qi Tang 小承氣湯
### Minor Rhubarb Combination
### Minor Reorder *Qi* Decoction

## Indications:
For the treatment of mild-pattern *yang ming fu* organ excess heat syndrome.

May be used for patients experiencing tidal fevers that dissipate, then return, especially accompanied by delirium, constipation, focal distention, and abdominal fullness with no palpable abdominal hardness.

**Tongue:**   red "old-looking" tongue, with a dirty and dry yellow coating
**Pulse:**   slippery and rapid

## Clinical Applications:
1. This formula treats *yang ming fu* organ disease, characterized by obvious distention, fullness, and excess with slight dryness.
2. Currently used for early-stage dysentery with distention, pain in abdomen and tenesmus. Also used for food poisoning, vomit, diarrhea, abdominal pain, high blood pressure, brain nerve heat and obesity.

## Ingredients:
1. da huang   12.0
2. hou po   6.0
3. zhi shi   6.0

## Functions:
Purges clumped heat to initiate bowel movements; disperses focal distention and eliminates fullness.

## Modifications:
1. For fire heat with fullness and focal distention: add *huang lian* and *huang qin*.
2. For food accumulation pain: add *cang zhu* and *chen pi*.
3. For blood deficiency with high heat: add *dang gui* and *sheng di huang*.
4. For external heat with dry thirst: combine with *Huang Lian Jie Du Tang*.
5. For internal heat with fire stagnation: combine with *Da Chai Hu Tang*.
6. For blood deficiency with irritable heat: combine with *Si Wu Tang*.

## Cautions and Contraindications:
Use only when necessary for weak patients with tonics. Not to be administered during pregnancy.

## Administration:
Take with cool water, after meals.

Source: *Shang Han Lun* (傷寒論)

# Xiao Feng San 消風散
Tangkuei and Arctium Formula
Eliminate Wind Powder (from Orthodox Lineage)

## Indications:
For the treatment of wind rash or damp rash caused by wind-heat or wind-dampness with pre-existing damp-heat.

May be used for patients experiencing itchy, weepy, red skin lesions over a large part of their body, especially those that become oozy after scratching.

**Tongue:** yellow or white coating
**Pulse:** forceful, floating, and rapid

## Clinical Applications:
1. This formula is used for treating wind rash and damp rash. Rashes can occur when wind-heat or wind-dampness invades the body and contends with pre-existing damp-heat.
2. Key symptoms include itchy, weepy, and red skin lesions over a large part of the body.
3. May include hives in large, red rashes which cause severe itching. Rashes due to wind-heat or damp heat may suddenly come and go. In severe cases, the rash can possibly include swelling of the face and lips.
4. Various stubborn skin diseases, urticaria, eczema, psoriasis, allergic dermatitis, drug eruption, diaper rash, sweat rash and neurodermatitis, itchy skin, and skin diseases that are prone to deterioration in the summer.

## Ingredients:

| | | | | | | | | |
|---|---|---|---|---|---|---|---|---|
| 1. | jing jie | 2.50 | 6. | cang zhu | 2.50 | 11. | shi gao | 2.5 |
| 2. | fang feng | 2.50 | 7. | chan tui | 2.50 | 12. | gan cao | 1.25 |
| 3. | dang gui | 2.50 | 8. | hu ma ren | 2.50 | 13. | mu tong | 1.25 |
| 4. | sheng di huang | 2.50 | 9. | niu pang zi | 2.50 | | | |
| 5. | ku shen | 2.50 | 10. | zhi mu | 2.50 | | | |

## Functions:
Nourishes the blood, disperses wind, clears up heat and eliminates dampness.

## Modifications:
1. For excess wind-heat, body heat, toxins, and thirst: add *jin yin hua* and *lian qiao*.
2. For excess damp heat: add *di fu zi, che qian zi,* and *zhi zi*.
3. For excess heat in the blood: add *chi shao, mu dan pi,* and *zi cao*.
4. For oozy eczema: add *yi yi ren*.

## Cautions and Contraindications:
Not to be used for patients with *qi* or blood deficiency.

## Administration:
Take with warm water, after meals.

Source: *Wai Ke Zheng Zong* (外科正宗)

# Xiao Huo Luo Dan 小活絡丹
Myrrh and Aconite Formula
Minor Invigorating Collaterals Special Pill

## Indications:
For the treatment of wind-cold damp *bi* syndrome. Also used for the treatment of wind stroke (*zhong feng*).

May be used for patients experiencing chronic pain, weakness, and numbness of the extremities, also for fixed or migrating pain in the bones and joints with reduced range of motion due to wind-cold-damp obstruction.

**Tongue:**     pale, dull-dark or purple with white and greasy coating
**Pulse:**      wiry and tight, or deep and moderate.

## Clinical Applications:
1. This formula is most commonly used for *bi* syndrome, which is related to wind-cold-damp. After the onset of wind-stroke, damp-phlegm and lifeless blood can obstruct the channels and collaterals. The limbs feel restrained, the flexion and extension are hindered, and numbness and pain can set in.
2. Currently, it is also used for hemiplegia and other sequelae, such as can occur after a cerebrovascular accident. Also may be used for rheumatic and rheumatoid arthritis, osteoarthritis, sciatica and peripheral nervous disorders due to wind-cold-damp and blood stasis.

## Ingredients:
| | | | | | |
|---|---|---|---|---|---|
| 1. | chuan wu (zhi) | 4.6 | 4. | di long | 4.6 |
| 2. | cao wu (zhi) | 4.6 | 5. | ru xiang | 1.7 |
| 3. | tian nan xing (zhi) | 4.6 | 6. | mo yao | 1.7 |

## Functions:
Dispels wind, eliminates dampness, transforms phlegm, expels internal stagnation, warms the channels, disperses the cold, unblocks the collaterals, and alleviates pain.

## Cautions and Contraindications:
Not to be used in cases with *yin* deficiency and/or deficient heat. Not to be taken during pregnancy. This formula is quite potent; it may be better to use only for those with strong body constitutions.

## Administration:
Take with cool wine, before meals.

Source: *Tai Pin Hui Min He Ji Ju Fang* (太平惠民和劑局方)

# Xiao Ji Yin Zi 小薊引子

Cephalanoplos Decoction

## Indications:

For the treatment of bloody *lin* syndrome: characterized by bloody, frequent, difficult, burning and painful urination or simple blood in the urine with thirst and irritability.

**Tongue:**      red; thin, yellow coating
**Pulse:**       rapid, forceful

## Clinical Applications:

1. This formula is used for treating blood in the urine due to excessive heat in the lower *jiao*.
2. Currently used for urinary tract infections (UTIs), polycystic kidney, renal cysts, and sickle-cell disease.

## Ingredients:

1.  xiao ji       5.0
2.  ou jie        5.0
3.  pu huang      5.0
4.  sheng di     20.0
5.  hua shi       5.0
6.  zhu ye        5.0
7.  mu tong       5.0
8.  zhi zi        5.0
9.  dang gui      5.0
10. zhi gan cao   5.0

## Functions:

Cools the blood, stops bleeding, promotes urination, and unblocks the symptoms of *lin* syndrome.

## Modifications:

1. For added strength in clearing heat and draining fire, omit *zhi gan cao* and add *sheng gan cao*.
2. For cases with burning pain, add *hu po* and *hai jin sha*.

## Cautions and Contraindications:

Chronic urinary bleeding due to *qi* deficiency.

## Administration:

Take with warm water, before meals.

Source: *Ji Sheng Fang* (濟生方)

# Xiao Jian Zhong Tang 小建中湯
Minor Cinnamon and Peony Combination
Minor Construct the Middle Decoction

## Indications:

May be used for the treatment of spasmodic pain, palpitations, and low-grade fever due to consumptive deficiency (*xu lao*) syndrome, characterized by:

1. Intermittent, spasmodic abdominal pain that is relieved by warmth and pressure.
2. Palpitations with an empty sensation and upset or lusterless complexion.
3. Sore extremities with non-specific discomfort, especially in the hands and feet, low-grade sensation of heat, and dry mouth and throat.

**Tongue:**   pale, white coating
**Pulse:**    thin, wiry, moderate

## Clinical Applications:

1. This formula can be used to treat conditions such as abdominal pain caused by a lack of regulation between the *ying* and *wei* energies, with spleen and stomach deficiency cold.
2. The formula is also currently used for gastritis, peptic ulcers, chronic hepatitis, neurasthenia, pernicious anemia and leukemia.
3. This is an important formula for improving pediatric physical weakness, including conditions such as nocturia, frequent urination, night crying or inflectional disease with abdominal pain. Also treats postpartum abdominal pain in women.

## Ingredients:

| | | | | | |
|---|---|---|---|---|---|
| 1. yi tang | 3.0 | 3. bai shao | 6.0 | 5. da zao | 3.0 |
| 2. gui zhi | 3.0 | 4. sheng jiang | 3.0 | 6. zhi gan cao | 2.0 |

## Functions:

Warms and tonifies the middle *jiao*, harmonizes and moderates spasmodic abdominal pain.

## Modifications:

1. For cases with severe *qi* deficiency marked by spontaneous sweating, fatigue, or intermittent low-grade fever, add *huang qi* (*huang qi jian zhong tang*) and *dang shen*.
2. For cases with blood deficiency marked by epigastric and abdominal cold pain, and for postpartum abdominal pain, add *dang gui* (*dang gui jian zhong tang*), *shu di* and *e jiao*.
3. For severe *qi* deficiency: add *huang qi* and *ren shen*.
4. For severe blood depletion: add *dang gui* and *chuan xiong*.
5. For lung deficiency or irritation: add *mai men dong* and *wu wei zi*.
6. For female exhaustion depletion: combine with *Si Wu Tang*.
7. For male exhaustion depletion: combine with *Si Jun Zi Tang*.
8. For essence depletion: combine with *Jin Suo Gu Jing Wan*.

## Cautions and Contraindications:

Not to be used for *yin* deficiencies and excess fire, vomiting, fullness and distention in the epigastrium and abdomen.

## Administration:

Take with warm water, as needed.

Source: *Shang Han Jin Gui Fang* (傷寒金櫃方)

# Xiao Luo Wan 消瘰丸
Scrophularia and Fritillaria Combination
Reduce Scrofula Pill

## Indications:
Scrofula (*Luo Li* syndromes).

Nodules on the side of the neck with firm and rubbery consistency accompanied by dry mouth and throat.

**Tongue:** red
**Pulse:** rapid, slippery or wiry pulse

## Clinical Applications:
1. This formula is used for scrofula due to liver and kidney *yin* deficiency that causes phlegm fire accumulation..
2. Scrofulous swellings, phlegm nodules, hyperthyroid, inflamed thyroid, and lymph node swellings.
3. Currently used in treating cervical lymphadenopathy, lymphadenitis, simple goiter, thyroiditis, and hyperthyroidism.

## Ingredients:
1. mu li       9.0
2. xuan shen   6.0
3. bei mu      3.0

## Functions:
Clear heat, transform phlegm, soften hardness, and dissipate nodules.

## Modifications:
1. For large and very hard nodules, increase the dosage of *mu li* and add *kun bu, hai zao*, and *xia ku cao*.
2. For severe dry throat and mouth, increase the dosage of *xuan shen* and add *zhi mu* and *mu dan pi*.

## Cautions and Contraindications:
Congealing nodules due to cold or inflamed and ulcerated nodules.

## Administration:
Take with warm water, after meals.

Source: *Yi Xue Xin Wu* (醫學心悟)

# Xiao Qing Long Tang 小青龍湯
## Minor Blue Dragon Combination
## Minor Blue-Green Dragon Decoction

### Indications:
For the treatment of exterior wind-cold with interior congested cold fluids syndrome. May be used for patients experiencing aversion to cold and fever without sweating. Symptoms may include coughing, wheezing, copious white sputum that is watery or bubbly; a stifling sensation in chest, generalized sensation of heaviness and body aches, lack of thirst and possibly edema in the face and limbs.

**Tongue:**    Moist coating
**Pulse:**    Floating (superficial), tight

### Clinical Applications:
1. This is a common formula used for releasing wind-cold from the exterior and transforming congested fluids in the interior.
2. Currently used for acute or chronic bronchitis, bronchial asthma, senile emphysema, or flu due to exterior cold with interior congested fluids. Also used for acute or chronic nephritis caused by water spilling out of the skin, edema and hyperacidity caused by stomach *qi* rebelling.

### Ingredients:
| | | | | | |
|---|---|---|---|---|---|
| 1. | ma huang | 4.0 | 5. | wu wei zi | 1.5 |
| 2. | gui zhi | 4.0 | 6. | bai shao | 4.0 |
| 3. | gan jiang | 4.0 | 7. | zhi ban xia | 4.0 |
| 4. | xi xin | 1.5 | 8. | zhi gan cao | 4.0 |

### Functions:
Releases exterior wind-cold, disperses the cold, calms asthma, warms the lungs, and transforms congested fluids.

### Modifications:
1. For lung heat, and excessive thirst: add *shi gao* and *huang qin*.
2. For cough and asthma: add *hou po* and *xing ren*.
3. For skin edema: add *fu ling pi* and *sheng jiang pi*.
4. For severe exterior cold disorders, increase the dosage of *ma huang* and *gui zhi*.
5. For mild exterior cold, omit *gui zhi* and replace *ma huang* with *mi zhi ma huang*.
6. For cases with thirst, omit *ban xia* and replace with *tian hua fen*.
7. For cases with severe wheezing, add *xing ren*.

### Cautions and Contraindications:
Not to be used in cases with *yin* deficiency characterized by dry coughing without sputum; should not be used long-term. Cases with phlegm heat characterized by coughing with yellow and sticky sputum, thirst and yellow tongue coating. Use with caution for patients with hypertension.

### Administration:
Take with warm water, after meals.

Source: *Shang Han Lun* (傷寒論)

# Xiao Xian Xiong Tang 小陷胸湯
Minor Trichosanthes Combination
Minor Decoction (for Pathogens) Stuck in the Chest

## Indications:
Phlegm heat accumulation in the chest symptoms.

Focal distention (with or without nodules) in the chest and epigastrium that are painful upon palpation, possible cough with yellow and sticky sputum, constipation, and bitter taste in the mouth.

**Tongue:**    greasy, yellow coating
**Pulse:**    slippery, either rapid or floating

## Clinical Applications:
1. This formula is used for clumping in the chest caused by the sinking of pathogenic heat into the chest and epigastric where it mixes with phlegm and forms clumps.
2. The key symptoms are focal distention in the chest and epigastrium that are painful upon palpation.
3. Currently used in treating acute bronchitis, pleurisy, acute or chronic gastritis, intercostal neuralgia, cholecystitis, peptic ulcer, and angina pectoris.

## Ingredients:
1. huang lian    3.0
2. ban xia    12.0
3. gua lou shi    12.0

## Functions:
Clear heat, transform phlegm, expand the chest, and dissipate clumps.

## Modifications:
1. For severe hypochondriac pain, add *yu jin* and *chai hu.*
2. For sticky sputum that is difficult to expectorate, add *dan nan xing* and *chuan bei mu.*
3. For vomiting: add *zhu ru* and *sheng jiang.*

## Cautions and Contraindications:
Spleen and stomach deficiency or loose stools.

## Administration:
Take with warm water, before meals.

Source: *Shang Han Lun* (傷寒論)

# Xiao Xu Ming Tang 小續命湯
### Ephedra and Peony Combination
### Minor Extend Life Decoction

## Indications:
Wind stroke (*zhong feng*).

Hemiplegia, asymmetry of the face, slow and slurred speech due to external wind; usually accompanied by fever and chills. In severe cases there is loss of consciousness.

**Tongue:**    pale, thin white coating
**Pulse:**    deficient and floating.

## Clinical Applications:
1. This formula is used for hemiplegia due to external wind stroke.
2. Also used for wind-cold damp *Bi* syndrome marked by pain with numbness or inability only in upper extremities.
3. Central and peripheral facial paralysis, sequelae of cerebrovascular accident, urticaria, and rheumatoid arthritis.
4. Stroke, cerebral hemorrhage, unconsciousness, depression, numbness, sensory palsy, muscle palsy, speech disorder, and high blood pressure.

## Ingredients:

| | | | | | |
|---|---|---|---|---|---|
| 1. fang feng | 3.0 | 6. bai shao | 2.0 | 11. pao fu zi | 1.0 |
| 2. gui zhi | 2.0 | 7. ren shen | 2.0 | 12. da zao | 1.0 |
| 3. ma huang | 2.0 | 8. gan cao | 2.0 | 13. sheng jiang | 6.0 |
| 4. xing ren | 2.0 | 9. huang qin | 2.0 | | |
| 5. chuan xiong | 2.0 | 10. fang ji | 2.0 | | |

## Functions:
Warms the channels, unblocks the *yang*, supports the righteous *qi* and expels wind.

## Modifications:
1. For facial asymmetry, add *wu gong* to dredge the channels and collaterals.
2. For cases with excessive sweating and an aversion to wind, omit *ma huang* and replace with *huang qi*.
3. For cases with difficult bowel movements: add *da huang* and *zhi shi*.

## Cautions and Contraindications:
Wind stroke due to internal liver wind or wind-damp heat *Bi* syndrome.

## Note:
This formula is a modification of Combined Cinnamon *Gui zhi Ma Huang Ge Ban Tang* (Twig and Ephedra Decoction) with *Shen Fu Tang* (Ginseng and Aconite Accessory Root Decoction).

## Administration:
Take with warm water, after meals.

Source: *Yi Fang ji Jie* （醫方集解）

# Xiao Yao San 逍遙散
## Tangkuei and Bupleurum Formula
## Rambling Powder

## Indications:
Used to treat liver *q* stagnation, blood deficiency, and transportation and transformation dysfunctions of the spleen: hypochondriac pain, headache, dizziness, dry mouth and throat, fatigue, and poor appetite, there may be alternating chills and fever, irregular menstruation, and breast distention.

**Tongue:**   pale and red
**Pulse:**   wiry and deficient

## Clinical Applications:
1. This formula is commonly used for regulating menstruation.
2. Currently used for chronic hepatitis, cirrhosis, gallstone, peptic ulcer, chronic gastritis, neurosis, menopausal syndromes, fibrocystic breasts, PMS, pelvic inflammation, and functional uterine bleeding.

## Ingredients:
1. chai hu        4.0
2. bai shao       4.0
3. dang gui       4.0
4. bai zhu        4.0
5. fu ling        4.0
6. zhi gan cao    2.0
7. wei jiang      4.0
8. bo he          2.0

## Functions:
Spreads liver *qi*, releases constraint, strengthens the spleen, and nourishes blood.

## Modifications:
1. For severe liver *qi* stagnation, add *xiang fu* and *chen pi*.
2. For severe blood deficiency, add *shu di* or *sheng di*.
3. For excess fire, add *mu dan pi* and *zhi zi*.
4. For headache and dizziness, add *chuan xiong* and *bai zhi*.
5. For irritability and thirst, add *huang qin* and *ren shen*.
6. For excessive thinking, combine with *Tian Wang Bu Xin Dan*.
7. For postpartum patients, combine with *Si Wu Tang*.

## Administration:
Take with warm water, as needed.

Source: *Tai Ping Hui Min He Ji Ju Fang* (太平惠民和劑局方)

# Xiao Zhi Wan 消痔丸
## Rehmannia and Scute Combination

**Indications:**

Internal and/or external hemorrhoids syndromes.

Constipation, hard and dry stool, irritability, and anus fistula.

**Clinical Applications:**
1. This formula is for freeing the bowel, purging fire and treating painful constipation with hemorrhoid or fistula symptoms.
2. Currently used in hemorrhoids, initial stage of anus fistula, and blood heat constipations.

**Ingredients:**
1. sheng di huang  4.8
2. huang qin  1.8
3. jin yin hua  1.2
4. zhi ke  1.2
5. qin jiao  1.2
6. fang feng  2.4
7. da huang  2.4
8. dang gui  2.4
9. cang zhu  2.4
10. di long  2.4
11. huai hua  2.4
12. chi shao  2.4

**Functions:**

Clear heat, cool blood and ease bowel movements.

**Administration:**

Take with warm water, after meals.

Source: *Yang Yi Da Quan* (瘍醫大全)

# Xie Bai San 瀉白散
Mulberry and Lycium Formula
Drain the White Powder

## Indications:
For the treatment of "smoldering fire syndrome" due to heat constrained in the lungs.

May be used for patients experiencing coughing or even shortness of breath (SOB), wheezing, five-center heat, irritability, fever with steaming sensation under the skin, which worsens in the late afternoon; red lips and cheeks and general excessive body heat.

**Tongue:**       red, yellow coating
**Pulse:**        thready and rapid

## Clinical Applications:
1. This formula is commonly used for lingering cough due to smoldering fire gradually injuring the *yin* stage. This is characterized by a high, clear sounding cough and absence of sputum, dry cough asthma.
2. Currently used for bronchitis, pertussis, initial stage of pulmonary TB, pleurisy, measles, pneumonia in the early stage, and upper respiratory tract bleeding.

## Ingredients:
1. sang bai pi    7.0
2. di gu pi       7.0
3. gan cao        3.5
4. geng mi        3.5
5. dan zhu ye     3.5

## Functions:
Cools and drains heat, expels phlegm, benefits the *qi* to reduce coughing and calm asthma.

## Modifications:
1. For fever aversion to cold: add *chai hu* and *shao yao*.
2. For severe cough and asthma: add *xing ren* and *jie geng*.
3. For irritability and thirst: add *mai men dong* and *wu wei zi*.
4. For cases with severe heat in the lungs: add *huang qin* and *zhi mu*.
5. For coughing due to dry-heat: add *gua lou pi* and *chuan bei mu*.

## Cautions and Contraindications:
Contraindicated for coughing and wheezing due to wind-cold, wind-heat, or damp-phlegm.

## Administration:
Take with warm water, after meals.

Source: *Qian Zhong Yang Fang* (錢仲陽方)

# Xie Huang San 瀉黃散
Siler and Licorice Formula
Drain the Yellow Powder

## Indications:
For the treatment of "smoldering fire syndrome" in the spleen and stomach.

May be used for patients experiencing dry mouth and lips, mouth ulcers, bad breath, irritability, thirst, frequent hunger, heat in the muscle layer, jaundice, heat in the limbs, and tongue thrusting in children.

**Tongue**: red
**Pulse**: rapid

## Clinical Applications:
1. This formula is commonly used for smoldering heat (fire); also used to treat yellowing of sclera due to excess spleen heat.
2. Currently used for aphthous ulcers, acute and chronic splenitis, gastroenteritis, gastrointestinal dilatation, gastrointestinal ulcers, gastrointestinal ptosis, and stomatitis, pharyngitis, excessive thirst, and general dyspepsia.

## Ingredients:
| | | | | |
|---|---|---|---|---|
| 1. shi gao | 1.5 | 4. huo xiang | 2.1 |
| 2. zhi zi | 3.0 | 5. gan cao | 3.0 |
| 3. fang feng | 12.0 | 6. zhi gan cao | 3.0 |

## Functions:
Clears smoldering fire to relieve muscle; regulates *qi* to harmonize the middle *jiao*.

Modifications:
1. For cases with severe jaundice, heat in the extremities: add *yin chen hao* and *huang qin*.
2. For severe irritability and thirst: add *zhi mu* and *jie geng*.
3. For severe mouth ulcers accompanied by bad breath: add *huang lian* and *sheng ma*.
4. For cases with severe heat: add *huang lian*.
5. For cases with irritability and restlessness: add *chi fu ling* and *deng xin cao*.

## Cautions and Contraindications:
Not to be used to treat stomach *yin* deficiency or tongue thrusting due to congenital *qi* deficiency.

## Administration:
Take with warm water, as needed.

Source: *Qian Zhong Yang Fang* (錢仲陽方)

# (San Huang) Xie Xin Tang （三黃）瀉心湯
## Coptis and Rhubarb Combination
## Drain the Epigastrium Decoction

### Indications:
For the treatment of excessive interior fire blazing causing reckless movement of the blood. May be used for patients experiencing the following symptoms:
1. Excessive heat, irritability, unconsciousness and delirium.
2. Vomiting of blood or nosebleeds.
3. Red and swollen eyes and ulceration of the tongue or mouth.
4. Dysentery, constipation, and/or jaundice, especially with blood and pus in stool.
5. Carbuncles or sores.

**Tongue:**   greasy, yellow coating
**Pulse:**   rapid, forceful

### Clinical Applications:
1. This is one of the strongest formulas for cases of constipation. It can alleviate red face due to blood rushing upward, as well as general irritability and excitement.
2. Currently used for hepatitis, cholecystitis, dysentery, conjunctivitis, stomatitis, vascular headaches and trigeminal neuralgia. To be used immediately after the onset of cerebral congestion or cerebral hemorrhage, or a few days after the onset.
3. Also used to treat general irritabilities after atherosclerosis and hypertension. Insomnia, skin disease, eye disease, neurasthenia, neurosis, schizophrenia, epilepsy, and even gynecological conditions with fire blazing upward.

### Ingredients:
1. da huang      9.0
2. huang lian    4.5
3. huang *qin*   4.5

### Functions:
Clears fire heat, relieves toxicity and dries dampness.

### Modifications:
1. For cases with bleeding: add *dang gui* and *sheng di huang.*
2. For severe thirst, dry heat: add *shi gao* and *zhi mu.*
3. For severe constipation: *zhi shi* and *hou po.*
4. For cases with damp heat that transforms into fire and injures the body's fluids, as indicated by dry mouth and tongue, add *tian hua fen, lu gen* and *sheng di huang.*
5. For cases when damp and heat are both prominent, evidenced by thick, yellow and greasy tongue coating, oppression in the chest and nausea: add *ban xia* and *hou po.*

### Cautions and Contraindications:
Not to be used for *yin* deficiency with excess fire.

### Administration:
Take with cool water for stop bleeding.
For sores and carbuncles, this formula can be applied topically in power form.

Source: *Jin Gui Yao Lue* (金櫃要略)

# Xin Yi Qing Fei Yin 辛夷清肺飲
Magnolia and Gypsum Combination
Magnolia Flower Drink to Clear the Lungs

## Indications:
Lung heat.

Nasal polyps, nasal congestion, rhinitis, or sinusitis.

**Tongue**: red tongue, white or yellow coating
**Pulse**: rapid

## Clinical Applications:
1. This formula is for treating nasal polyps that are the result of heat in the lungs.
2. The key symptoms are stuffy nose and nasal polyps.
3. Currently used in treating loss of smell (anosmia) due to nasal congestion, nasal heat sensation, thirst and other symptoms such as sinusitis, atrophic rhinitis, nasal polyps, rhinitis, or allergic rhinitis.

## Ingredients:
1. xin yi hua     2.0
2. huang qin     3.0
3. zhi zi     3.0
4. mai men dong     3.0
5. bai he     3.0
6. zhi mu     3.0
7. shi gao     3.0
8. gan cao     1.5
9. pi pa ye     3.0
10. sheng ma     1.0

## Functions:
Clear lung heat, disseminates Lung *qi*, and unblocks the nasal orifices.

## Modifications:
1. For cases with wind-cold cold: add *fang feng* and *qiang huo*.
2. For cases with wind-heat cold and irritability: add *huang lian* and *sheng di huang*.
3. For cases with wind-damp and body odors: add *yin chen hao* and *jin yin hua*.

## Administration:
Take with warm water, after meals.

Source: *Wai Ke Zheng Zong* （外科正宗）

# Xin Yi San 辛夷散
Magnolia Flower Formula
Magnolia Flower Powder

## Indications:
Nasal congestion in the initial stage of common cold, with clear nasal discharge.

Nasal congestion and pain, persistent, copious nasal discharge, loss of sense of smell, and wind-cold headache.

## Clinical Applications:
1. This formula is for treating nasal congestion, pain, copious nasal discharge, loss of sense of smell, and wind-cold headache.
2. This formula is for relieving wind and easing pain. As it is particularly strong for head disorders, it is effective for long-term use of colds, nasal congestion, and headaches.
3. Currently used in treating common cold, stuffy nose, headache, hypertrophic rhinitis, empyema, sinusitis, and nasal polyps.

## Ingredients:
1. xin yi hua      2.4
2. bai zhi         2.4
3. sheng ma        2.4
4. gao ben         2.4
5. fang feng       2.4
6. chuan xiong     2.4
7. xi xin          2.4
8. mu tong         2.4
9. gan cao         2.4
10. cha ye         2.4

## Functions:
Disperse wind-cold, dispel the damp and open the nasal orifice.

## Modifications:
1. For wind-cold with clear nasal discharge: add *jing jie* and *qiang huo*.
2. For wind-heat with nasal congestion: add *cang er zi* and *bo he*.
3. For wind-damp with nasal congestion with pus: add *cang zhu* and *lian qiao*.
4. For congestion pain with pus: combine with *Liang Ge San*.
5. For congestion and loss sense of smell with pus: combine with *Pai Nong San*.

## Administration:
Take with warm water, after meals.

Source: *Yi Fang ji Jie* (醫方集解)

# Xing Su San 杏蘇散
Apricot Seed and Perilla Formula
Apricot Kernel and Perilla Leaf Powder

**Indications:**
For the treatment of external wind-cold attacks, resulting in dryness.

May be used for patients experiencing slight headaches, excessive body heat, aversion to cold without sweating, coughing with watery sputum, stuffy nose, and/or dry throat.

| | |
|---|---|
| **Tongue:** | dry, white coating |
| **Pulse:** | wiry |

**Clinical Applications:**
1. This is the most widely used formula used for treating cool-dryness disorder and cough. This is externally contracted cool-dryness, which interferes with the dispersing and descending functions of the lungs, resulting in aversion to cold and body heat.
2. Currently used for chronic bronchitis, bronchiectasis, and emphysema due to cool-dryness with damp-phlegm stagnation.

**Ingredients:**

| | | | | |
|---|---|---|---|---|
| 1. zi su ye | 3.0 | 7. chen pi | 1.5 |
| 2. xing ren | 3.0 | 8. fu ling | 3.0 |
| 3. qian hu | 3.0 | 9. sheng jiang | 0.8 |
| 4. jie geng | 1.5 | 10. ge gen | 1.5 |
| 5. zhi ke | 1.5 | 11. gan cao | 0.8 |
| 6. ban xia | 3.0 | | |

**Functions:**
Gently disperses wind cool-dryness, ventilates lung *qi* and transforms phlegm.

**Modifications:**
1. For wind-cold pathogenic attack: add *fang feng* and *jing jie.*
2. For severe phlegmatic coughing and asthma: add *zi su zi* and *ting li zi.*
3. For dry throat and excessive thirst: add *huang qin* and *shi gao.*
4. For wind-cold cough and asthma: combine with *Di Chuan Tang.*
5. For cough due to fluid retention: combine with *Er Chen Tang.*
6. For wiry or tight pulse without sweating: add *qiang huo.*
7. For severe headaches: add *fang feng* and *chuan xiong.*
8. For frontal headaches: add *bai zhi.*

**Administration:**
Take with warm water, after meals.

Source: *Yi Zong Jin Jian* (醫宗金鑑)

# Xiong Gui Jiao Ai Tang (芎歸) 膠艾湯
## Tangkuei and Gelatin Combination
## Donkey-Hide Gelatin and Mugwort Decoction

## Indications:
For the treatment of deficiencies in the *chong* and *ren* channels as well as *beng lou* syndrome.

Indications include: abdominal pain with uterine bleeding, excessive menstruation, menstruation with constant spotting, postpartum bleeding or bleeding during pregnancy, bleeding after miscarriage, situations where the blood is pale and thin without clots, especially if accompanied by weakness, soreness of the lower back, or a dull complexion.

**Tongue**:     pale; thin, white coating
**Pulse**:       thin, frail

## Clinical Applications:
1. This is a formula used for conditions of blood stasis that tend toward cold, and is especially useful in treating irregular menstruation with anemia.
2. Currently used for functional uterine bleeding, pregnancies with risk of miscarriage, postpartum uterine bleeding or menopausal bleeding, bleeding caused by endometriosis, or hemorrhoid bleeding.
3. Other symptoms include: hematuria, or blood in urine, internal bleeding caused by external trauma, habitual miscarriages; deficiency bleeding caused by uterine cancer, oral bleeding, or kidney stones.

## Ingredients:
| | | | | | |
|---|---|---|---|---|---|
| 1. | e jiao | 2 | 5. | sheng di huang | 5 |
| 2. | ai ye | 3 | 6. | chuan xiong | 2 |
| 3. | dang gui | 3 | 7. | gan cao | 2 |
| 4. | bai shao | 4 | | | |

## Functions:
Nourishes blood, stops bleeding, regulates menstruation and calms the fetus in pregnancy.

## Modifications:
1. For an unstable fetus: add *huang qin* and *bai zhu*.
2. For waist and abdominal pain: add *zhi shi* and *hou po*.
3. For basic spotting: add *pao jiang, di yu tan,* and *ai ye tan.*
4. For pain during pregnancy: add *Bao Chan Wu You Fang.*

## Cautions and Contraindications:
Contraindicated for occasional uterine bleeding due to heat.

## Administration:
Take with warm water, before meals.

Source: *Jin Gui Yao Lue* (金櫃要略)

# Xiong Gui Tiao Xue Yin 芎歸調血飲
Ligusticum and Rehmannia Combination
Chuanxiong and Tangkuei Drink to Regulated the Blood

## Indications:
Postpartum symptoms of *qi* and blood depletion.

Lochia retention, prolonged bleeding, irritability, asthmatic breathing, abdominal pain, dizziness, tinnitus, and fever.

## Clinical Applications:
1. This formula is for treating postpartum disorders characterized by deficiency of *qi* and blood and weakened spleen and stomach.
2. The key symptoms are prolonged lochia, excessive postpartum bleeding, spontaneous sweating, dry mouth, irritability, abdominal pain, hypochondriac fullness and distention, dizziness, blurry vision, and tinnitus.
3. This formula is also used in the treatment of menstrual irregularities marked by both deficiency and blood stasis as well as the sequelae of trauma or surgery.
4. Currently used in treating functional uterine bleeding, abdominal pain before menstruation or poor menstrual flow, chronic pelvic inflammatory disease, neuropathic headache, spleen and stomach bloating and nausea and vomiting.
5. Any other postpartum conditions: postpartum neurosis, insufficient milk, beriberi, edema, anemia, and lochia.

## Ingredients:

| | | | | | |
|---|---|---|---|---|---|
| 1. dang gui | 2.4 | 6. chen pi | 2.4 | 11. da zao | 1.3 |
| 2. chuan xiong | 2.4 | 7. wu yao | 2.4 | 12. sheng jiang | 1.2 |
| 3. shu di huang | 2.4 | 8. xiang fu | 2.4 | 13. gan cao | 1.2 |
| 4. bai zhu | 2.4 | 9. mu dan pi | 2.4 | 14. gan jiang | 2.4 |
| 5. fu ling | 2.4 | 10. yi mu cao | 2.4 | | |

## Functions:
Harmonize the liver and spleen; sooth the liver and resolve *qi* stagnation; tonify the *qi* and nourish blood; transform stasis and generate the new.

## Modifications:
1. For severe *qi* and blood deficiency: add *ren shen* and *huang qi* or combine with *Dang Gui Bu Xue Tang.*
2. For vexation-heat thirst and dry mouth: add *sheng di huang* and *huang qin.*
3. For headache and dizziness: add *bai zhi* and *huang qi.*
4. For deficiency startle, unsettled spirit: add *suan zao ren, yuan zhi*, and *mai men dong.*
5. For severe constipation: combine with *Zhe Chong Wan.*

## Cautions and Contraindications:
Excess heat condition.

**Note:**

This formula is similar to *Sheng Hua Tang* (*Tangkuei* and Ginger Combination), but it is more focused on tonifying *qi* and blood and is less able to move blood and dispel stasis.

**Administration:**

Take with warm water, as needed.

Source: *Wan Bing Hui Chun* (萬病回春)

# Xuan Fu Dai Zhe Tang 旋覆代赭湯
## Inula and Hematite Combination
## Inula and Hematite Decoction

## Indications:

For the treatment of stomach *qi* deficiency with turbidity-phlegm obstructing the interior syndrome.

May be used for patients experiencing the constant need to belch, as well as hiccupping, regurgitation, nausea and vomiting, and hard epigastric focal distention.

**Tongue**:    white, slippery coating
**Pulse**:    wiry, deficient

## Clinical Applications:

1. This formula is used for phlegm turbidity obstructing the interior, especially together with weak and deficient stomach *qi*.
2. Currently used for functional gastric neurosis, chronic gastritis, gastric dilatation, peptic ulcers, partial pyloric obstruction, spasm of the gastroesophageal junction and nervous hiccoughs. May also treat borborygmus, acid regurgitation, vomiting, constipation, abdominal fullness, and hyperperistalsis.

## Ingredients:

| | | | | | |
|---|---|---|---|---|---|
| 1. | xuan fu hua | 3.6 | 5. | ren shen | 2.4 |
| 2. | da zhe shi | 1.2 | 6. | gan cao | 3.6 |
| 3. | ban xia | 3.6 | 7. | da zao | 2.4 |
| 4. | sheng jiang | 6.0 | | | |

## Functions:

Augments the *qi* and harmonizes the stomach; directs the rebellious *qi* downward and transforms phlegm.

## Modifications:

1. For severe hypochondriac focal distention: add *huang lian* and *huang qin*.
2. For severe belching: add *zhi shi* and *jie geng*.
3. For severe nausea and vomiting:  add *fu ling* and *chen pi*.
4. For cases without stomach *qi* deficiency: omit *ren shen* and *da zao*, and increase *dai zhe shi* dosage.
5. For copious sputum: add *fu ling* and *chen pi*.

## Administration:

Take with warm water, after meals.

Source: *Shang Han Za Bing Lun* (傷寒雜病論)

# Xue Fu Zhu Yu Tang 血府逐瘀湯
Persica and Carthamus Combination
Drive Out Stasis in the Mansion of Blood Decoction

## Indications:
For the treatment of blood and *qi* stagnation in the chest.

May be used for patients experiencing pain in the chest and hypochondriac region, chronic, stubborn headaches with a fixed, piercing quality, chronic, incessant hiccupping, a choking sensation when drinking, dry heaves, depression or low spirits accompanied by a sensation of warmth in the chest, palpitations, insomnia, restless sleep, irritability, extreme mood swings, and evening tidal fever.

**Tongue**:  dark-red, dark spots on the sides of the tongue, dark or purplish lips.
**Pulse**:  choppy or wiry, tight.

## Clinical Applications:
1. This formula is used to treat blood stasis in the "mansion of blood", with acute impairment of blood flow in the area above the diaphragm; the key symptoms are chronic, stubborn pain in the chest area, especially with a fixed and stabbing quality.
2. Currently used for patients with coronary artery disease - angina pectoris, rheumatic heart diseases, costochondritis, and post-concussion syndrome: headaches, migraines, and depression, as well as hallucinations, headaches, dizziness, insomnia, and forgetfulness.

## Ingredients:
1. tao ren        6.0
2. hong hua       4.5
3. dang gui       4.5
4. chi shao       3.0
5. sheng di       4.5
6. chuan xiong    2.3
7. niu xi         4.5
8. chai hu        1.5
9. jie geng       2.3
10. zhi ke        3.0
11. gan cao       1.5

## Functions:
Invigorates the blood, dispels blood stasis, moves the *qi*, and alleviates pain.

## Modifications:
1. For cases with hypertension: add *gao ben*.
2. For female blood stagnation, amenorrhea or dysmenorrhea: add *yi mu cao* and *ze lan*.
3. For immobile sub-costal and abdominal mass: add *yu jin* and *dan shen*.
4. For amenorrhea or dysmenorrhea, omit *jie geng* and add *xiang fu* and *yi mu cao*.

## Related Formulations

### Tong Qiao Huo Xue Tang 通竅活血湯
Unblock the Orifices and Invigorate the Blood Decoction

Invigorates the blood, dispels blood stasis, and opens the orifices. For accumulation of blood stasis in the head, face, and upper part of body, which may cause headache and vertigo, chronic tinnitus, hair loss and dark "brandy" nose.

**Ingredients**: *she xiang, tao ren, hong hua, chuan xiong, chi shao, cong bai, da zao, sheng jiang* and wine.

### Ge Xia Zhu Yu Tang 膈下逐瘀湯
Drive Out Stasis from Below the Diaphragm Decoction

Invigorates the blood, dispels blood stasis, moves the *qi*, alleviates pain. For blood stasis and liver *qi* stagnation in the area below the diaphragm with palpable abdominal masses accompanied by fixed pain or abdominal masses which are visible when lying down.

**Ingredients:** *wu ling zhi, dang gui, chuan xiong, tao ren, mu dan pi, chi shao, wu yao, yan hu suo. gan cao, xiang fu, hong hua,* and *zhi ke.*

## Cautions and Contraindications:
Not to be taken during pregnancy. Use caution for all kinds of active hemorrhagic disorders, or bleeding diathesis. This formula is a blood mover, which could easily to damage the righteous *qi*, and therefore should not be taken for a long time.

## Administration:
Take with warm water, after meals.

Source: *Yi Lin Gai Cuo* (醫林改錯)

# Yang He Tang 陽和湯
Balmy Yang Decoction

## Indications:
For the treatment of *yin* gangrene syndromes.

May be used for patients experiencing localized, painful swellings without pronounced heads, and which blend into the surrounding tissue and do not affect the texture or color of the skin and which are not hot to the touch; also accompanied by lack of thirst.

**Tongue:**     very pale
**Pulse:**      submerged, thin, forceless

## Clinical Applications:
1. This formula is used for *yin* gangrene and carbuncles due to *yang* and blood deficiency with cold coagulation in the muscles, sinews, bones, or vessels.
2. Currently used in treating thromboangiitis, gangrene, chronic osteomyelitis, chronic lymphnoditis, gravity abscesses, rheumatoid arthritis, bone and joint tuberculosis.

## Ingredients:
1. shu di         30.0
2. lu jiao jiao    9.0
3. pao jiang       1.5
4. rou gui         3.0
5. ma huang        1.5
6. bai jie zi      6.0
7. gan cao         3.0

## Functions:
Warms the *yang*, tonifies the blood, disperses cold, unblocks stagnation.

## Modifications:
For severe *qi* deficiency: add *huang qi* and *ren shen.*

## Cautions and Contraindications:
Use caution for patients with *yang* syndromes, *yin* deficiency, or chronic ulceration.

## Administration:
Take with warm water, as needed.

Source: *Wai Ke Quan Sheng Ji* (外科全生集)

# Yang Xin Tang 養心湯

### Astragalus and Zizyphus Combination
### Nourish the Heart Decoction from Comprehensive Collection

## Indications:
Heart deficiency and insufficiency of blood with unsettled spirit.

Weak constitution or debility in post-illness, palpitations with anxiety, insomnia, and forgetfulness, easily frightened or racing heart, anxiety, and dream-disturbed sleep.

| | |
|---|---|
| **Tongue:** | slightly red and not as dry |
| **Pulse:** | deficient, frail or fine |

## Clinical Applications:
1. This formula is for treating heart deficiency and insufficiency of blood with unsettled spirit.
2. The key symptoms are a wan and withered complexion, a tongue that is only slightly red and not as dry, and a pulse that is deficient and frail rather than fine. Also fright with palpitations, night sweats, insomnia, fever and irritability, deficiency heat, sores, deficiency heart blood, restlessness, insomnia and dreaminess.
3. Currently used in treating weak heart, neurasthenia, anemia, insomnia, hyperactivity and palpitations, mental restlessness, and forgetfulness, palpitation, nocturnal emission insomnia, excessive dreaming, and irritability.

## Ingredients:

| | | | | | | | |
|---|---|---|---|---|---|---|---|
| 1. | zhi huang qi | 3.0 | 6. | ban xia (qu) | 3.0 | 11. ren shen | 2.0 |
| 2. | fu ling | 3.0 | 7. | bai zi ren | 2.0 | 12. rou gui | 2.0 |
| 3. | fu shen | 3.0 | 8. | suan zao ren | 2.0 | 13. zhi gan cao | 1.0 |
| 4. | dang gui | 3.0 | 9. | wu wei zi | 2.0 | 14. sheng jiang | 1.0 |
| 5. | chuan xiong | 3.0 | 10. | yuan zhi | 2.0 | 15. da zao | 1.0 |

## Functions:
Nourish the heart and harmonize, tonify the blood; transform phlegm and clear *qi*; calm the spirit and settle the will.

## Modifications:
1. For cases with fever irritable, thirst: add *mai men dong* and *zhu ru.*
2. For cases with irritable heat and insomnia: add *zhi mu* and *huang bai.*
3. For cases with forgetfulness and frighten palpitation: add *shi chang pu* and *shao yao.*

## Administration:
Take with warm water, after meals.

Source: *Zheng Zhi Zhun Sheng* (證治準繩)

# Yang Xue Chuang Jin Jian Bu Wan 養血壯筋健步丸
### Eucommia and Rehmannia Formula

## Indications:
Liver-kidney deficiency and *yin* deficiency with internal heat, nerve pain, and pain in muscles sinews, and joints.

Bone density loss, sore, weak knees and lower back, or atrophy of the sinew and bones.

## Clinical Applications:
1. This formula is for treating liver and kidney deficiency and *yin* deficiency with internal heat.
2. The key symptoms are weak knees and lower back, atrophy of the sinews and bones, wasting of leg muscles and feet, and difficulty in walking.
3. Currently used in osteoporosis, leg muscle atrophy, and weakness of knees.

## Ingredients:

| | | | | | |
|---|---|---|---|---|---|
| 1. | shu di huang | 3.20 | 11. | wu wei zi | 0.80 |
| 2. | huang qi | 0.80 | 12. | fang ji | 0.40 |
| 3. | bai zhu | 0.80 | 13. | huang bai | 1.60 |
| 4. | huai niu xi | 1.60 | 14. | gou qi zi | 1.20 |
| 5. | bu gu zhi | 0.80 | 15. | qiang huo | 0.24 |
| 6. | gui ban | 0.80 | 16. | cang zhu | 1.60 |
| 7. | du zhong | 1.60 | 17. | ren shen | 1.60 |
| 8. | shan yao | 0.80 | 18. | bai shao | 1.20 |
| 9. | fang feng | 0.48 | 19. | tu si zi | 0.80 |
| 10. | dang gui | 1.60 | | | |

## Functions:
Strengthen sinews and bones, benefit lower back and knees eliminate soreness, nourish *yin*, clear heat and stop pain.

## Administration:
Take with warm water, after meals.

Source: *Gu Jin Yi Jian* (古今醫鑒)

# Yang Yin Qing Fei Tang 養陰清肺湯
## Ophiopogon and Scrophlaria Formula
### Nourish the *Yin* and Clear the Lungs Decoction

**Indications:**

Diphtheria (白喉 *Bai Ho*) – white throat.

A swollen and sore throat, noisy breathing resembling wheezing, dry nose and lips; there may also be fever and cough.

**Clinical Applications:**

1. This formula is for treating lung and kidney issues from a combination of a weak body constitution and overconsumption of spicy food and/or exposure to dry weather.
2. The key symptoms are 'white throat' (*Bai Ho*) or diphtherial disorder, which usually develops in those with constitutional *yin* deficiency and internal accumulated heat who contract epidemic toxin (*Du Yi*).
3. Currently used in diphtheria, tonsillitis, pharyngitis, and the side effects of radiation therapy to tumors of the head and throat.

**Ingredients:**

| | | | | | |
|---|---|---|---|---|---|
| 1. | sheng di huang | 6.0 | 5. | chuan bei mu | 2.4 |
| 2. | xuan shen | 4.5 | 6. | mu dan pi | 2.4 |
| 3. | mai men dong | 3.6 | 7. | sheng gan cao | 1.5 |
| 4. | bai shao | 2.4 | 8. | bo he | 1.5 |

**Functions:**

Nourish *yin*, clear lung heat, release toxin to benefit the throat; clear inflammation, expel phlegm and relieve cough.

**Modifications:**

1. For cases with severe *yin* deficiency: add *shu di huang*.
2. For cases with severe dryness: add *tian men dong*, *zhi mu*, and *lu gen*.
3. For cases with severe swelling and painful throat: add *she gan*, *jie geng*, *bai jian can* and *ma bo*.

**Cautions and Contraindications:**

Diphtheria is a very serious, even life-threatening disease, and extreme care must be exercised. In China, this formula is for breathing difficulty.

**Administration:**

Take with warm water, after meals.

Source: *Chong Luo Yu Yao* (重樓玉鑰)

# Yi Gan San 抑肝散
Bupleurum Formula
Restrain the Liver Powder

## Indications:
Deficiency heat in the liver channel.

Spasms, feverishness, frightpalpitations, fever and chills, or vomiting of watery-phlegm sputum and saliva, abdominal distention, reduced appetite, and restless sleep.

## Clinical Applications:
1. This formula is for treating deficiency heat in the liver channel.
2. The key symptoms are spasms, feverishness, fright palpitations, fever and chills, or vomiting of watery-phlegm sputum and saliva, abdominal distention, reduced appetite, and restless sleep.
3. Currently used in treating nervousness and hysteria. It can also be applied to children's night crying and night terrors, insomnia, short-tempered and easily angered nature, aggressiveness, impatience, clenching and grinding teeth while sleeping, epilepsy and seizure disorders.
4. Unexplained fever, menopausal disorders, gynecomastia and nervousness.

## Ingredients:
| | | | | | | |
|---|---|---|---|---|---|---|
| 1. | chai hu | 2.0 | | 5. | bai zhu | 4.0 |
| 2. | gan cao | 2.0 | | 6. | fu ling | 4.0 |
| 3. | chuan xiong | 3.2 | | 7. | gou teng | 4.0 |
| 4. | dang gui | 4.0 | | | | |

## Functions:
Clear the liver heat, sooth the liver and regulate the liver blood and *qi*.

## Modifications:
1. For irritable insomnia: add *suan zao ren* and *bai zi ren.*
2. For abdominal bloating, fullness and distention: add *zhi shi* and *hou po.*
3. For physical body tired and fatigue: add *ren shen* and *huang qi.*
4. For vomiting phlegm fluid: combine with *Wen Dan Tang.*
5. For frightened palpitation, chills and fever: combine with *Xiao Chai Hu Tang.*

## Note:
This formula is similar to *Xiao Yao San* (*Tangkuei* and Bupleurum Formula); however, *Yi Gan San* primarily addresses liver *qi* stagnation with liver wind symptoms such as spasms, seizures, headache, and dizziness.

## Administration:
Take with warm water, after meals.

Source: *Zheng Zhi Zhun Sheng* (證治準繩 )

# Yi Guan Jian 一貫煎
### Linking Decoction

## Indications:
For the treatment of syndromes related to liver and kidney *yin* deficiency with liver *qi* stagnation.

May be used for patients experiencing chest and pain in the hypochondriac area, epigastric and abdominal distention, acid regurgitation, bitter taste or dry mouth and throat.

**Tongue**:     red, dry tongue
**Pulse**:     thin, frail or deficient and wiry

## Clinical Applications:
1. This formula is used for liver and kidney *yin* deficiencies which can bring about epigastric and hypochondriac pain.
2. Currently used to treat peptic ulcers, chronic hepatitis, chronic gastritis, liver pain due to fatty liver, and nervous exhaustion with insomnia and dreams.

## Ingredients:
1. sheng di huang    8.0
2. bei sha shen      4.0
3. mai men dong     4.0
4. dang gui (shen)   4.0
5. gou qi zi         4.0
6. chuan lian zi      2.0

## Functions:
Enriches the *yin* and spreads the liver *qi*.

## Modifications:
1. For constipation: add *gua lou ren, yu li ren* and *huo ma ren.*
2. For deficiency heat sweating: add *di gu pi* and *shi hu.*
3. For coughs with profuse sputum: add *bei mu.*
4. For severe thirst: add *shi hu.*
5. For atrophy of lower extremities: add *niu xi* and *yi yi ren.*
6. For hypochondriac distention and pain with masses: add *bie jiao* and *ji nei jin.*
7. For bitter taste in the mouth: add *huang lian* or *huang qin* and *tian hua fen.*

## Cautions and Contraindications:
Contraindicated for excessively damp phlegm accumulations.

## Administration:
Take with cool water, after meals.

Source: *Liu Zhou Yi Hua* (柳州醫話)

# Yi Qi Cong Ming Tang 益氣聰明湯

Ginseng, Astragalus, and Pueraria Combination
Augment *Qi* and Clear the Metal Decoction 323

### Indications:
Wind-heat blazing upward disturbing the upper orifices.

Superficial visual obstructions, cloudy vision, diminished visual acuity, and deafness and ringing of the ears.

| | |
|---|---|
| **Tongue**: | pale, thin white |
| **Pulse**: | thin and weak |

### Clinical Applications:
1. This formula is for treating wind-heat blazing upward caused headache, blurry vision, and dizziness.
2. The key symptoms are early onset of cataracts, tinnitus, deafness, hearing loss, and degradation of vision.
3. Currently used in treating deafness, tinnitus, and early stage of cataracts, diminished vision, and floaters. Also neurological tinnitus, cerebral anemia, and frontal neuralgia.
4. Cataracts, amblyopia, floaters, tinnitus, deafness, visual impairment, and memory loss.

### Ingredients:

| | | | | | |
|---|---|---|---|---|---|
| 1. | huang qi | 6.0 | 5. | bai shao | 2.4 |
| 2. | ren shen | 6.0 | 6. | huang bai | 2.4 |
| 3. | ge gen | 3.6 | 7. | sheng ma | 1.8 |
| 4. | man jing zi | 3.6 | 8. | gan cao | 1.2 |

### Functions:
Benefit the *qi,* raise the clear *yang,* and brighten the eyes, dispersing wind and clear heat.

### Modifications:
1. For blurry vision: add bai *ju hua* and *gou qi zi.*
2. For wind-cold common cold: add *fang feng* and *qiang huo.*
3. For deficiency cataracts: combine with *Zi Shen Ming Mu Tang.*

### Cautions and Contraindications:
This is not for acute inflammation of eyes and ears diseases or dampness conditions.
Avoid the greasy, raw, cold food.

### Administration:
Take with warm water, after meals.

Source: *Yi Fang ji Jie* (醫方集解)

# Yi Yi Ren Tang 薏苡仁湯
## Coix Combination
### Coicis Decoction from Enlightened Physicians

## Indications:
Wind-damp-cold *bi* symptoms.

Swelling and painful numbness and difficulty in moving hand and foot joints.

**Tongue:** glossy coating
**Pulse:** slippery

## Clinical Applications:
1. This formula is for treating pain and swelling of the joints that has not responded to treatment or was improperly treated at the acute stage and is beginning to show chronic signs.
2. The key symptoms are worsening in damp or cold weather, a glossy tongue fur, and pain predominantly in the lower body, which are signs that cold and damp are the root of the disorder.
3. Currently used in treating subacute and chronic early joints arthritis.
4. Pain in hands and feet, numbness, difficulty in stretching and flexing. Damp-*Bi* stroke, paralysis, joint muscle spasm, and intestinal carbuncle mastitis.
5. Rheumatism arthritis, rheumatoid arthritis, muscular rheumatism, pulmonary edema, pleurisy, chronic nephritis, and beriberi.

## Ingredients:
| | | | | | | |
|---|---|---|---|---|---|---|
| 1. | yi yi ren | 10.0 | | 5. | gui zhi | 1.6 |
| 2. | bai shao | 3.0 | | 6. | bai zhu | 2.0 |
| 3. | dang gui | 3.0 | | 7. | gan cao | 1.4 |
| 4. | ma huang | 1.6 | | 8. | sheng jiang | 1.0 |

## Functions:
Disperse wind and dispel damp, tonify the *qi* and activate blood and relieve pain.

## Modifications:
1. For irritable heat and pain: add *zhi* mu and *huang* bai.
2. For aversion to cold and pain: add *fu zi* and *di long*.
3. For severe dampness and swelling: add *fang ji*, *tao ren*, and *fu ling*.

## Note:
Both this formula and *Ma Xing Yi Gan Tang* treat damp-cold inflammatory joint disorders.
1. *Ma Xing Yi Gan Tang* (Ephedra and Coix Combination) treats mild and initial stage disorders.
2. *Gui Zhi Shao Yao Zhi Mu Tang* (Cinnamon and Anemarrhena Combination) treats the disorder that has become entrenched and has existed long enough to damage *yin* and generate blood stasis.
3. *Yi Yi Ren Tang* treats a more severe and chronic pattern, but the patient is still able to walk.

## Administration:
Take with warm water, either before or after meals.

Source: *Ming Yi Zhi Zhang Fang* （明醫指掌方）

# Yi Zi Tang 乙字湯
## Cimicifuga Combination
## Decoction "B"

### Indications:
Stagnation and heat in the lower body – intestine.

Intestinal wind, bleeding hemorrhoids or fistulas, prolapsed rectum, uterine bleeding, bleeding during childbirth, or blood stagnation with abdominal pain; also for itching or pain in or around the vagina caused by heat accumulation.

### Clinical Applications:
1. For treating intestinal wind and bloody stool from bleeding of the lower intestines. Anal disease with a tendency to constipation and a small amount of bleeding, even local pain.
2. The key symptoms are bleeding hemorrhoids or fistulas, profuse uterine bleeding or spotting, excessive bleeding during childbirth, or blood stasis abdominal pain.
3. Currently used in treating hemorrhoids pain, anal laceration, bleeding rectum prolapse, and female genital itching.
4. Or for nerve pain caused by mistakenly treated skin diseases that drove toxicity internally.

### Ingredients:
| | | | | | |
|---|---|---|---|---|---|
| 1. | dang gui | 6.0 | 4. | gan cao | 3.0 |
| 2. | chai hu | 6.0 | 5. | sheng ma | 2.0 |
| 3. | huang qin | 3.0 | 6. | da huang | 1.5 |

### Functions:
Clear heat and drain stagnation, stop bleeding, ease the bowel movement, cool the blood.

### Modifications:
1. For cases with constipation: increase the dosage of *da huang* and *zhi shi.*
2. For cases with hemorrhoid pain: add *wu yao* and *xiang fu.*
3. For cases with rectum prolapse and bleeding: add *di yu tan*, *sheng di huang*, and *huang lian.*
4. For cases with vaginal itching pain: add *jin yin hua* and *lian qiao.*
5. For female blood stagnation in the lower *jiao*: combine with *Gui Zhi Fu Ling Wan.*

### Cautions and Contraindications:
Pregnancy or no constipation tendency.

### Note:
This formula and *Huai Hua San* (Sophora Flower Formula) both treat heat accumulation in the lower body with bleeding from the rectum or uterus. *Yi Zi Tang* is better at draining stasis and raising the *yang*. *Huai Hua San* is better at clearing heat and astringing bleeding.

### Administration:
Take with warm water, before meals or empty stomach.

Source: *Yuan Nan Yang* (原南陽)

# Yin Chen Hao Tang 茵陳蒿湯
Capillaris Combination
Artemisia *Yinchenhao* Decoction

## Indications:
For the treatment of damp-heat or *yang*-type jaundice (*huang dan*). May be used for patients experiencing whole-body jaundice with bright yellow color, especially in sclera and skin, slight abdominal distention, difficulty urinating, excessive thirst, and sweating in the head, but not in the body.

**Tongue:**  yellow, greasy coating
**Pulse:**  slippery and rapid

## Clinical Applications:
1. This formula is very effective in treating *yang*-type or damp-heat jaundice, as indicated by whole-body jaundice with bright yellow-orange color caused by damp-evil and heat accumulation in the middle *jiao*; patient shows no sweating or sweating only from the head, not below the neck.
2. This formula may be used in treating acute hepatitis, hepatic necrosis, cirrhosis, cholecystitis, cholelithiasis, malaria, typhoid fever, leukemia, and allergic dermatitis; other applications: include urticaria, pruritus, endophthalmitis, tongue sores, and eye pain.

## Ingredients:
1. yin chen hao     12.0
2. zhi zi     6.0
3. da huang     4.0

## Functions:
Clears heat, dissipates dampness, and reduces jaundice, promoting sweating.

## Modifications:
1. For difficult bowel movements: add *zhi shi* and *hou po.*
2. For slow or difficult urination: add *fu ling* and *cang zhu.*
3. For thirst fullness distention: add *huang lian* and *huang qin.*
4. For cases with more heat and less damp: add *long dan cao* and *huang bai.*
5. For cases with more damp and less heat: add *fu ling, zhu ling* and *ze xie.*
6. For cases with hypochondriac pain: add *chai hu* and *chuan lian zi.*

## Cautions and Contraindications:
Not for treating *yin-type* jaundice or jaundice in which cold-dampness predominates; not to be taken during pregnancy.

## Administration:
Take with warm water, after meals.

Source: *Shang Han Lun* (傷寒論)

# Yin Chen Wu Ling San 茵陳五苓散

Capillaris and Poria Five Formula

Virgate Wormwood and Five-Ingredient Powder with Poria 729

## Indications:
Internal and external jaundice due to damp-heat.

Yellow skin, difficulty urinating, irritability, body cold and fever, loss of appetite, loose stools, and yellow urine which is difficult and short.

| | |
|---|---|
| **Tongue:** | greasy coating |
| **Pulse:** | slow |

## Clinical Applications:
1. This formula is for treating damp-heat jaundice when there is more damp than heat and urine is inhibited.
2. The key symptoms are jaundice, difficulty urinating, irritability and slightly pale skin tone.
3. Currently used in treating jaundice, hepatitis, nephritis, peritonitis, dysuria, fever, thirst, ascites, and cholestatic jaundice.

## Ingredients:
1. yin chen hao   16.0
2. ze xie           2.5
3. fu ling          1.5
4. zhu ling         1.5
5. bai zhu          1.5
6. gui zhi          1.0

## Functions:
Eliminate heat, bring down jaundice, promote sweating and move the water.

## Modifications:
1. For cases with thirst and irritability: add *zhi zi* and *cang zhu.*
2. For cases with difficulty urinating: add *mu tong* and *sheng jiang.*
3. For cases with fever and a desire to drink: add *shi gao* and *zhi mu.*

## Cautions and Contraindications:
*Yang* jaundice.

## Administration:
Take with warm water, after meals.

Source: *Jin Gui Yao Lue* (金匱要略)

# Yin Qiao San 銀翹散
## Lonicera and Forsythia Formula

### Indications:
Early stage of food retention disease: fever, slight or no sweating, slight or no aversion to wind-cold, headache, thirst, cough, and sore throat.

**Tongue**: thin white or thin yellow coating with a red tongue tip
**Pulse**: floating or superficial and rapid

### Clinical Applications:
1. This is the standard moderate, pungent, and cool formula. It is used in the early stage of wind-warm febrile diseases.
2. Currently used for flu, acute tonsillitis, measles, epidemic parotitis, acute endometritis, and early stage encephalitis or meningitis due to wind-heat in the *wei* stage.

### Ingredients:

| | | | | | |
|---|---|---|---|---|---|
| 1. | jin yin hua | 20.0 | 6. | dan dou chi | 10.0 |
| 2. | lian qiao | 20.0 | 7. | lu gan | 10.0 |
| 3. | bo he | 12.0 | 8. | dan zhu ye | 9.0 |
| 4. | niu bang zi | 12.0 | 9. | jie geng | 10.0 |
| 5. | jing jie | 9.0 | 10. | gan cao | 10.0 |

### Functions:
Disperses exterior wind-heat, clears interior heat, and relieves toxicity.

### Modifications:
1. For severe thirst, add *tian hua fen*.
2. For severe sore throat, add *ma bo* and *xuan shen*.
3. For prominent coughing, add *xing ren*.
4. For stifling sensation in the chest, add *huo xiang* and *yu jin*.
5. For cough with sore throat, add *sang bai pi* and *di gu pi*.
6. For aversion to wind and headache, add *fang feng* and *cong bai*.
7. For irritability and thirst, add *mai men dong* and *shi gao*.
8. For wind-heat and thirst, combine with *Bai Hu Tang*.

### Cautions and Contraindications:
Should not be used when a patient has damp heat or wind damp.

### Administration:
Swallow with warm water, after meals.

Source: *Wen Bing Tiao Bian* (溫病條辨)

# You Gui Wan 右歸丸
Eucommia and Rehmannia Formula
Restore the Right (Kidney) Pill

## Indications:

For the treatment of kidney *yang* deficiency, with waning of the *ming men* fire. May be used for patients experiencing cold due to spleen and stomach deficiency, exhaustion from long-term illness, aversion to cold, coolness of the extremities, impotence, spermatorrhea, aching and weakness in the lower back and knees, infertility, loose stools, especially with undigested food, incontinence, and edema in lower extremities.

**Tongue:**     pale; thin, white coating
**Pulse:**      deep, slow, faint

## Clinical Applications:

1. This is one of the best formulas for treating kidney-*yang* deficiency with insufficient *ming men* fire, most often seen in the elderly and those suffering chronic diseases.
2. Currently used to treat lower back pain, osteoporosis, infertility, and leukopenia. Also used for chronic nephritis, hypertension, neurasthenia, limb burnout, decreased sperm count, low endocrine function, aplastic anemia, kidney *yang* deficiency, diabetes, leukorrhea and proteinemia. It can promote the secretion of the adrenal gland to support righteous energy and expel evil.

## Ingredients:

| | | | | | | |
|---|---|---|---|---|---|---|
| 1. fu zi | 1.10 | 5. shan zhu yu | 2.20 | 9. du zhong | 2.20 |
| 2. rou gui | 1.10 | 6. shan yao | 2.20 | 10. dang gui | 0.16 |
| 3. lu jiao (jiao) | 0.16 | 7. gou qi zi | 2.20 | | |
| 4. shu di huang | 4.40 | 8. tu si zi | 2.20 | | |

## Functions:

Warms and tonifies the kidney *yang*, replenishes the essence (*jing*), and tonifies the blood.

## Modifications:

1. For patterns of true cold and false heat, and for kidney *yang* deficiency, exhibited by feebleness and exhaustion: add *you gui yin* (restore the right [kidney] drink): *shu di, shan yao, shan zhu yu, gou qi zi, zhi gan cao, du zhong, rou gui* and *zhi fu zi.*
2. For cases with *qi* deficiency: add *ren shen* and *huang qi.*
3. For weakness in the lower back and legs: add *niu xi, xu duan* and *he shou wu.*
4. For premature ejaculation: add *ba ji tian, rou cong rong* and *jiu cai zi.*
5. For chronic coughing and asthma: combine with *Xin Su Yin.*
6. For lacking blood and leukorrhea: combine with *Wan Dai Tang* or *Li Zhong Tang.*
7. For dizziness and irritability: combine with *ban xia, bai zhu* and *tian ma tang.*
8. For spontaneous spermatorrhea, or loose stool: add *bu gu zhi.*
9. For constant abdominal pain; add *wu zhu yu.*

## Cautions and Contraindications:

Not to be used for kidney deficiency with cloudy urination.

**Administration:**
Take with warm water, before meals.

Source: *Jing Yue Quan Shu* (景岳全書)

# Yu Nu Jian 玉女煎
## Rehmannia and Gypsum Combination
### Jade Woman Decoction

## Indications:

For the treatment of excessive stomach heat with *yin* deficiency due to excess stomach fire, which injures the kidney *yin*.

May be used for patients experiencing frontal headaches, toothaches, loose teeth, bleeding gums, irritability, fever and thirst.

**Tongue:**    dry, red color, yellow coating
**Pulse:**    floating, slippery, deficient, and large

## Clinical Applications:

1. This formula nourishes the *yin* and drains fire excess from the stomach. It is used for bleeding gums and *xiao ke* syndrome.
2. Currently used for toothaches, gingivitis, diabetes, stomatitis, glossitis, blood in the vomit and bloody stool.

## Ingredients:

1. sheng shi gao    10.0
2. shu di    10.0
3. zhi mu    4.0
4. mai men dong    5.0
5. niu xi    4.0

## Functions:

Clears the stomach of excess heat and nourishes kidney *yin*.

## Modifications:

1. For severe toothache: add *huang lian* and *gan cao*.
2. For irritable thirst: add *tian men dong* and *sheng di huang*.
3. For severe vomiting with blood: add *zhi zi* and *hei jiang*.
4. For severe swollen gum: combine with *Gan Lu Yin*.
5. For severe mouth ulcer pain: combine with *Qing Wei San*.
6. For cases with blazing fire: add *zhi zi* and *di gu pi*.
7. For excess blood heat or severe bleeding: omit *shu di* and replace with *sheng di* and *xuan shen*.

## Cautions and Contraindication:

Use with caution for patients with diarrhea.

## Administration:

Take with cool water, after meals.

Source: *Jing Yue Quan Shu* (景岳全書)

# Yu Ping Feng San 玉屏風散
Astragalus and Siler Formula
Jade Windscreen Powder

## Indications:
For the treatment of *wei qi* deficiency syndrome, with spontaneous sweating.

May be used for patients experiencing spontaneous sweating with aversion to the cold, aversion to drafts, pale complexion, and recurrent cold.

**Tongue**:     pale; white
**Pulse**:     floating, deficient, and soft

## Clinical Applications:
1. This formula is used for exterior deficiency with weak and unstable *wei qi,* or immune response.
2. Currently used for acute upper respiratory tract infections, bronchitis, allergic rhinitis, autonomic dystonia, and nephritis, or for patients with recurring colds. May be taken after the measles, where the body can still keep the residual heat.

## Ingredients:
1. huang qi     15.0
2. bai zhu     5.0
3. fang feng     5.0

## Functions:
Augments the *qi*, stabilizes the exterior, and stops sweating.

## Modifications:
1. For cases with wind-cold: add *cang zhu* and *qiang huo.*
2. For cases with fatigue related to *qi* deficiency: add *ren shen* and *gan cao.*
3. For cases with dizziness caused by blood deficiency: add *dang gui* and *chuan xiong.*
4. For persistent sweating, add *fu xiao mai, mu li* and *ma huang gen.*
5. For patients who easily catch colds: combine with *Gui Zhi Tang.*
6. For patients who are overly fatigued: combine with *Xiao Jian Zhong Tang.*

## Cautions and Contraindications:
Contraindicated for patients with night sweats due to *yin* deficiency or excess heat.

## Administration:
Take with warm water, after meals.

Source: *Shi Yi De Xiao Fang* (世醫得效方)

# Yu Quan Wan 玉泉丸
Jade Source Combination
Jade Spring Pill

## Indications:
Wasting and thirsting disorder (*xiao ke* 消渴).

Irritability with thirst, frequent urination, dry mouth, increased appetite, and weight loss.

**Tongue**:  red and dry
**Pulse**:  large and rapid

## Clinical Applications:
1. This formula is for treating wasting and thirsting disorders.
2. The key symptoms are irritability, thirst, and dry mouth, frequent urination, increased appetite, loose stool, fatigue and weight loss. It is the upper, central and lower "*xiao*", in fact it is simply *yin* depletion, *yang* hyperactivity, parching of fluids by excess heat.
3. Currently used in treating post-febrile diseases with body heat, thirst, and five-center vexation heat; diabetes and hyperglycemia.

## Ingredients:
1. gua lou gen     4.5
2. ge gen          4.5
3. mai men dong    3.0
4. ren shen        3.0
5. fu ling         3.0
6. wu mei          3.0
7. gan cao         3.0
8. huang qi (sheng)  1.5
9. huang qi (zhi)    1.5

## Functions:
Generate fluid and quench the thirst; benefit the *qi* and nourish the *yin*.

## Modifications:
1. For cases with *yin* deficiency: add *sheng di huang*.
2. For cases with *qi* deficiency: add *ren shen* and *shan yao*.
3. For cases with strong heat in upper *xiao*: add *shi gao* and *zhi mu*.

## Note:
*Yu Quan Wan* and *Liu Wei Di Huang Wan* (Rehmannia Six Formula) form a good combination to treat diabetes-like disorders.

## Administration:
Take with warm water, after meals.

Source: *Gu Jin Yi Tong* (古今醫統)

# Yue Bi Jia Zhu Tang 越婢加朮湯
### Atractylodes Combination
Maidservant from Yue's Decoction plus Atractylodes

## Indications:
*Feng shui* (wind water) edema.

Wind-water in the exterior, swelling in the upper body, mild edema in lower limb joints, inhibited urination, thirst, a mild fever, and spontaneous sweating.

**Pulse:**      floating and slippery, or submerged

## Clinical Applications:
1. This formula is for treating wind-water edema.
2. The key symptoms are water swollen in the upper body and lower limbs, mild edema, sore and heavy limbs, reduced urination, fever and chills.
3. Currently used in treating acute nephritis, arthritis, rheumatoid, beriberi edema, paralysis of lower extremities, difficulty urinating. And skin eczema fever, nocturia. Conjunctivitis pain with tears and swollen eyes.

## Ingredients:
| | | | | | |
|---|---|---|---|---|---|
| 1. | ma huang | 7.2 | 4. | da zao | 2.4 |
| 2. | shi gao | 9.6 | 5. | gan cao | 2.4 |
| 3. | sheng jiang | 3.6 | 6. | bai zhu | 4.8 |

## Functions:
Dispel wind and clear heat, induce sweating and moves water.

## Modifications:
1. For cases with yellowish skin: add *yin chen hao* and *zhi zi*.
2. For cases with severe edema: add *fang ji, zhu ling,* and *fu ling*.
3. For cases with irritable thirsty desire to drink water: add *zhi mu* and *huang bai*.
4. For cases with cough and *qi* rebelling: add *ban xia*.

## Note:
1. This formula is modified from *Yue Pi Tang* (Maidservant from Yue's Decoction) with the addition of *bai zhu*.
2. A reference claims this formula was used to treat a maid from "*Yue*". Another reference claims that the pathogen in this pattern is trapped in the flesh just as a "maidservant" is trapped by the social standing.
3. Both this formula and *Fang Ji Huang Qi Tang* (Stephania and Astragalus Combination) treat wind-water. *Yue Bi Jia Zhu Tang* treats wind-water that is located in the exterior with heat. *Fang Ji Huang Qi Tang* treats a deficiency pattern.

## Administration:
Take with warm water, as needed.

Source: *Jin Gui Yao Lue* (金匱要略)

# Yue Ju Wan 越橘丸
### Cyperus and Atractylodes Combination
### Escape Restraint Pill

## Indications:
For the treatment of stagnation syndrome (*yu zheng*).

May be used for patients experiencing focal distention, a stifling sensation in the chest and abdomen, fixed pain in the hypochondriac region, belching, vomit, acid regurgitation, reduced appetite, and indigestion.

## Clinical Applications:
1. This formula is used to treat the "six constraints:" *qi*, blood, phlegm, fire, food and dampness, due to middle *jiao qi* stagnation.
2. Currently used for peptic ulcers, chronic gastritis, infectious hepatitis, cholecystitis, gallstones, intercostal neuralgia, neurosis, and dysmenorrhea. Neurodegitic gastroenteritis, gastrointestinal ulcers, gastrointestinal dilation, gastrointestinal prolapse, and hysteria.

## Ingredients:
1. cang zhu       5.0
2. chuan xiong    5.0
3. xiang fu       5.0
4. zhi zi        5.0
5. shen qu       5.0

## Functions:
Move the *qi* and releases stagnations.

## Modifications:
1. For indigestive food: add *chen pi* and *hou po*.
2. For belching acid regurgitation: add *ban xia* and *fu ling*.
3. For hypochondriac distention: add *chai hu* and *huang qin*.
4. For severe *qi* constraint: increase dosage of *xiang fu*, add *mu xiang, zhi ke* and *hou po*.
5. For severe blood constraint: increase dosage of *chuan xiong,* and add *tao ren* and *hong hua*.
6. For severe dampness constraint: increase dosage of *cang zhu*, add *fu ling* and *ze xie*.
7. For severe food constraint: increase dosage of *shen qu*, add *shan zha* and *mai ya*.
8. For severe phlegm constraint: add *ban xia* and *gua lou*.

## Cautions and Contraindications:
Not to be used for general stagnation due to deficiency.

## Administration:
Take with warm water, after meals.

Source: *Dan Xi Xin Fa* (丹溪心法)

# Zeng Ye Tang 增液湯
Increase the Fluids Decoction

## Indications:
For the treatment of *yang ming* febrile disease. Symptoms include constipation, fluid damage, and excessive thirst.

| | |
|---|---|
| **Tongue:** | red, dry coating |
| **Pulse:** | thin, slightly rapid or weak, forceless |

## Clinical Applications:
1. This formula is used for dry intestines or constipation due to damage of the body's internal fluids, usually from warm-febrile disease. The key symptom is excessive thirst and constipation due to exhaustion of the fluids. Therefore, this formula is thought to "increase the fluids to float the boat."
2. Currently used for anal fissures, hemorrhoids, chronic pancreatitis, pharyngitis, recurrent aphthous ulcers and diabetes due to *yin* and fluid deficiency.

## Ingredients:
1. xuan shen       30.0
2. mai men dong   24.0
3. sheng di        24.0

## Functions:
Generates fluids, moistens dryness, and unblocks the bowels.

## Modifications:
1. For severe dry heat caused by damaged *yin* and fluid, add *sheng da huang* and *mang xiao.*
2. For toothache, add *mu dan pi, bu gu zhi* and *lu feng fang.*
3. For bleeding hemorrhoids, add *Huai Hua San.*

## Administration:
Take with warm water, as needed.

Source: *Wen Bing Tiao Bian* (溫病條辨)

# Zhe Chong Yin 折衝飲

Cinnamon and Persica Combination
Drink to Turn Back the Penetrating (Vessel)

## Indications:
Blood stasis in the lower abdomen.

Menstrual pain, delayed menstruation, menstrual stagnation, post-miscarriage blood stasis pain and bleeding, and abdominal accumulations.

## Clinical Applications:
1. This formula is for treating female blood stasis in the lower abdomen, or women with abdominal pain.
2. The key symptoms are menstrual pain, menstrual stagnation, and abdominal accumulations (including fibroid tumors). Irregular menstruation, painful menstruation, blood stasis, abdominal accumulations, amenorrhea or postpartum or post-miscarriage bleeding or pain.
3. Currently used in treating pelvic inflammatory disease, inflammation of the fallopian tubes, uterine leiomyoma, chronic metritis miscellaneous abdominal masses, endometritis, or dysfunctional uterine bleeding.

## Ingredients:

| | | | | |
|---|---|---|---|---|
| 1. | mu dan pi | 2.4 | 6. dang gui | 4.0 |
| 2. | chuan xiong | 2.4 | 7. yan hu suo | 2.0 |
| 3. | bai shao | 2.4 | 8. huai niu xi | 2.0 |
| 4. | gui zhi | 2.4 | 9. hong hua | 1.2 |
| 5. | tao ren | 4.0 | | |

## Functions:
Invigorate and nourish the blood, transform accumulation and dissipate stagnation.

## Modifications:
1. For cases with menstrual blood stagnation: add *san leng* and *e zhu*.
2. For cases with painful menstruation: add *xiang fu* and *ai ye*.
3. For cases with menstrual dizziness: add *ren shen* and *huang qi*.
4. For cases with wind-cold and painful menses: combine with *Xiao Chai Hu Tang*.
5. For cases with postpartum abdominal pain: combine with *Sheng Hua Tang*.

## Cautions and Contraindications:
Pregnancy.

## Administration:
Take with warm water, before meals.

Source: *Fu Bao Chan Lun Fang* (婦寶產論方)

# Zhen Gan Xi Feng Tang 鎮肝熄風湯
### Hematite and Scrophularia Combination
### Sedate the Liver and Extinguish Wind Decoction

## Indications:
For the treatment of internal wind stroke or similar wind-type stroke syndrome.

Symptoms the patient may experience include dizziness, vertigo, distending sensation in the eyes, tinnitus, headaches with feverish or heat sensation, restlessness and flushed face as if intoxicated, possible frequent belching, progressive motor dysfunction of the body, and even development of facial asymmetry. In severe cases there may also be severe vertigo, falling down, and sudden loss of consciousness that persists over a long period, possibly coming to senses, and possibly unable to fully recover.

**Pulse:**         wiry, long and forceful

## Clinical Applications:
1. This formula is often used to treat wind stroke caused by excessive *qi* gushing upward, whether before, during, or after the onset of stroke, if the syndrome is due to liver *yin* and fluid deficiency with liver *yang* rising.
2. The key symptoms are dizziness, vertigo, distending sensation in the eyes, tinnitus, headache with feverish sensation, and upset feeling with heat sensation and flushed face.
3. Currently used in treating hypertension, vascular headaches, trigeminal neuralgia, post-concussion syndrome, cerebral arteriosclerosis, coronary artery disease or migraines due to liver wind and *yin* fluid deficiency with liver *yang* rising.

## Ingredients:
| | | | | | | | | |
|---|---|---|---|---|---|---|---|---|
| 1. | huai niu xi | 10.0 | 5. | gui ban | 5.0 | 9. | yin chen hao | 2.0 |
| 2. | dai zhe shi | 10.0 | 6. | bai shao | 5.0 | 10. | chuan lian zi | 2.0 |
| 3. | long gu | 5.0 | 7. | xuan shen | 5.0 | 11. | mai ya | 2.0 |
| 4. | mu li | 5.0 | 8. | tian men dong | 5.0 | 12. | gan cao | 1.5 |

## Functions:
Sedates the liver, extinguishes wind, nourishes the *yin* and anchors the yang.

## Modifications:
1. For sensations of heat in the chest: add *shi gao* (30).
2. For congestion with profuse sputum: add *dan nan xing.*
3. For deficient proximal pulse when pressed firmly: add *shu di* and *shan zhu yu.*

## Cautions and Contraindications:
Use caution for treating patients with spleen *qi* deficiency.

## Administration:
Take with warm water, as needed.

Source: *Yi Xue Zhong Zhong Can Xi Lu* (醫學衷中參西錄)

# Zhen Ren Huo Ming Yin 真人活命飲
### Angelica and Mastic Combination

## Indications:
Initial stage of carbuncle and promote suppuration.

## Clinical Applications:
1. This formula is for treating the beginning of carbuncle.
2. The key symptoms are redness, swelling and pain, purulent disease, promote pus discharge function.
3. Currently used in treating the initial stage of carbuncle, swelling, toxins, and pus that have not dissipated; it will dissipate if the pus is not formed yet; it will suppurate if already pustulated. This works with all *yin* or *yang* types of sores.
4. If it has suppurated, do not take this formula.

## Ingredients:
1. jin yin hua     6.0
2. chen pi     1.4
3. dang gui     1.4
4. fang feng     1.4
5. bai zhi     2.0
6. gan cao (jie)     2.0
7. bei mu     2.0
8. gua lou gen     2.0
9. ru xiang     2.0
10. mo yao     1.0
11. zao jiao ci     1.0

## Functions:
Disperse stagnation and dissipate swelling; transform pus and generate flesh.

## Modifications:
1. For wind-cold swelling pain: add *fang feng* and *qiang huo*.
2. For wind-heat swelling pain: add *lian qiao* and *huang qin*.
3. For aversion to cold swelling pain: add *huang qi* and *ren shen*.
4. For red, swelling, heat, and pain: combine with *Huang Lian Jie Du Tang*.
5. For not yet ripened pus swelling: combine with *Tuo Li Xiao Du Yin*.
6. For swelling pus not suppurated: combine with *Pai Nong San*.

## Cautions and Contraindications:
If it has suppurated, do not take this formula.

## Administration:
Take with warm water, as needed.

Source: *Yi Fang ji Jie* (醫方集解)

# Zhen Ren Yang Zang Tang 真人養臟湯
### True Man's Decoction to Nourish the Organs

## Indications:
For the treatment of chronic diarrhea or dysentery.

May be used for patients experiencing chronic, unremitting diarrhea or dysentery to the point of incontinence, and, in severe cases, prolapsed rectum; may be accompanied by abdominal pain, a cramping sensation around the navel, reduced appetite, and tenesmus; also soreness of the lower back, and lack of strength in the legs.

| | |
|---|---|
| **Tongue**: | pale, white coating |
| **Pulse**: | slow, thin |

## Clinical Applications:
1. This formula is used for spleen and kidney deficiency cold, accompanied with chronic diarrhea or dysentery.
2. Currently used for chronic colitis, chronic dysentery, and ulcerative colitis.

## Ingredients:
1. ying su ke       15.0
2. rou dou kou       6.0
3. he zi            12.0
4. ren shen         18.0
5. bai zhu           9.0
6. dang gui         18.0
7. bai shao         15.0
8. rou gui           3.0
9. mu xiang          4.5
10. zhi gan cao      6.0

## Functions:
Constricts the intestines, stops diarrhea, warms up the middle *jiao*, and tonifies deficiencies.

## Modifications:
1. For severe kidney and spleen *yang* deficiency cold, add *pao fu zi*.
2. For a prolapsed rectum, add *sheng ma* and *huang qi*.

## Cautions and Contraindications:
Not to be used for patients with damp-heat dysentery; while taking, avoid cold, raw, fishy and greasy food.

## Administration:
Take with warm water, before meals.

Source: *Tai Ping Hui Min He Ji Ju Fang* (太平惠民和劑局方)

# Zhen Wu Tang 真武湯
Ginger, Aconite, Poria, and Peony Combination
True Warrior Decoction

## Indications:

For the treatment of water retention due to spleen and kidney *yang* deficiency: may result in urinary difficulty, deep aches and heaviness in the extremities, abdominal pain, loose stool or diarrhea. May also result in generalized edema, a heavy sensation in the head, and palpitations.

May be used for patients experiencing excessive sweating in *tai yang* disease, which depletes the *yang* and body fluid; may be accompanied by fever that doesn't dissipate after sweating and palpitations, dizziness, vertigo, shivering, with an unsteady appearance and the feeling of being unstable on the feet.

**Tongue:**    white, slippery coating, or swollen with teeth marks
**Pulse:**      submerged, thin, and forceless

## Clinical Applications:

1. This formula is used for kidney and/or spleen *yang* deficiency, especially with retention of pathogenic water. It is especially useful for cases in which the protective *yang qi* is depleted by excessive sweating.
2. The key symptoms are urinary difficulty, heavy-feeling extremities, loose stool, or edema in the limbs.
3. Currently used in treating chronic nephritis, rheumatic valvular heart disease, congestive heart failure, ascites, hypothyroidism, chronic bronchitis, intestinal tuberculosis, Meniere's disease or post-concussion headaches, and acute febrile diseases.

## Ingredients:

| 1. fu zi | 2.0 | 3. fu ling | 6.0 | 5. bai shao | 6.0 |
|---|---|---|---|---|---|
| 2. bai zhu | 6.0 | 4. sheng jiang | 6.0 | | |

## Functions:

Expels the cold to tonify *qi*, warms the *yang* and promotes urination, strengthens spleen and moves internal water.

## Modifications:

1. For dizziness and palpitations: add *ren shen* and *gui zhi*.
2. For painful extremities: add *xi xin* and *ma huang*.
3. For difficulty with urination: add *ze xie* and *rou gui*.
4. For water retention or edema: combine with *Ji Sheng Shen Qi Wan*.
5. For coughing, add *gan jiang, xi xin* and *wu wei zi*.
6. For severe diarrhea: omit *bai shao* and add *gan jiang* and *yi zhi ren*.
7. For vomiting: add *wu zhu yu* and *ban xia*.

## Cautions and Contraindications:

Not to be taken during pregnancy.

## Administration:

Take with warm water, as needed.

Source: *Shang Han Lun* (傷寒論)

# Zheng Gu Zi Jin Dan 正骨紫金丹
### Calamus and Carthamus Formula
### Bone-Setter's Purple-Gold Special Pill

## Indications:
Fall-hit traumatic injury which can be second- and third-stage trauma.

An injury where swelling has mostly receded, and the symptom is pain.
Blood stasis is prominent in this pattern.

## Clinical Applications:
1. This formula is for treating pain and blood stasis due to trauma. Also, it combines blood movers with pain-relieving *qi* movers, and strengthens the bone.
2. The key symptoms are strained or sprained muscles and sinews or broken bones. After the swelling and inflammation of the first stage of trauma have decreased, stasis is a main condition, both due to the trauma itself and to the immobility during recovery.
3. Currently used in treating sprains, strains, fractures, bruises, and tissue damage created bruising, swelling and pain.

## Ingredients:

| | | | | | | |
|---|---|---|---|---|---|---|
| 1. | ding xiang | 2.0 | | 7. | dang gui | 4.0 |
| 2. | mu xiang | 2.0 | | 8. | lian zi | 4.0 |
| 3. | xue jie | 2.0 | | 9. | fu ling | 4.0 |
| 4. | er cha | 2.0 | | 10. | bai shao | 4.0 |
| 5. | da huang (shu) | 2.0 | | 11. | mu dan pi | 1.0 |
| 6. | hong hua | 2.0 | | 12. | gan cao | 0.6 |

## Functions:
Invigorate the blood, dispel stasis, eliminate stagnation, and alleviate pain.

## Modifications:
1. For more severe swelling pain: add *ru xiang*, *mo yao*, and *san qi.*
2. For bone fracture: add *gu sui bu* and *xu duan.*
3. For injury in lower limbs: add *niu xi.*
4. For injury in upper limbs: add *sheng ma*, *gui zhi*, and *jie geng.*

## Cautions and Contraindications:
Pregnancy.

## Administration:
Take with warm water or warm yellow rice wine, as needed.

Source: *Yi Zong Jin Jian* (醫宗金鑑)

# Zhi Bai Di Huang Wan 知柏地黃丸
## Anemarrhena, Phellodendron, and Rehmannia Formula

## Indications:
Used to treat *yin* deficiency with vigorous fire patterns: night sweats, chronic throat dryness and soreness, there may also be feverish palms and soles, lower back pain, wasting and thirsting disorder, and difficult urination.

**Tongue**: dry tongue with no coating
**Pulse**: large only in the rear position

## Clinical Applications:
1. This is the basic formula for *yin* deficiency with vigorous fire, which is marked by night sweats, steaming bone disorder, irritability, tidal fever, and chronic urinary tract infection (UTI).
2. Currently used for chronic nephritis, hypertension, diabetes, hyperthyroidism, menopausal syndrome, insomnia, and chronic prostatitis.

## Ingredients:

| | | | | | |
|---|---|---|---|---|---|
| 1. | shu di huang | 24.0 | 5. | mu dan pi | 9.0 |
| 2. | shan zhu yu | 12.0 | 6. | fu ling | 9.0 |
| 3. | shan yao | 12.0 | 7. | zhi mu | 6.0 |
| 4. | ze xie | 9.0 | 8. | huang bai on | 6.0 |

## Functions:
Enriches *yin*, causes fire to descend, moistens dryness, and benefits *qi*.

## Modifications:
1. For shortness of breath and asthma, add *hou pu* and *bei mu*.
2. For excess phlegm cough, add *fu ling* and *chen pi*.
3. For irritability and heat, add *mai men dong* and *di gu pi*.
4. For wind-cold asthma, combine with *Ma Huang Tang*.
5. For damp-heat asthma, combine with *Liang Ge San*.
6. For phlegm asthma, combine with *Er Chen Tang*.

## Cautions and Contraindications:
This formula has cloying properties and should be used cautiously in cases with indigestion, diarrhea due to spleen deficiency, or a white and greasy tongue coating.

## Administration:
Swallow with warm water or lightly salted warm water, after meals.

Source: *Yi Fang Ji Jie* (醫方集解)

# Zhi Gan Cao Tang 炙甘草湯
Licorice Combination
Honey-Fried Licorice Decoction

## Indications:
This decoction is used in the treatment of the following:

1. ***Qi* and blood deficienc**y: characterized by knotted pulse (*jie mai*), or intermittent pulse (*dai mai*), palpitations with anxiety, irritability, insomnia, emaciation, shortness of breath (SOB), constipation, and dry mouth and throat.
2. **Lung atrophy due to consumption**: characterized by a dry cough with little to no sputum, especially with threadlike blood visible in sputum, emaciation, shortness of breath, insomnia with restlessness, night sweats, or spontaneous sweating, dry mouth, dry stool, or intermittent low fever.

**Tongue:**  pale, shiny
**Pulse:**  irregular, slow-irregular or thin, faint, forceless, or rapid

## Clinical Applications:
1. This is the principal formula for the treatment of irregular pulses with throbbing palpitation and a dry cough.
2. Currently used for supraventricular arrhythmia, rheumatic heart disease, mitral valve prolapse, hyperthyroidism, pulmonary tuberculosis, emphysema, and neurasthenia. Other symptoms can include nutritional decline, dry skin, and fatigue; elderly and weak patients have dry fluid and constipation, neuropathic heart disease, ocular protrusion of thyroid (Bassedu's disease), and bedridden heat.

## Ingredients:

| | | | | | | | | |
|---|---|---|---|---|---|---|---|---|
| 1. | zhi gan cao | 3.0 | 4. | da zao | 3.0 | 7. | huo ma ren | 3.0 |
| 2. | sheng di hüang | 1.2 | 5. | mai men dong | 2.5 | 8. | gui zhi | 2.5 |
| 3. | ren shen | 1.5 | 6. | e jiao | 1.5 | 9. | sheng jiang | 2.5 |

## Functions:
Augments the *qi* and tonifies the blood, nourishes the *yin* and restores the pulse.

## Modifications:
1. For irritability and palpitations: add *huang qi* and *wu wei zi.*
2. For overfatigue exhaustion: add *tian men dong* and *shu di huang.*
3. For lung atrophy cough: add *jie geng* and *zhi shi.*
4. For vomiting and excessive belching: combine with *Wen Dan Tang.*
5. For severe *yin* deficiency dry cough: omit *sheng jiang, gui zhi* and *qing jiu.*

## Administration:
Take with warm water, after meals.

Source: *Shang Han Lun* (傷寒論)

# Zhi Suo Er Chen Tang 枳縮二陳湯
## Aurantium Immaturus and Amomum Combination

## Indications:
Fluid-phlegm accumulation in the chest that penetrates to the back with severe pain.

Pain in the epigastrium or diaphragm caused by reversal cold with retching and vomiting.

## Clinical Applications:
1. This formula is for treating fluid and phlegm accumulation in the area around the diaphragm that yields pain in the ribcage and epigastrium.
2. The key symptoms are retching, nausea, or vomiting.
3. Currently used in treating gastritis, stomach pain, stenosis, cardiac neuralgia, stomach fluid retentions, gastric dilation gastritis, angina, intercostal neuralgia, gastric ulcers, or pleurisy.

## Ingredients:
1. ban xia          2.2
2. fu ling          2.2
3. xiang fu         1.5
4. hou po           1.5
5. yan hu suo       1.5
6. chen pi          1.5
7. sha ren (suo)    1.1
8. hui xiang        0.8
9. mu xiang         0.8
10. zhi shi         1.1
11. cao dou kou     0.8
12. sheng jiang     1.5

## Functions:
Transform phlegm, move the *qi*, dispel cold, and relieve pain.

## Note:
This formula is basic from *Er Chen Tang* with the addition of *xiao hui xiang, yan hu suo, gan jiang*, and *xiang fu* to move *qi* and ease the pain; and also adding *zhi shi (suo), sha ren, mu xiang, huo po, cao dou kou* to move phlegm and *qi*.

## Cautions and Contraindications:
Chest/back pain not caused by phlegm-fluid accumulations.

## Administration:
Take with warm water, before meals.

Source: *Wan Bing Hui Chun* (萬病回春 )

# Zhi Sou San 止嗽散
Citrus and Aster Formula
Stop Coughing Powder

## Indications:
For the treatment of coughing, especially as the sequela of external wind-cold attacks.

May be used for patients experiencing coughing with or without slight chills and fever with an itchy throat and phlegm that is difficult to expectorate.

**Tongue:**    thin, white coating
**Pulse:**    moderate, floating or thin and rapid pulse

## Clinical Applications:
1. This formula is used for lingering coughs due to external wind attack.
2. Currently used in treating upper respiratory tract infections, acute or chronic bronchitis, and early-stage pneumonia. Treats headaches, coughs from the common cold, particularly in patients younger in age or of weak constitutions cough.

## Ingredients:
1. zi wan   5.0
2. bai bu   5.0
3. bai qian   5.0
4. jie geng   5.0
5. chen pi   2.5
6. jing jie   5.0
7. gan cao   2.0

## Functions:
Extinguishes and dissipates external wind, ventilates lungs, stops coughing, and transforms phlegm.

## Modifications:
1. For cough with excess phlegm: add *ban xia, fu ling* or *Er Chen Tang.*
2. For difficulty expectorating: add *she gan* and *niu pang zi.*
3. For damp-heat cough: add *qian hu* and *bai dou kou.*
4. For aversion to cold and headache: add *bai zhi* and *xi xin.*
5. For severe external wind-cold cough: add *fang feng, zi su ye* and *sheng jiang.*
6. For phlegm-damp coughs with profuse, sticky sputum: add *ban xia, fu ling* and *sang bai pi.*
7. For dry coughs due to liver fire attacking lungs: add *gua lou, bei mu* and *zhi mu.*
8. For chronic bronchitis: add *ban xia, fu ling, xing ren* and *zi su zi.*
9. For lung-TB coughs with excess phlegm: add *sang bai pi, di gu pi, sha shen* and *huang lian.*

## Cautions and Contraindications:
Not to be used for chronic coughs due to *yin* deficiency.

## Administration:
Take with warm water, after meals.

Source: *Yi Xue Xin Wu* (醫學心悟)

# Zhi Zi Chi Tang 栀子豉湯

Gardenia and Soja Combination
Gardenia and Prepared Soybean Decoction

## Indications:

Unformed constrained heat lingering in the chest and diaphragm.

Fever, irritability, insomnia with tossing and turning in bed, a stifling sensation in the chest, and a soft epigastrium when palpated.

**Tongue:**  slightly yellow coating
**Pulse:**  slightly rapid pulse, or a strong, floating pulse at the distal position

## Clinical Applications:

1. This formula can be used to treat irritability due to lingering heat. Usually, symptoms are indicated in the aftermath of a febrile disease or during a relapse.
2. Currently used for respiratory tract infection, fever of unknown origin, and autonomic dystonia. Also hypertension and coronary artery disease.
3. Acute hepatitis, esophagitis, esophageal stricture, insomnia, endostomatitis, hemorrhoids, and itching of porta hepatis.
4. Hemorrhages from the upper part of the body including upper GI bleeds, nosebleeds, and bronchiectasis.
5. Upper gastrointestinal disorders including esophagitis, esophageal strictures, peptic ulcers, acute gastritis, and bile reflux gastritis.
6. The formula has also been used to treat hypertension and coronary artery disease.

## Ingredients:

1. zhi zi       7.5
2. dan dou chi   10.0

## Functions:

Clear heat and alleviate restlessness and irritability.

## Modifications:

1. For cases with lingering wind-heat in the exterior, add *niu bang zi* and *bo he.*
2. For bitter taste in the mouth, yellow tongue and severe interior heat, add *huang qin* and *lian qiao.*
3. For nausea, vomiting, greasy tongue coating and severe dampness, add *ban xia* and *huo xiang.*
4. For cases with alcohol jaundice with irritability and chest heat pain: add *da huang* and *zhi shi.*

## Cautions and Contraindications:

Spleen and stomach *Yang* deficiency marked by loose stools.

## Administration:

Take with warm water, after meals.

Source: *Shang Han Lun* (傷寒論)

# Zhu Ling Tang 豬苓湯
Polyporus Combination
Polyporus Decoction

## Indications:
For the treatment of water and heat clumping in the urinary tract or bladder (cold enters *yang ming* or *shao yin* and transforms into heat).

Patients may be experiencing the following:
1. ***Shang-han yang-ming* syndrome:** characterized by difficulty urinating, fever, thirst, irritability, insomnia, persistent cough, nausea and diarrhea.
2. ***Shao-yin* syndrome or bloody *lin* syndrome:** difficult, weak, dripping, or painful urination, especially with distention or pain in the lower abdomen, accompanied by thirst and red in the urine.

**Tongue:**    red, dry, or slightly yellow coating
**Pulse:**    thready and rapid, or superficial

## Clinical Applications:
1. The key symptoms are difficulty urinating, excessive thirst, fever with red tongue and rapid pulse. Generally, this formula promotes urination and stops bleeding.
2. Currently used in treating cystitis, urethritis, UTIs, nephritis, bloody urine, urgency, dysuria hemorrhagic shock, cirrhosis or insomnia.

## Ingredients:
1. zhu ling   5
2. ze xie   5
3. fu ling   5
4. hua shi   5
5. e jiao   5

## Functions:
Promotes urination drains dampness, clears heat and nourishes the dryness.

## Modifications:
1. For irritable thirst: add *shi gao* and *zhi mu*.
2. For red urine, pain: add *sheng di huang* and *mu tong*.
3. For frequent need to urinate: add *cang zhu* and *bai zhu*.
4. For kidney or bladder stones: combine with *shao yao gan cao tang*.
5. For hot *lin* syndrome, add *zhi zi* and *che qian zi*.
6. For bloody *lin* syndrome, add *bai mao gen* and *da xiao ji*.

## Cautions and Contraindications:
Contraindicated for internal excess heat, injuring the *yin* and body fluids, or for excessive dampness conditions.

## Administration:
Take with warm water, before meals.

Source: *Shang Han Lun* (傷寒論)

# Zhu Ru Wen Dan Tang 竹茹溫膽湯
Bamboo and Ginseng Combination

## Indications:
Post-illness insomnia syndromes.

Damp accumulation causes insomnia, fright, heat in the chest, cough and palpitations, and nervousness and hypersensitivity.

**Tongue:** greasy coating

## Clinical Applications:
1. This formula is for treating phlegm accumulation with heat insomnia.
2. The key symptoms are insomnia, disturbed sleep, fright palpitations, and irritability. Also nausea and vomiting associated with phlegm and suppressed heat in the middle burner.
3. Currently used in treating typhoid fever heat, restless sleep, palpitation, irritability and insomnia caused by excessive phlegm.

## Ingredients:
| | | | | | | |
|---|---|---|---|---|---|---|
| 1. chai hu | 1.9 | 6. ren shen | 0.8 | 11. gan cao | 0.4 |
| 2. zhu ru | 2.7 | 7. chen pi | 1.2 | 12. sheng jiang | 0.8 |
| 3. jie geng | 2.7 | 8. ban xia | 1.2 | 13. da zao | 0.4 |
| 4. zhi shi | 2.7 | 9. fu ling | 1.2 | | |
| 5. huang lian | 0.8 | 10. xiang fu | 1.2 | | |

## Functions:
Clear heat, transform phlegm; move the *qi* and calm spirit (*shen*).

## Modifications:
1. For cases with fright palpitation: add *shi chang pu.*
2. For cases with severe heat: add *zhi zi.*

## Note:
This formula is *Wen Dan Tang* (Poria and Bamboo Combination) with the addition of *chai hu, jie geng, huang lian, ren shen* and *xiang fu.* It is for long-term *shen* disorder and phlegm accumulation with heat.

## Administration:
Take with warm water, after meals.

Source: *Wan Bing Hui Chun* (萬病回春)

# Zhu Ye Shi Gao Tang 竹葉石膏湯
Bamboo Leaves and Gypsum Combination
Lophatherus and Gypsum Decoction

## Indications:
For the treatment of residual heat and *qi* fluid damage in the late stages of *yang ming* syndrome (*shan han* diseases), *qi*-level (*wen ben* diseases), and summer heat diseases.

May be used for patients experiencing fever with profuse sweating, irritability, and thirst; may be accompanied by vomiting, a stifling sensation in the chest, nausea, insomnia, dry mouth, and a strong desire to drink.

**Tongue**:   red with little coating
**Pulse**:    deficient, rapid or surging big and forceless

## Clinical Applications:
1. This formula can be used anytime during the course of a febrile disease where there is injury to the *qi* and *yin* with unabated fever with sweating, thirst, dryness and nausea. This is a nourishing, cooling formula that relieves heat and soothes a big, forceless pulse.
2. Currently used for infectious diseases such as pharyngitis, nephritis, or diabetes.

## Ingredients:
| | | | |
|---|---|---|---|
| 1. zhu ye | 2.0 | 5. ban xia | 4.0 |
| 2. shi gao | 16.0 | 6. zhi gan cao | 2.0 |
| 3. ren shen | 3.0 | 7. jing mi | 6.0 |
| 4. mai men dong | 6.0 | | |

## Functions:
Clears heat, generates vital fluids, augments the *qi* and harmonizes the stomach.

## Modifications:
1. For cases with cough and difficulty breathing: add *xing ren.*
2. For deficiency irritable thirst: add *huang qi* and *wu wei zi.*
3. For summer heat thirst: add *xiang ru* and *zhi mu.*
4. For post-illness thirst: add *shao yao* and *chai hu.*
5. For residual heat after wind-cold: combine with *Sheng Ma Ge Gen Tang.*
6. For female patients with deficiency heat: combine with *Si Wu Tang.*
7. For cases with stomach *yin* deficiency and oral ulcerations: add *tian hua fen* and *shi hu.*
8. For intense, blazing stomach fire with persistent hunger: add *tian hua fen* and *zhi mu.*

## Administration:
Take with warm or cool water, after meals.

Source: *Shang Han Lun* (傷寒論)

# Zi Cao Gen Mu Li Tang 紫草根牡蠣湯
## Arnebia and Oyster Shell Combination

### Indications:
Syphilitic sores with chronic ailments and stubborn sores.

Malignant sores and tumors, mastitis, stubborn skin lesions, enlarged lymph nodes and pruritus.

### Clinical Applications:
1. This formula is for treating deep-seated malignant sores whose prolonged existence has weakened *qi* and blood.
2. Currently used in treating carcinomas of the lymph system and breasts, and also for syphilitic sores.
3. Breast cancer, mastitis, cervical lymphadenopathy, lung gangrene, intestinal ulcer, systemic lymphoid tumor, black flesh tumor, syphilitic skin disease, syphilitic papules, and unexplained skin disease.

### Ingredients:
1. dang gui          4.0
2. bai shao          2.4
3. chuan xiong       2.4
4. zi cao gen        2.4
5. da huang          1.2
6. ren dong hua      1.2
7. sheng ma          1.6
8. huang qi          1.6
9. mu li             3.2
10. gan cao          0.8

### Functions:
Clear heat, resolve toxin, uplift *Yang*, dissipate swelling, and dispel malignant sores.

### Modifications:
1. For stagnation swollen pain: add *ru xiang* and *mo yao*.
2. For wind-damp swollen: add *bai zhi* and *bai zhu*.

### Administration:
Take with warm water, as needed.

Source: *Zheng Li Xin Shu* (徵癘新書)

# Zi Shen Ming Mu Tang 滋腎明目湯
## Chrysanthemum Combination
### Enrich the Kidneys and Improve Vision Decoction

## Indications:
Diminished eye vision caused by liver and kidney *yin* and blood deficiency.

Visual loss, visual dizziness, eyes that tire easily, dry eyes, excessive tearing, and cataracts.

## Clinical Applications:
1. This formula is for treating eye disorders in older or weak patients who display obvious signs of blood deficiency and heat.
2. Currently used in treating nervous exhaustion, diminished visual acuity, tired eyes, trouble seeing, blurred vision, itchy tears, mydriasis, cataract, etc.
3. Conjunctivitis or sties, pain or swelling following surgery or other invasive procedures at or near the eyes.

## Ingredients:
| | | | | | | | | |
|---|---|---|---|---|---|---|---|---|
| 1. | chuan xiong | 2.4 | 6. | ren shen | 1.2 | 11. | ju hua | 1.2 |
| 2. | dang gui | 2.4 | 7. | jie geng | 1.2 | 12. | gan cao | 1.2 |
| 3. | bai shao | 2.4 | 8. | zhi zi | 1.2 | 13. | man jing zi | 1.2 |
| 4. | shu di huang | 2.4 | 9. | bai zhi | 1.2 | 14. | cha ye ye | 1.2 |
| 5. | sheng di huang | 2.4 | 10. | huang lian | 1.2 | 15. | deng xin cao | 1.2 |

## Functions:
Enrich the *yin* and nourish the blood; tonify the *qi*, clear heat and brighten eyes.

## Modifications:
1. For dizziness vision: add *huang qi* and *gou qi zi.*
2. For eyes fatigue: add *fu ling* and *bai zhu.*
3. For eye pain tearing: add *fang feng* and *qiang huo.*
4. For cataract blurred vision: combine with *Ba Wei Di Huang Wan.*
5. For blurred vision: combine with *Liu Wei Di Huang Wan.*

## Note:
This formula is also known as *Shen Qi Ming Mu Tang* (Kidney *Qi* Eye-Brightening Decoction).

## Administration:
Take with warm water, after meals.

Source: *Wan Bing Hui Chun* (萬病回春)

# Zi Wan Tang 紫菀湯
## Aster Combination

### Indications:
Deficiency chronic lung cough from wasting-heat.

Both *qi* and *yin* deficiency, labored breathing, fatigue, night sweats, or tidal fevers and thirst. Coughing up bloody sputum, fever, and difficulty breathing.

### Clinical Applications:
1. This formula is for treating deficiency chronic lung cough from consumption-heat (*Lao Re* 勞熱).
2. The key symptoms are cough, fevers, night sweating, fatigue, and labored breathing from both *qi* and *yin* deficiency.
3. Currently used in treating lung atrophy, prolonged cough due to labor-heat, blood in sputum, pulmonary atrophy, pulmonary abscesses.

### Ingredients:
1. zi wan        4.0
2. e jiao        4.0
3. zhi mu        4.0
4. bei mu        4.0
5. jie geng      2.0
6. ren shen      2.0
7. fu ling       2.0
8. zhi gan cao   2.0
9. wu wei zi     1.5

### Functions:
Nourish the lung, stop the cough; clear heat, transform phlegm.

### Modifications:
1. For lung atrophy with abscess: add *ting li zi* and *da zao*.
2. For coughing up phlegm with blood: add *zhu ru* and *sheng di huang*.
3. For chronic dry cough: add *mai men dong* and *zhi shi*.
4. For severe abscess from lung atrophy: combine with *Pai Nong San*.
5. For coughing up bloody sputum from lung atrophy: combine with *San Huang Xie Xin Tang*.

### Cautions and Contraindications:
Excess lung heat.

### Note:
Both this formula and *Mai Men Dong Tang* (Ophiopogon Combination) treat lung deficiency and consumptive disorders.

*Mai Men Dong Tang* treats these disorders from *yin* deficiency of the stomach and lung, *Zi Wan Tang* treats conditions due to a deficiency in the lung of both *qi* and *yin*.

### Administration:
Take with warm water, after meals.

Source: *Yi Fang ji Jie* (醫方集解)

# Zi Yin Di Huang Wan 滋陰地黃湯
## Rehmannia, Bupleurum, and Scute Formula

**Indications:**

Various eye disorders related to blood and *yin* failing to nourish the heart and liver.

**Clinical Applications:**

1. This formula is for treating blood deficiency and kidney *yin* deficiency that leave the heart undernourished. Lack of nourishment to the heart produces heart fire that rises and affects the eyes (liver wood).
2. The key symptom is blurry vision.
3. Currently used in treating clouded vision or dilated pupils.

**Ingredients:**

1.  shu di huang      3.3
2.  sheng di huang    2.5
3.  chai hu           2.7
4.  huang qin         1.7
5.  dang gui          1.7
6.  tian men dong     1.0
7.  di gu pi          1.0
8.  wu wei zi         1.0
9.  huang lian        1.0
10. ren shen          0.7
11. gan cao           0.7
12. zhi ke            0.7

**Functions:**

Nourish blood and *yin*, disperse internal wind; tonify *qi*, drain fire.

**Cautions and Contraindications:**

Avoid pungent, spicy and hot food to generate fire; and cold, raw food to damage spleen-stomach.

**Administration:**

Take with warm water, after meals.

Source: *Yi Fang ji Jie* (醫方集解)

# Zi Yin Jiang Huo Tang 滋陰降火湯
## Phellodendron Combination
### Decoction to Enrich *Yin* and Direct Fire Downward

## Indications:
*Yin* deficiency fire cough, and asthma.

Cough that may or may not be productive, wheezing, night sweats, dry mouth, fever, coughing of blood, wasting and thirsting, and steaming bones.

## Clinical Applications:
1. This formula is for treating *yin* deficiency fire that causes cough, asthmatic breathing, night sweats, dry mouth, fever, coughing of blood, dispersion thirst, or steaming bones.
2. The symptoms also include dry or sore throat or throat sores.
3. Currently used in treating pulmonary tuberculosis, pneumonia, pleurisy, acute or chronic bronchitis, pharyngitis, laryngitis, renal tuberculosis, pyelitis, diabetes and perimenopausal syndrome and/or gonorrhea.

## Ingredients:

| | | | | | | | |
|---|---|---|---|---|---|---|---|
| 1. bai shao | 2.5 | 6. mai men dong | 2.0 | 11. zhi gan cao | 1.0 |
| 2. dang gui | 2.5 | 7. sheng di huang | 1.5 | 12. sheng jiang | 3.0 |
| 3. shu di huang | 2.0 | 8. chen pi | 1.5 | 13. da zao | 2.0 |
| 4. bai zhu | 2.0 | 9. zhi mu | 1.0 | | |
| 5. tian men dong | 2.0 | 10. huang bai | 1.0 | | |

## Functions:
Enrich the *yin*, nourish the blood, and direct fire downward.

## Modifications:
1. For cases with blood heat vomit: add *huang lian*, *huang qin*, and *zhi zi*.
2. For cases with *yin* deficiency steaming bone syndromes: add *chai hu* and *di gu pi*.
3. For cases with strong fire heat: add *sha shen* and *wu wei zi*.
4. For cases with severe night sweat: add *mu li*, *suan zao ren*, and *fu xiao mai*.

## Cautions and Contraindications:
Avoid pungent, spicy and hot food to raise the fire.

## Note:
The formula is similar to *Zhi Bai Di Huang Wan* (Anemarrhena, Phellodendron, and Rehmannia Formula) in function but is more focused on deficiency heat that attacks the lung.

## Administration:
Take with warm water, as needed.

Source: *Shen Shi Zuen Sheng Shu* (沈氏尊生書)

# Zuo Gui Wan 左歸丸
Cyathula and Rehmannia Formula
Restore the Left (Kidney) Pill

## Indications:
For the treatment of true *yin* deficiency with essence and marrow depletion syndromes.

May be used for patients experiencing dizziness, vertigo, soreness and weakness in the lower back and knees, spontaneous or nocturnal emissions, spontaneous sweating, including night sweats, and dry mouth and throat with general body fluid depletion.

**Tongue**: red, shiny or peeled
**Pulse**: rapid, thin

## Clinical Applications:
1. This formulation directly nourishes the *yin*, and is used for true *yin* deficiency, especially with kidney essence deficiency and *ying-wei* deficiency.
2. Neurasthenia insomnia, convulsions, atherosclerosis, *yin* deficiency-type hypertension, frequent urination, blurred vision, rheumatoid arthritis, neuralgia, and chronic nephritis; can also be used to prevent uremia.
3. It calms and protects the liver, regulating metabolism, promotes the formation of immunoglobulin, and promotes the secretion from the adrenal gland, supporting righteous energies and expelling evil.

## Ingredients:
1. shu di          4.0
2. shan zhu yu      2.0
3. shan yao         2.0
4. gou qi zi        2.0
5. gui ban jiao     2.0
6. lu jiao jiao     2.0
7. tu si zi         2.0
8. niu xi           1.5

## Functions:
Enriches the *yin*, tonifies the kidney, replenishes essence, and benefits the marrow.

## Modifications:
**Zuo Gui Yin** 左歸飲 Restore the Left (Kidney) Drink: add for mild *yin* deficiency cases.
Ingredients: *shu di, shan yao, gou qi zi, zhi gan cao, fu ling* and *shan zhu yu.*

1. For tidal fever with steaming bone disorder: add *di gu pi.*
2. For cases of constipation: omit *tu si zi* and add *rou cong rong.*
3. For sore throat and coughs with phlegm: add *mai men dong* and *sha shen.*
4. For irritable insomnia: add *dan shen, huang qin, huang bai* and *zhi mu.*

5.  For abdominal acute pain: add *shao yao* and *hou po*.
6.  For low sperm count: add nu *zhen zi* and *hai lian cao*.
7.  For blood deficiency or dry stagnation: add *dang gui* and *mu dan pi*.
8.  For soreness and weakness in lower back and knees: add *du zhong, xu duan* and *gu zhi zi*.
9.  For joints injury: add *san qi, ru xiang* and *mo yao*.
10. For unsettled heart and spirit: combine with *Suan Zao Ren Tang* or *Tian Wan Bu Xin Dan*.

## Cautions and Contraindications:
Not to be used for patients with spleen *qi* deficiency or acute diarrhea.

## Administration:
Take with warm water, after meals.

Source: *Jing Yue Quan Shu* (景岳全書)

# Zuo Jin Wan 左金丸
## Left Metal Pill

### Indications:
For the treatment of liver fire attacking the stomach.

May be used for patients experiencing pain and distention in the hypochondriac area, indeterminate gnawing hunger, acid regurgitation, vomiting, epigastric stifling sensation, distention, belching, and bitter taste in the mouth.

**Tongue**:  red color, yellow coating
**Pulse**:  wiry, rapid

### Clinical Applications:
1. This formula is used for rebellious *qi* and fire rushing upward, causing nausea and acid regurgitation, associated with heat. It may also be used in treating hernia disorders caused by disturbed the liver channel.
2. Currently used for gastritis, peptic ulcers, esophageal reflux and esophageal inflammation.

### Ingredients:
1. huang lian          60.0
2. wu zhu yu          10.0

### Functions:
Clears liver heat, drains stomach fire; moves *qi* downward and stops nausea.

### Modifications:
1. For cases with severe hypochondriac pain, combine with *Si Ni San* formulation (*chai hu, bai shao, zhi shi* and *zhi gan cao*).
2. For cases with severe acid regurgitation, add *hai piao xiao* and *duan wa leng zi.*

### Cautions and Contraindication:
Not to be used for acid regurgitation due to stomach cold caused by deficiency.

### Administration:
Take with warm water, before meals.

Source: *Ji Bing Zhuan Ke Lu Ru* (疾病專科錄入)

# Index of Common Names

# Index of Ingredients:

# Index of Symptoms

296

cold beverages
 desire to drink, 118
cold coagulation, 40, 183, 237
cold damage, 83
 internal, 196
cold drink
 desire for, 122
 pain, 117
cold drinks injury, 22
cold invading the channels, 40
cold pain, 31, 151, 152
cold sensation, 11, 69, 73
cold-phlegm, 50
colds
 susceptibility to, 252
colitis, 13, 29, 78, 101, 135, 146
 allergic, 174
 chronic, 174, 188, 260
 ulcerative, 65, 180, 260
collapse from roundworm syndromes, 200
collateral vessels, 54
collaterals
 qi and blood obstruction in, 151
colon
 cancer, 59, 65
coma, 82
common cold, 18, 22, 58, 64, 71, 97, 106,
 110, 141, 213, 229
 initial stage, 229
 no sweating, 89
 warm-wind, 139
 wind-cold, 243
Common cold
 wind, 45
complexation
 yellow, 195
complexion
 black or bluish, 20
 dull, 231
 lusterless, 218
 pale, 185, 190, 252
 pale yellow, 135
 pallid, 61, 163, 171
 sallow, 163
 shiny, 190
 upset, 218
 wan, 61
 wan and withered, 238
compulsive disorders, 46
concussion
 post, syndrome, 258

congested fluids syndrome, 198
congestion, 33, 97
 with profuse sputum, 258
congestive heart failure, 198, 201, 261
conjunctivitis, 57, 88, 114, 139, 202, 205,
 227, 272
 chronic, 200
conjunctivitis pain, 254
conjunctivitis-like disorders, 205
connective tissue disorders, 63
consciousness
 loss of, 46, 82, 222, 258
 vague and restless, 27
constipation, 19, 26, 27, 36, 46, 59, 67, 69,
 72, 75, 80, 91, 96, 102, 107, 116, 118,
 120, 128, 130, 132, 133, 144, 162, 171,
 180, 184, 186, 207, 214, 221, 224, 227,
 234, 242, 245, 256, 264, 276
 blood deficiency, 91
 blood heat, 224
 common cold, 130
 due to hypertension, 130
 elderly, 186
 febrile disease, 186
 habitual, 91, 130
 habitual atonic, 69
 hemorrhoid, 91
 in the elderly, 264
 painful, 224
 postpartum, 91
 post-surgical, 91
 severe, 227
 with fistula symptoms, 224
 with hemorrhoid symptoms, 224
constitution
 blood deficient, 42
 deficient, 28
 weak, 46, 59, 185, 238, 240
consumptive deficiency, 218
control oneself, inability to, 56
convulsions, 46, 47, 82, 112, 119, 276
 pediatric, 78
 persistent, 46
 with shrieking, 46
 yelling, animal sounds, 47
cool-dryness
 disorder, 230
 externally contracted, 230
coolness
 lingering, 158
coronary artery disease, 156, 235, 258, 267

318

*purgatives, premature use, 19*

*purpura, 61, 123, 187, 195*

*purulence*

*purulent disease, 100, 164, 259*

*pus*

*pustules, 29*

*pyelitis, 121, 275*

*pyelonephritis, 135, 172*

*pyloric obstruction*

*qi*

incoherent, 67
laconic, 14
slow, 222
slurred, 222

*sperm count*
low, 103, 249, 277

*spermatorrhea, 25, 53, 75, 129, 140, 163, 249*
spontaneous, 249
without dreams, 75

*spirit*
cloudy, 165
disturbance, 98
lassitude of, 86, 117
low, 98
unsettled, 238, 277
weakness of, 98

*spitting up fluids, 78*

*spitting up phlegm, 120*

*spleen*
bloating, 232
cold-damp with fluid in, 192
damaged, 207
deficiency, 39, 43, 84, 85, 104, 115, 129, 148, 171, 190, 201, 263
deficiency fatigue, 163
deficiency, cold/damp, 190
deficiency, preexisting, 165
deficiency, with damp, 208
earth, 158
excess heat, 226
failing to control the blood, 61
failure to transport water, 198
fluid depletion, 91
fluid transport difficulty, 81
heat accumulation, 122
inability to transform, transport fluids, 192
qi and blood deficiency, 61
qi deficiency, 85
regulation, 172
transformation dysfunction, 223
transportation dysfunction, 223
unable to control blood, 61
unable to distribute fluids, 91
yang deficiency, 81, 88, 261

*spleen and kidney*
deficiency cold, 260

*spleen and kidney qi*
deficiency, 199

*spleen and kidney yang*
deficiency, 261

*spleen and stomach*
dampness obstructing, 101
deficiency, 106, 249
deficiency cold, 218

disharmony between, 208
qi, 50
qi deficiency, 14
qi deficiency, 84
qi deficiency, 148
qi deficiency, 171
weakness, 106
weaknessl, 105
yin and qi damage, 130

*spleen and stomach qi*
damage during summer heat, 192
damage during summer stroke, 192
deficiency, 211

*spleen and stomach yang*
deficiency, 119

*spleen constraint pattern, 91*

*spleen qi, 56*
deficiency, 103, 171, 258, 277

*spleen yin deficiency, 158*

*splenitis*
acute, 226
chronic, 226

*spontaneous emission, 85, 103*

*sputum*
blood in, 142, 273
copious, 138, 177, 193, 210, 234
copious, thick, yellow, 45
difficult to exectorate, 45
purulent, 210
sticky, difficult to expectorate, 221
thick and yellow, 127
threadlike blood in, 264
with pus, 191

*St deficiency, 35*

*stagnation*
dry, 277
food, 50
to dissipate, 100

*steaming bone, 25, 72, 111, 275*
severe, 158
warm to touch, 158

*steaming bone disorder, 263, 276*

*stenosis, 265*

*stifling sensation, 200*

*stomach*
abscess, 100
bleeding, 176
bleeding ulcer, 61
bloating, 81, 232
blockage, 55
cold vomit, 171
damaged, 207
damp heat, 65

329